The Treasure-Seekers

The Men Who Built Home Oil

Philip Smith

Macmillan of Canada/Toronto

CANADIAN CATALOGUING IN PUBLICATION DATA

Smith, Philip, 1925–
The treasure-seekers

Includes index.
ISBN 0-7705-1661-0

1. Home Oil Company—History. 2. Petroleum industry and trade—Canada—History. I. Title.

HD9574.c24H66   338.7'62'233820971   c78-001585-1

49,350

Printed in Canada for
The Macmillan Company of Canada Limited
70 Bond Street
Toronto M5B 1X3

Contents

Acknowledgements

In writing this book, I relied heavily on personal interviews with those who participated in some of the events it describes, and with relatives and close associates of the two men chiefly involved, Jim Lowery and R. A. Brown, Jr. My thanks go to all those who responded so generously to my requests for sometimes large amounts of their time. In alphabetical order, they include: Mr. Justice Gordon H. Allen, Calgary; Dr. Don Armstrong, Montreal; Senator Jack Austin, Ottawa; Mrs. Joan (Macdonald) Banks, Vancouver; George J. Blundun, Calgary; Edmund C. Bovey, Toronto; Mrs. R. A. (Genny) Brown and Donald S. Brown, Calgary; R. M. Brown and Mrs. Kay (MacAdams) Cameron, Vancouver; David Campbell, Toronto; Robert W. Campbell, John Carr, and George Cloakey, Calgary; James D. Cochrane, Toronto; Rowan Coleman, Montreal; Mrs. Ruby Cook and S. G. (Sam) Coultis, Calgary; Arthur H. Crockett and Duncan Derry, Toronto; M. A. (Red) Dutton and George Fong, Calgary; Mrs. Jean (Lowery) Frost, Vancouver; John Galloway, Calgary; Bart W. Gillespie, Santa Paula, California; Max Govier, James H. Gray, and Glenn Holmes, Calgary; Jack Horner, Ottawa; George V. F. Hudson, Vancouver; R. E. Humphreys, Calgary; Dr. W. F. James and Donald M. Johnston, Toronto; Earl Joudrie, Ashland, Kentucky; Edwin L. Kennedy, New York City; the late R. H. B. Ker, Victoria, B.C.; James W. Kerr, Toronto; S. Aubrey Kerr, Calgary; Mrs. Thelma Kingston, Campbellford, Ontario; Frank Knight, Vancouver; W. L. Kurtze, Calgary; Theo Link, Victoria; Milton Lipton, New York City; Earl Lomas, Mrs. Harold R. Lowery, Boyd Lowery, Bruce A. Macdonald, and W. D. C. Mackenzie, Calgary; Benton Mackid, Sidney, B.C.; J. C. McCarthy and J. K. McCausland, Toronto; Mr. Justice N. D. McDermid, Graham C. McIvor, and the Hon. C. C. McLaurin, Calgary; Senator E. C. Manning, Ottawa; R. J. Michaelides, Toronto; George de Mille, Calgary; Mrs. Lois Mostyn-Brown and Cecil H. Munro, Calgary; Carl O. Nickle, the Hon. Marsh M. Porter, and Robert G. Price, Calgary; Hank Romaine, New York City; Bart Rombough, Calgary; John Scrymgeour, Bermuda; W. B. Shelly, Toronto; A. M. (Scotty) Shoults and Stuart Smith, Vancouver; Hubert Somerville, Edmonton; the late J. Grant Spratt, Milton H. Staples, Q.C., and John Stephen, Calgary; N. Eldon Tanner, Salt Lake City, Utah; Austin Taylor, Vancouver; J. Ross Tolmie, Ottawa; J. Page R. Wadsworth, Toronto; Ralph Will, Calgary; David Williams, Jr., Tulsa, Oklahoma; W. H. and R. Zimmerman, Toronto.

In addition to the above, I am grateful to the many present and former members of the staff of Home Oil Co. Ltd. who not only gave me the benefit of their recollections but often went to great pains to track down answers to questions which, at least in the early stages of the research, were by no means as specific as I— and doubtless they—would have wished. My over-all debt to the company will be evident to the reader, and I am glad to say that while its management gave me unrestricted access to all its minute books and files, no attempt was made to direct my research or control the use to which it was put.

Among other documentary sources consulted were various publications of the Alberta government, particularly *The History of Alberta Oil*, by F. K. Beach and J. L. Irwin, of the old Department of Lands and Mines; *The Great Canadian Oil Patch*, by Earle Gray, published by Maclean-Hunter Ltd., Toronto; *Oil in Canada West— The Early Years*, by George de Mille, printed by Northwest Printing and Lithographing Ltd., Calgary; *History of Oil Well Drilling*, by J. E. Brantly, published by the Energy Research and Education Foundation/Gulf Publishing; and *Edmonton: A History*, by James Grierson MacGregor, Hurtig Publishers, Edmonton.

I am indebted also to the Glenbow-Alberta Institute, where Sheilagh Jameson in particular was invariably helpful, and to the staffs of the following libraries: University of Calgary; *The Financial Post*, Toronto; Imperial Oil Ltd. in Toronto and Calgary; *The Vancouver Sun*; and *The Calgary Herald*, where Ron Nowell, of that newspaper's business reporting staff, cheerfully assisted me with some of the research.

Philip Smith

Introduction

The oil business has been described as "playing games with the hidden history of the earth, at a million dollars a throw". More commonly, it is known as "legitimized gambling".

What sort of man is drawn to this game? What are its rules and how is it played? What are the risks of failure? How great the rewards of success? In this book, by telling the story of the founding of one oil company and its by no means uninterrupted growth—its history encompasses near-fatal disasters as well as spectacular successes—I hope to provide some answers to those questions.

Actually, the description of the oil business in the first sentence above is now somewhat out of date. There was a time, when money bought more than it does today, when you could drill an oil well in Alberta for less than $50 thousand. Home Oil Co. Ltd. went into business in 1925 with $150 thousand, scraped together a few hundred dollars at a time from a list of backers ranging from prosperous members of Vancouver's business elite to Alberta storekeepers.

By 1972, the cost of a typical Alberta well had indeed risen to a million dollars. But only six years later, in 1978, it was more than four million. And as man reaches ever farther afield in his search for the slippery treasure that turns the wheels of the modern world, the costs mount astronomically: a single well in the Beaufort Sea or the North Sea can easily cost twelve million, or eighteen million, or even more.

The expenditure of all this money, notwithstanding the scientific advances made in the field of petroleum exploration in the past half-century, does not guarantee that your well will strike oil—any more than it did in the old days, when wells were sometimes drilled on the advice of a water-witcher.

Partly because of this element of risk, partly because of the high stakes needed to get into the game, but mostly because petroleum in its many guises so dominates our lives, the oil business is the biggest business of all. And for a variety of reasons—among them the historical accident that the oil was laid down in the rock beneath our feet many millions of years before man walked the earth, without regard to the geographical and political divisions he has imposed on its surface—most of that business has come to be concentrated in the hands of a few huge international, indeed supranational, corporations.

Such are the rewards of the game to the successful, however, that there have always been Davids to challenge the Goliaths. Hundreds of oil companies have been founded in Canada through the years. Many were mere stock promotions which soon disappeared without trace, and without even trying to find oil. Others tried to find it, and went broke in the process. Some found oil on their first attempt and enjoyed varying periods of prosperity before being swallowed up by larger companies. Only a handful found oil, survived, grew, and retained their original identity.

These so-called "independent" companies—by which is usually meant a company restricted to the finding and development of oil, without the vast resources for its refining and marketing owned by the majors—have played an important role in the Canadian oil industry. They have drilled well over half of all the exploratory wells in the country through the years, and they pride themselves on their "wildcat" status. (The term "wildcat" probably derived from a saying popular among early U.S. drillers who broke away from established oil areas to try their luck in some unexplored wilderness. They were going, they used to say, "out among the wildcats". The "wildcatter" is an unusual breed of man, to whom the taking of risks is as natural—and essential—as breathing.)

Home Oil Co. Ltd. is among the oldest and most successful of these independent companies. It has been Canadian-owned since its formation, and its ownership, if not control, has always been widely dispersed among ordinary members of the public: it had almost ten thousand shareholders before the Great Crash of 1929 and it has just over that number now, with much of its equity held by institutions, such as insurance companies and pension funds, whose investments represent the savings of thousands of Canadians in all walks of life.

Notwithstanding this wide ownership, Home Oil owes its success, and the retention of its identity, to two strong, individualistic, and at times idiosyncratic, men—of different generations and different character, but alike in their qualities of enterprise, foresight, and leadership.

Major Jim Lowery was an Ontario farm boy who emigrated to Alberta at the age of twenty-one in 1905 and tried his hand at a wide variety of ventures with enthusiasm but indifferent success until, at the age of forty, he set about rounding up the money to found Home Oil. He knew nothing about the oil business when he entered it, but he piloted Home through its first twenty-five years and by the end of the Second World War had built it into the largest independent company in the country.

R. A. Brown, Jr., unlike Lowery, was born into the oil business; his father was one of the best-known oil entrepreneurs of Lowery's generation. By his early twenties, Bob Brown, Jr., was already forming oil companies and developing the capacity for financial tightrope walking which would make him a legend in the world of Canadian business. As Jim Lowery reached the age at which he had to pass on the torch, Bob Brown picked it up, purchasing control of Home by secretly buying its shares on the open market.

Jim Lowery had an unusual corporate philosophy: he never at any time owned more than a thousand or so shares of Home, believing that if he had a large personal stake in the company it might impair his objectivity in carrying out his responsibilities to its shareholders. In contrast, Bob Brown did not believe in running any company he could not control. And while his control of Home was sometimes threatened, he had the instincts of the "wildcatter" in abundance and during his twenty years at the helm the company grew and prospered and made some of the most important oil and gas discoveries in Alberta.

For a variety of reasons, neither man made the kind of huge fortune he might have piled up in the heyday of the oil business in the United States. Jim Lowery may or may not have been a millionaire for a brief period in his middle life—but whatever he made he soon lost. Bob Brown became a millionaire very quickly, and lived like one. But he was seldom out of hock to the banks and toward the end of his life he lost his biggest gamble of all and found himself facing bankruptcy, his personal debt a staggering $26 million.

Through the years, of course, many other men contributed their talents and skills to the building of Home Oil, which in 1979 celebrates the fiftieth anniversary of the granting of its present charter. But to an extent seldom found in other large companies today, the story of Home is the story of Jim Lowery and R. A. Brown, Jr., and how they played the game.

Part One

CHAPTER ONE

"Hustling Jimmie Lowery" Gets on His Way

James Robert Lowery arrived in Alberta at an exhilarating time. It was 1905, and the territory first trodden by a white man only a century and a half earlier had just been granted what the more vociferous of its citizens had long demanded—its status as a fully fledged province of Canada. The new province's population numbered between 160,000 and 173,000—settlers were flocking in so fast no one could keep an exact count. But everyone took great pride in the knowledge that the population had more than doubled since the popular if somewhat dissipated Edward VII had succeeded to his mother Victoria's throne four years earlier, and it would no doubt soon double again.

The magnet drawing newcomers from all over eastern Canada, Europe, and the United States was the deep, rich soil that covers much of Alberta's 255,000 square miles. The development of a strain of wheat suited to both the requirements of European millers and the short growing season on the prairies—No. 1 hard—had already established a thriving export trade for Canada. It could be shipped from the Canadian west to the English port of Liverpool for twenty-one cents a bushel and by 1905 American farmers were becoming restive about the formidable competition of their rivals to the north: early that year, Congress held some hearings into the problem which were reported at length in the *Weekly Herald* of Calgary under the headline "CANADA'S WHEAT OUTPUT REGARDED AS A MENACE". To the hopeful settlers filling up the Canadian west, this was no menace at all, and those few who had the time or the opportunity to read the newspapers found in them no issues more threatening than the endlessly contentious questions of separate schools and provincial rights. The terrible blood-letting of the Great War that was to break out within a decade could not even be imagined. True, Russia and Japan were at war, but that was far away on the other side of the world and now that the little Japanese admiral Togo had vanquished the Russian fleet in the greatest sea battle since Trafalgar, presumably the Czar would sue for peace.

Of much greater interest to the new arrivals was the bumper harvest of 1905, and the apparently limitless prospects for many more in the future. If he was over eighteen and willing and able-bodied enough to work it, a settler could have a quarter-section of land—160 acres—for a mere ten-dollar registration fee. That was only half of what it would cost him to buy the best "blue or black fine worsted suit", which even in those early days of mass-merchandising he would find advertised as being in the true "twentieth-century style". All over the province, the 160-acre homesteads were being occupied as fast as government surveyors, working overtime, could map them. More than 3,000 were taken up in the area around Edmonton during 1905, and it was in Edmonton that Jim Lowery, a twenty-one-year-old schoolteacher from Ontario, had chosen to begin his quest for whatever treasure this new land might provide.

But it was not the prospect of clearing bush and growing wheat that attracted the young Jim Lowery. He had formed a distaste for working in fields while growing up on his father's farm at Wellman's Corners, near Campbellford, in the dairy country beside the Trent River, north of Lake Ontario and to the east of Toronto. Many years later, his youngest sister recalled that whenever Jim was assigned to tend the vegetable garden he would assemble a band of boys to help him and then keep them so amused with his stories that they would fail to notice he himself was doing no more hoeing than the overseer on a cotton plantation.

Jim was the third of ten children born to John Boyd Lowery and Rachel Whitton—which made him a second cousin to young Charlotte Whitton, who went on to become probably the liveliest mayor in the history of Ottawa. Jim and Charlotte were life-long friends and bore a family resemblance, not only in appearance but in their peppery personalities. The senior Lowery was a farmer whose prize-winning cheeses eventually won him a post as government cheese inspector, in which capacity he moved to Frankford, near Belleville, where the family's red-brick home, turreted in typical Ontario style, still stands.

In later years, Jim Lowery was widely admired for his quick, intuitive mind. But he was only an average student in the high school at Stirling, and one year even had to repeat his math. Nevertheless, he was able to get a job teaching school in nearby North

Hastings county, where he demonstrated his horse-trading instincts by compounding an innocuous mixture of water and soap suds and selling it to the locals as fly repellent.

There was some confusion in the Lowery family over whether their Protestant forebears hailed from Ireland or northern England. They could, of course, have come from both, since so many Irish crossed the narrow sea to England during Victoria's reign that the port of Liverpool was sometimes slightingly described as "the capital of Ireland". At any rate, Jim Lowery always considered himself to be Irish, and one of his later associates recalled him as "that wild, red-headed Irishman—a real Blarney-stone type". Certainly he was renowned for his occasional flashes of "Irish temper". One of these flashes was narrowly averted when, having decided that Ontario had become altogether too settled and tame for a man of ambition, he was boarding the train for Edmonton at Belleville. The conductor tried to insist that an orange crate he was man-handing up the steps should travel in the baggage car. Lowery protested indignantly that the crate contained a "lunch" his mother had packed for him. He was a stubborn man even then, and not the kind to lose an argument. But with his round face and dis-armingly innocent eyes, neither was he a man anyone stayed mad at for very long. The conductor soon relented and the "lunch", which included some of his mother's canned chicken and his father's cheese, sustained the eager emigrant all the way across the continent.

In Edmonton he found an industrious if somewhat boisterous community confident that once Ottawa had rejected the claims of that upstart rival, Calgary, 180 miles to the south, their city would take its rightful place as capital of the new province. After all, Edmonton had grown up around posts established by the Hudson's Bay Company and its rival, the North West Company, as long ago as 1795, and for years it had been an important trading centre and stopping place on the water route from eastern Canada to the west coast, the only trans-Canada highway of its day. Why, as early as 1825—when Calgary was nothing but buffalo pasture—a *road* had been built to link Edmonton with Fort Assiniboine, eighty miles to the northwest. One of the first pack trails in the whole west, it enabled the fur traders to use the Saskatchewan River on their journeys across the continent, a saving of many days over the former route to the north, by way of the Athabasca, Beaver, and Churchill rivers.

But then, in 1881, came the blow under which Edmontonians were still smarting: the appalling news leaked out that because the Dominion government feared that Americans from below the 49th parallel would take over the empty prairies of southern Alberta and Saskatchewan unless something was done to establish the Canadian presence there, the Canadian Pacific Railway was going to by-pass Edmonton and take the southern route through Calgary. With this stimulus, Calgary's population soon shot past Edmonton's, and the gateway to the north was no longer the entrepôt of the west. Its merchants recouped some of their confidence—and replenished their tills—in the late nineties, when they outfitted the hundreds of gold-seekers who set off from Edmonton up the Klondike Trail. And between 1895 and 1904, when it was incorporated, the city's population grew from 1,165 to 8,350. Now, in 1905, Sir Wilfrid Laurier himself had presided over a great celebration held there to mark the inauguration of the new province—"I see everywhere hope," he had said—and Edmontonians at last had their own rail link with the east; the first Canadian Northern Railway train steamed in that November, and in due course the line was pushed through to the west coast, giving Canada its second transcontinental railroad.

James Robert Lowery's arrival on this bustling scene coincided almost exactly with the first appearance there of a novelty still known as the "horseless carriage". A man named Morris had startled his neighbours in 1904 with his first outing in a two-cylinder "autocar". By the next year there were half a dozen of these contraptions clanking their smelly way through the horse-drawn wagons that crowded the streets. But they were still mere curiosities, marginally useful toys, perhaps. No one foresaw that they were destined to mould an entirely different America, or that their endless appetite for the undiscovered riches far beneath Alberta's deep soil would one day give the new province a prosperity headier even than the most ardent booster could envisage in 1905.

Actually, though it seems unlikely that Jim Lowery would have known of them at that stage of his career, there were already some indications to the knowledgeable that Alberta was sitting on a hidden store of petroleum, the fascinating "rock oil" which, while it had not yet come to dominate the economy of the world, had founded handsome fortunes in other places where it had been discovered. The existence of strange tar sands along the Athabasca

River had been known for almost two centuries, ever since Henry Kelsey, governor of the Hudson's Bay Company, had sent a Cree Indian named Wa-pa-su into the Athabasca country to try to establish trade with the Indians there. Wa-pa-su made two long journeys west of Hudson Bay and when he returned to the east from the second, in 1719, he presented Governor Kelsey with a lump of oil-saturated sand he had chipped from the cliffs overlooking the river. Kelsey recorded his acquisition of "that Gum or Pitch that flows out of the Banks of that River" in his journal, thus becoming the first man to write, however unknowingly, about Alberta oil. Peter Pond, the tough Yankee fur trader, visited the Athabasca country in 1778 and found the bitumen flowing from the ground useful for caulking canoes. Among later travellers who probably also used it for that purpose was Alexander Mackenzie, the first white explorer to penetrate the barrier of the Rockies, but for many years thereafter the "black pitch" was considered just one more useless phenomenon of nature.

In 1875, however, George M. Dawson, a geologist assigned by Her Majesty's North American Boundary Commission to study what was then still the Northwest Territories, said of this phenomenon, "Where bitumen exists in such abundance on the surface there is every possibility that flowing wells might be obtained without going to any great depth." Dawson, who subsequently joined the Geological Survey of Canada and was its director from 1895 to 1901, conducted valuable pioneer studies of the geology of the west and in 1888 produced a resources map outlining areas of Alberta in which petroleum might reasonably be expected to exist.

The Geological Survey did some of the earliest drilling in Alberta, on behalf of the CPR, though its target was not oil but coal, and more particularly water, to power the steam locomotives. In 1883, a well it sank in search of water at Langevin Station, a stop on the line northwest of Medicine Hat, now known as Alderson, struck natural gas. The gas caught fire almost immediately and burned down the derrick, but another well drilled near by a year afterward went on producing a small flow of gas until 1954. When a similarly fortuitous set of circumstances occurred at Medicine Hat itself in 1890, the far-sighted villagers resolved to take advantage of the discovery. Within a few years six more successful wells were supplying the whole city with gas for use in houses and street lamps (which were kept burning all day because that was cheaper than paying someone to shut them off) and to burn lime to make plaster—the first industrial application of natural gas in Alberta. Medicine Hat's unusual good fortune intrigued the British poet Rudyard Kipling when he toured Canada in 1907, and prompted his famous remark that the city had "all Hell for a basement".

These accidental discoveries encouraged intentional attempts to find gas elsewhere in the province, including one by the city of Calgary, which sank a well in 1895 in what is now the downtown area, using taxpayers' money—and prompting thereby a number of protests in the press against this "waste of public funds". All these early attempts failed, as did the first well sunk in search of oil, near Pincher Creek, south of Calgary close to the U.S. border. Interest in this area stemmed from a casual remark in 1884 by John Baring, of the prominent London banking firm Baring Brothers, who seems to have been on a visit to inspect ranching prospects and was presumably taking the opportunity to get in a spot of fishing. After examining some rock outcrops beside a creek, Baring delivered his opinion that if a man were to drill there he might find oil. A local promoter named Fernie (for whom the town of Fernie, British Columbia, was named) tapped some of his friends for money and formed the Southern Alberta Development Company. Its well, sunk in 1891, suffered the fate of so many others that followed: it struck water instead of oil.

Two years later, no doubt inspired by Dawson's faith and the occasional discovery in Alberta of places where oil actually oozed out of the ground, the Dominion government appropriated $7,000 to drill a well at the town of Athabasca, north of Edmonton. It was abandoned in 1894, having penetrated 1,770 feet into the ground without striking oil. Three years later, the government rig was moved about eighty-five miles down the Athabasca River to a place called Pelican Portage and a new attempt to find oil was made. This one encountered a flow of natural gas so strong that the driller reported he could not have dropped a cannon ball down the pipe. Such was the force of the escaping gas, in fact, that it was twenty-one years before the technique was available to shut it off, and during that period several million cubic feet of gas roared uselessly into the air every day.

Notwithstanding these disappointments, and since it was already reaping revenue from oil production in Ontario, the Dominion government in 1898 introduced the first regulations governing petroleum prospecting and production in Alberta, reserving to itself a 2.5 per cent royalty on the sale price of any oil found there.[1] For a time, this seemed as if it might have been a prescient move, for the locals around Pincher Creek had never given up their hopes for that area and in 1902 a company named the Rocky Mountain Development Company struck the first oil ever found in Alberta, on Cameron Brook, which cuts through what is now the Waterton Lakes National Park. In its first flush of enthusiasm, the company laid out a townsite which it named Oil City, and a short-lived real estate boom followed. But even though other companies joined in the rush to drill, the oil never flowed in commercial quantities and the search was eventually given up—until Gulf Oil discovered the large Pincher Creek gas field in 1948.

Alberta's oil industry, then, when Jim Lowery arrived on the scene, could not even have been said to be in its infancy; to all but the most optimistic it must have seemed an infant stillborn. And it would be twenty years before its development gave Lowery the opportunity he had come to the west to seek. In the meantime, his ambition was to be in business for himself. He indignantly rejected the first job he was offered, in a funeral parlour—he said he'd rather die himself—and somehow procured the buttermilk concession at the local exhibition. Then he did accept a job, as circulation manager for the *Edmonton Journal*; but before long he resigned to join forces with a colourful local character named John Michaels, one of the many friends he was quickly making in his new surroundings. A contract to distribute the *Journal* that Lowery had negotiated gave their operation a sound base and they were soon earning more than any of the paper's salaried employees. Michaels went on to use his famous Mike's News Stand, which is still an Edmonton institution, as a springboard for a remarkable variety of business and philanthropic enterprises. But Lowery's ambition wouldn't let him settle down at that early stage. For the next ten years he moved restlessly around trying his hand at a succession of ventures which did little more than widen the circle of friends who were attracted by his generosity and good humour.

He twice opened grocery stores in Edmonton and one summer, sensing that there was going to be a shortage of potatoes, toured the farms around the city buying up whole crops and ensuring himself a brief but profitable corner in the market. In 1907, he moved to Kitscoty, a small settlement near Lloydminster, on the province's border with Saskatchewan, to open a hardware store in partnership with John Dale, a boyhood friend. This enterprise seems to have flourished, even though its proprietors once became so caught up with the activities of a hockey team they were sponsoring that a clerk absconded with the takings.

In his frequent letters home, Lowery wrote so glowingly about his new life that in due course all three of his surviving brothers followed him to the west. Tragically, the first to join him—Charlie, his junior by two years—developed appendicitis soon after his arrival. Jim took him to hospital in Edmonton but his appendix ruptured and he died within a few days—though not before his brother's roguish eye had been caught by one of his nurses, a girl named Ethel Whyte from Brandon, Manitoba.

Somewhere along the way in Kitscoty Lowery had taken up a homestead; in the light of his subsequent career he undoubtedly viewed it more as an investment than an opportunity to follow in his father's footsteps. In 1909, he ran for election to the Alberta Legislature as a Conservative and was beaten—the Liberals were firmly in control of Alberta from 1905 to 1921. After the election, he scrawled a note on the back of one of his posters and sent it to the nurse he had met two years before. "Dear Miss Whyte," it read, "That's what I was up for but was unfortunate enough to be the Conservative candidate and there were only two of that stamp elected in Alberta so I guess I got mine. . . . Well, I did not send you this to show you how much better-looking I was getting but . . . it struck me that you had never sent me any condolences over my defeat so I thought I would jar your memory. Write soon (if you are not married)."

Conservatives were so rare in Alberta in those days that according to a popular wisecrack they were protected under the Game Act. But privately Lowery ascribed his defeat to the fact that his opponent was "a college man" and forthwith resolved to continue his own education. He had saved enough to return to the east, where he hoped to study law at Queen's University in Kingston, not far from his home. The citizens of Kitscoty were sorry to see him go and presented him with a gold watch.

In May 1910 he qualified for university by passing his senior matriculation examination at the University of Toronto with third-class honours in English, and Greek and Roman history. After a year at Queen's he returned to Edmonton, presumably because his money had run out. The real estate boom in that city was in full swing during 1911 and 1912 and the energetic Lowery made enough money selling lots to marry Ethel, whom he had courted largely by mail, and return to Queen's for a further instalment of his education.

This time, he seems to have left without completing his second year because in 1913 he was back in Kitscoty running for election again as "the people's candidate" for the riding of Alexandra. His message to the electors spelled out the Conservative platform as: "Provincial control of natural resources [the rights to which had been retained by Ottawa]; good roads and plenty of them; systematic drainage; rapid railway construction and operation of all lines constructed; cheaper money for settlers; a business administration of provincial affairs; and an accounting and auditing of provincial finances."

Alberta election campaigns were just as invigorating then as they are now, and Lowery's speaking style—which could never be described as a model of precision—left him wide open for a political cartoonist who drew a map of the province that showed the candidate for Alexandra standing with his feet planted firmly among the burgeoning buildings of Edmonton while off to the right three indignant citizens pointed at him accusingly from hamlets identified as Oxville, Kitscoty, and Lloydminster. At different times, it seems, Lowery had promised to live in all three places. An accompanying article said: "As an Edmonton town-lotter, Mr. Lowery naturally feels strange to Alexandra, and . . . it will be very hard for him to live in these three places at once. Mr. Lowery announces that he has a college education. . . . This should not be held against him. Many a good man has lived his college education down. The University of Life soon teaches him what's what."

Lowery survived the attack, though narrowly: he was elected by a mere three votes. During the next few years he fulfilled at least one of his election promises—he lived in Lloydminster, where he went into partnership with a man named Murray Miller in a company billed as "Lowery and Miller, the Land Men. Farm lands, loans, and insurance". Henceforth he confined his academic studies to extramural courses at the University of Alberta, where he wrote his bar examinations successfully in 1923—after absorbing some of the more bitter lessons offered by the "University of Life" as an infantry officer during the First World War.

Commissioned in the 151st Battalion in November 1915, he sailed with it the following year to England where at his age—he was now thirty-two—he could probably have remained throughout the war, training reinforcements and occasionally shepherding drafts across the English Channel to the fighting in France: officers assigned to this duty were scornfully referred to as "Cook's tourists". Instead, on one such visit to France Lowery wangled a posting to the crack 49th Battalion (famous during the Second World War as the Loyal Edmonton Regiment), reverting in rank from captain to lieutenant to do so. Wounded in the knee during the infamous slaughter of Vimy Ridge in 1917, he was left lying helpless on the field of battle where more than 11,000 of his fellow Canadians were killed or wounded. And to his everlasting indignation he was shot again, through the hand, as he was being carried off on a stretcher hours later.

Discharged as a result of his wounds in March 1918, he returned to Lloydminster with the rank of major and became a dedicated member of the Great War Veterans' Association, in which capacity—and as an MLA, since he had been returned to the Legislature during a wartime election in which serving members were unopposed by general agreement—he was summoned to Ottawa for the national conference held to consider "soldier problems" after that war. Predictably, for one of his mercurial temperament, he soon became disillusioned with politics. He was particularly incensed, for instance, when the Liberal Premier, Charles Stewart, suggested after the armistice that it would not be wise to demobilize all the returning veterans right away, that they would be better kept occupied building railways or doing other such useful jobs to prevent "dislocation in absorbing them into the work force". After the 1921 election in which the Liberals were turned out—though by the United Farmers of Alberta rather than the Conservatives—Major Lowery, as he was now known, never ran for public office again.

Instead he busied himself with his real estate business and rapidly became one of the leading lights of Lloydminster's small "establishment". Urged to take over the town's moribund Board of Trade he plunged into its affairs with all his booster's enthusiasm, arranged for booklets to be issued extolling the area's unrivalled prospects, and prevailed upon various eminent personages, including both provincial and federal ministers, to address the Board's functions. But by 1923, still as restless as ever at the age of thirty-nine, he decided it was once more time to move on. The Board saluted its retiring president that November with a farewell dinner and the gift of a leather suitcase, and several speakers praised his efforts on behalf of their town. Gordon Cook, a cousin of Lowery's from Campbellford who had come out in 1907 to work in the hardware store at Kitscoty, recalled their boyhood together and said the Major had "gone as hard at the ball game then as he has at the Board", and Bill Holland, a rival real estate man, sang a song of his own composition in praise of "Hustling Jimmie Lowery".

In response, the Major made one more speech in celebration of Lloydminster, "the brightest spot in Canada today". The Board's members, he said, should do all in their power to persuade the CPR to use some of the vacant property in the east end as a divisional point, and make sure their town got its share of the following year's immigrants, "particularly those coming from Denmark", who presumably embodied qualities Lowery always admired: industriousness and probity. Then, having acknowledged the Board's gift as an appropriate one, since it seemed he would be "living out of a trunk" for a while, Lloydminster's most popular citizen left for Edmonton once again, installed Ethel and their young daughter Jean in a boarding house that had seen better days when it was the home of Senator Lougheed, grandfather of the present Alberta premier, and went to work as Alberta agent for the Mutual Life Insurance Company of New York—which many years later would by coincidence become an important source of financial support for the company he was about to found.

CHAPTER TWO

Turner Valley:
"The Wildest Kind of Delirium"

It may be scant consolation to a present-day Albertan battling a blizzard, but tropical plants once flourished in his province, and camels and elephants roamed there until fairly recent times—geologically speaking. Long before that—for much of the past two billion years, in fact—the province was repeatedly submerged beneath first the Pacific Ocean, then the Arctic, and finally the Gulf of Mexico. These warm arms of the sea advanced and retreated as the shape of the land changed, and each time the waves washed in they brought with them, over hundreds of millions of years, countless colonies of tiny plants and marine creatures, from unicellular organisms to primitive versions of the fish and clams and crabs we know today. As generations of these creatures died they sank to the bottom and were covered by successive sedimentary layers of sand and mud which gradually solidified into layers of rock. Somehow, under forces that are even now not clearly understood—some combination of bacterial action, heat, and pressure—their remains decayed to form the petroleum which, until modern times, was locked in the rock as oil or gas or a combination of both.

Petroleum engineers speak of their stock in trade as existing in "reservoirs", a misleading term to the layman since it suggests vast underground ponds of oil just waiting for someone to stick in a hose and siphon it out. Actually, oil and gas are distributed within layers of porous rock virtually indistinguishable to the untrained eye from any other rock, held there under pressure and sealed in by non-porous layers of rock above them. The greater the depth of the well, the greater the pressure. But the oil or gas can be extracted from the ground only when a number of conditions are met: the pores in the rock must be large enough, and the porous layer sufficiently extensive, to hold oil or gas in commercially worthwhile quantities; the pores must be connected—a measure of the rock's permeability—so that the oil or gas can flow through them; and the pressure must be such that when the porous layer is broached by the drilling bit the oil or gas will be forced through the rock to the base of the well. From there, the lighter-than-air gas will rise automatically to the surface up a well which nowadays may be more than three miles deep; oil, being heavier, may need to be pumped up the well, but occasionally it is held under such pressure that it will gladden the oil man's heart by gushing to the surface under its own volition.

There are known today to be many kinds of geological structures, or "traps", in which petroleum can accumulate, but the first seekers after oil could only rely on surface indications of its presence: oil or "gum" seeping out of the ground, perhaps, or a certain type of rocky outcrop at a bend in a creek. Most early wells were drilled on nothing more substantial than a hunch; some were "witched" by water-diviners; a few were actually drilled on sites that came to their backers in dreams—dreams of one sort or another having always been a mainspring of the oil industry.

For the first scientific description of a structure likely to produce oil in commercial quantities North American drillers were indebted to another member of Canada's Geological Survey, a chemist named Thomas Sterry Hunt. As early as 1850, Hunt drew attention to some "gum beds" in Enniskillen Township, near Lake Erie in western Ontario, where a year later a man named Charles Nelson Tripp incorporated the first oil company in North America—and possibly in the world—to produce asphalt. Even though a sample of his asphalt won an honourable mention at the Universal Exhibition in Paris in 1885, Tripp later got into financial difficulties and was bought out by James Miller Williams, a prosperous manufacturer of railway cars. Williams and Tripp dug a forty-nine-foot well by hand and secured the first commercial production of crude oil in North America in 1858, so the Canadian oil industry is older than Confederation itself.

But as so often happens, this Canadian achievement went unnoticed in the larger world outside and a well drilled the following year at Titusville, in Pennsylvania, on the opposite side of Lake Erie, is popularly supposed to have given birth to the North American oil industry. Seventy feet deep, this well was sunk by "Colonel" Edwin L. Drake—actually, he seems to have been a former railroad conductor. It produced only eight to ten barrels of oil a day. But it set off a tremendous boom, and within a year wildcatters had drilled hundreds of wells across the United States and found oil in West Virginia, Kentucky, Ohio, and Kansas. Within two years, the infant U.S. oil industry was producing at the rate of more than two million barrels a year, far outstripping its Canadian counterpart, centred on the boom town of Petrolia which soon grew up near the Enniskillen gum beds. Ontario, even though by 1870 it was exporting some oil to Europe, could not keep pace with the U.S. competition: its peak production was less than 900,000 barrels, in the year 1894. (The barrel was early standardized at 42 U.S. gallons, or approximately 35 Imperial gallons.)

As the U.S. wildcatters fanned out across the continent they began to put into practice, with conspicuous success, the theory Hunt postulated in 1861. This was that petroleum accumulations would be found in "anticlines", places where a layer of porous rock arches upward like a road crossing a railway on a hump-backed bridge. Where these humps were overlaid by non-porous rock, Hunt predicted, they would have filled up with oil and gas under pressure from below.

His theory dominated oil exploration for years and some of the world's best-known oil fields were found through its application. And it was a classic anticline—in Turner Valley, about thirty-five miles south of Calgary—that plunged Alberta into its first oil boom. The valley, a fifteen-mile-long stretch of rolling foothills rangeland within sight of and parallel to the Rockies, took its name from two brothers, Robert and James Turner, who settled at Millarville in 1886 to raise cattle and Clydesdale horses. They soon owned most of the land in the neighbourhood—but no doubt to their everlasting chagrin had sold it by the time the oil boom raised its price to thousands of dollars an acre.

In 1888, a cowboy named John Ware, who had the unusual distinction for those parts of being black, stopped to water his horse at a pond on Sheep Creek, which runs through the valley. Puzzled when the horse refused to drink, he dismounted and found the water covered with an oil that smelled of sulphur. Rashly perhaps, Ware tossed a match into the pond and was shaken when it erupted into flames.

Elsewhere in the valley, gas seepages also startled the unsuspecting from time to time. In 1904, the *Weekly Herald* of Calgary recorded the nerve-wracking experience of a party of prospectors who had uncovered a vein of coal on Sheep Creek. When one of them lit his pipe during a work break one day, there was an explosion and "some of the shanty and scaffolding caught fire." The men were hard put to extinguish the blaze and in the view of the writer the gas that had caused it was an indication that "the geological formation around Calgary is very favourable to the presence of natural gas and other coal products." To bolster his theory that oil and gas must be present thereabouts, he offered the fact that coal existed in many adjacent districts and continued: "Right south of the Canadian line lie the Wyoming coal and oil fields, and still further south in a straight line is the largest natural gas field in the world, Texas. The students of the petroleum industry know that these deposits extend north and south over the entire continent, though dipping deeper in some places than others."

The supposed link between coal and petroleum was a common one in those days, and understandable: it was the distillation of kerosene, or "coal oil", from asphalt by a little-known Nova Scotian, Dr. Abraham Gesner, that paved the way for the oil age. Like many others in the first half of the nineteenth century, Gesner was looking for a substitute for the whale oil used in lamps, which was becoming prohibitively expensive as the great whaling fleets roved the oceans chasing their quarry into near-extinction. His and other discoveries led to a flourishing manufacturing industry that was already producing lighting oil and lubricants from coal when the first oil wells came along to supply it with a more convenient raw material for the same products. The tremendous thirst for gasoline did not develop until the oil industry was already well established—and it was just beginning when William S. Herron, a rancher in the Okotoks district, decided to follow up the phenomena of Sheep Creek.

An enterprising and hard-working man, Herron had come to Okotoks in 1901 from Northern Ontario, where he began work as a cook in a lumber camp at sixteen and by the age of twenty had his own lumbering operation with 150 employees. From that he branched out as a railroad contractor and on the side did some prospecting around Cobalt—in later life he used to hint darkly that he had lost valuable mineral claims there to rivals with friends in high places. Having thus missed one prospective fortune, he was determined to take advantage of any other opportunity that came his way. And since running a 950-acre ranch did not exhaust his considerable energy he dabbled in other ventures such as breaking horses and hauling coal with his team from a small pit near the town of Turner Valley to a power plant at Okotoks. While thus engaged, one day in 1911, he came across gas escaping from the ground near a crossing on Sheep Creek. He collected a sample of the gas and sent it for analysis to an uncle in the oil business in Pennsylvania. As he had hoped, it was petroleum, not marsh gas.

Having assembled the petroleum and natural gas rights to more than 7,000 acres of Turner Valley, Herron set about raising the financing required to drill a well. Apparently blessed with some of the instincts of Phineas T. Barnum, he organized a fishing trip on Sheep Creek for two prominent Calgary figures—R. B. Bennett, a rising young lawyer who would in due course become Prime Minister of Canada, and Archibald W. Dingman, another Ontario entrepreneur who had some experience in the Pennsylvania oil fields and was the first man to supply natural gas to Calgary. Both were duly impressed when Herron applied a match to his gas seepage and cooked their lunch on its flames.

Dingman, who had founded companies in Toronto before moving west—one made soap and another bicycle brakes—quickly put together a syndicate of Calgary businessmen who subscribed $150,000 to form a company called Calgary Petroleum Products Ltd. Herron put in some of his land in return for $22,000 cash and a twenty-five per cent interest in the company and it started drilling—the technical term is "spudded in"—its first well in January 1913. The site, recommended by Chester A. Naramore, an American geologist, was beside the Sheep River near the present town of Turner Valley. And on May 14, 1914, the Dingman No. 1 well roared to life with a flow of natural gas saturated with a light oil the colour of straw.

Throughout 1913, progress reports from the well had aroused growing interest in Calgary. First, traces of gas were found at 467 feet; then, from a little over a thousand feet deeper into the earth, a quantity of "high-grade oil" was brought to the surface in a bailer. By October, a local newspaper was predicting that "there exists in southern Alberta an oil field second to none in North America". In November, Dingman wrote to the *Herald* protesting against "some of the absolutely irresponsible and ridiculous statements" which were being published. His letter utterly failed to dampen the universal frenzy to get in on the coming bonanza. And when the Dingman well finally did strike it rich the city exploded into what the *Herald* later described as "the wildest and most irresponsible kind of delirium". Every storefront on the main street was taken up by hucksters selling oil stock and the sidewalks were jammed by excited citizens clamouring for their wares. Banners suspended from second-storey windows proclaimed the virtues of oil companies no one had ever heard of before, but the crowds were so anxious to buy their shares that the salesmen used laundry baskets to gather in the cash.

For a shyster promoter, forming an oil company in those days was childishly simple. The mineral rights to ninety-five per cent of the land in Alberta were held not by the farmers who owned the surface rights but by the Crown.[1] The Dominion Land Agent's office in Calgary granted petroleum and natural gas leases on a first-come, first-served basis to anyone who could scrounge the $5 filing fee and a rental payment of twenty-five cents an acre for the first year. For $45, an unscrupulous promoter could thus pick up the mineral rights to 160 acres he had never seen, much less explored for indications of oil. He would then "organize" a company, transfer his leases to it in return for any number of shares he chose, and peddle the shares for whatever price his glib tongue could extract from the eager buyers.

So it is not surprising that more than five hundred oil companies were floated in Calgary during 1914. Bankers estimated later that the public, ordinary, hard-working labourers, clerks, shopkeepers, and housewives, withdrew more than $1 million from savings accounts to buy oil shares—handsomely engraved documents, certainly, but most of them good for nothing except papering rooms, if the "investor" cared to be reminded of his folly. For only one in ten of the new companies bothered to erect a derrick, and fewer still actually got around to drilling a well: by 1920, six years later, there were only eight producing wells in the whole valley—and the future would show they had barely scratched the surface of its riches. A few dedicated oil men remained convinced those riches existed, but the memory of the 1914 promoters' depredations lingered on and for years they found it all but impossible to raise the capital they needed to justify their faith.

The Dingman well and those that came after it in the early years of Turner Valley produced a mixture of light crude oil and natural gas containing a highly volatile liquid condensate variously described as naphtha or natural gasoline. Calgary Petroleum Products built an absorption plant in 1914 to extract the natural gasoline from the Dingman well's gas. Trucked to Okotoks in steel drums on wagons hauled by six-horse teams, it sold for more than $4 a barrel. But in 1920 the plant caught fire and was destroyed. The $70,000 loss almost bankrupted the company and the re-financing it made necessary was supplied by the Imperial Oil Company Ltd. It was agreed to set up a new, jointly owned company called Royalite Oil Company Ltd., after a popular brand of kerosene marketed by Imperial, which had begun life in 1880 as a merger of sixteen independent Ontario producing and refining companies desperate to meet the heavy competition they were encountering from U.S. rivals. The merger failed to stem the tide and in 1899, on the principle that if you can't lick 'em you'd better join 'em, Imperial merged with John D. Rockefeller's Standard Oil of New Jersey.

Upon its formation, Royalite undertook to build a new absorption plant to go on extracting the natural gasoline from the Dingman wells—there were now three of them, to be known from then on as Royalite No. 1, 2, and 3; to build a pipeline to deliver the wells' output of natural gas to Calgary; and to continue drilling on Herron's original leases. Fulfilling this latter obligation, Royalite spudded in a new well on September 17, 1921.

The Dingman discovery well had obtained its production—four million cubic feet of natural gas a day—at the 2,718-foot level. Royalite No. 4 blew in at 2,871 feet in November 1923, with a flow of seven million cubic feet a day. But after a few months of operation the gas pressure was falling off so rapidly it was decided to deepen the well. When the bit ground almost a thousand feet deeper into the earth without result, Imperial's management ordered the hole abandoned. Sam Coultis, a chemical engineer from Forest, Ontario, who had been put in charge of Royalite's operations, pleaded with his bosses for one more chance: the bit, he pointed out, had now entered a layer of limestone known as the Mississippian, laid down about 350 million years ago, and if Royalite did not explore its possibilities no other company was likely to. Imperial reluctantly agreed to let the drilling continue for at least a few more days—and ten feet further down, on the night of October 12, 1924, the well suddenly blew in at 3,740 feet with a spectacular daily flow of twenty-one million cubic feet of natural gas and six hundred barrels of what Coultis—at the age of ninety in 1977—recalled as "water-white gasoline". For the next decade, the condensate of the Mississippian lime, not crude oil, was to be the target for drillers in Turner Valley. Royalite No. 4—the "Wonder Well"—had ushered in a new Alberta boom.

As a sidelight to that era, it was in 1924 that President Coolidge granted a constitution to the first federal oil conservation authority established in the U.S. In a letter to Congress explaining his action, he pointed out that America's oil supply was kept up only by drilling thousands of new wells every year, and that a failure to bring in further production for a two-year period would slow down the wheels of industry and bring serious industrial depression. The development of aircraft, Coolidge added, was now such that the national defence would have to be supplemented by them. Aviation might indeed come to dominate national defence, so that the supremacy of nations might be determined by the possession of petroleum and its various products. Two years later, the conservation board he established estimated that U.S. oil reserves amounted to only six years' supply. Among other measures it suggested to stave off a threatened oil shortage was "the expansion of American holdings in foreign oil fields".

CHAPTER THREE

The Major
Finds His Backers

When Royalite No. 4 came in, Jim Lowery was forty, with a wife and child but without any visible resources. Perhaps that was why he never hung out his shingle as a lawyer, which would certainly have raised his income, at least in the long run. At any rate, he seemed to have little or nothing to show for all the years of wheeling and dealing in real estate and grocery stores. Then suddenly, in 1925, he found his métier. And during the next couple of years he would become one of the most successful oil men in the country: a promoter free of the opprobrium sometimes associated with that term, trusted and respected in the financial circles of Toronto, Montreal, and Vancouver; a beaming *bon vivant* who delighted in entertaining his friends in the lavish style of a millionaire.

He owed the transformation in his fortunes to William Mac-Adams, an itinerant newspaperman with a late-blooming entre-preneurial streak and a dry wit that reminded his friends of the U.S. humorist Will Rogers. MacAdams' father hailed from Petro-lia and in 1872 founded a newspaper in nearby Sarnia which was later merged into today's *Sarnia Observer*. Two of his sons followed him into the business side of the firm but young Bill, more adven-turous, ran away from home at the age of sixteen and wound up in British Columbia. The turn of the century found him editing the *Pay Streak*, a newspaper in Sandon, which is a ghost town now but was then at the height of a boom based on its lead and silver mines. He later turned up in Edmonton, where for a while he wrote the editorials for two rival newspapers, taking either side of an issue with equal ease in a trenchant prose that once brought him a five-day jail sentence for accusing a judge of being crooked. He served his sentence, sustained by hearty meals brought in to him by friends, but had the satisfaction of seeing the judge removed from office soon afterward.

One of his three sisters had married W. J. Hanna, a Sarnia lawyer who was at various times Provincial Secretary of Ontario, Dominion Food Controller in the First World War, and president of Imperial Oil. Perhaps through this connection, MacAdams moved back east to a variety of jobs with Imperial. One of them, he once told a friend, was acting as a sort of companion to John D. Rockefeller, in the hope that as they sat whittling on the porch the old man might let slip some business secrets that even his own management didn't know about. MacAdams was a good listener, the type of man who might sit in the corner of a noisy room all evening soaking up the conversation but rarely entering it himself—though when he did his contribution displayed a penetrating intellect. In later years, he used to sit in his study in the evenings, hat perched on the back of his head, reading everything from Gibbon to the *Saturday Evening Post*, for which he had occasionally written. But whenever his daughter entered the room he would jump up and sweep off his hat.

He had no previous experience in the oil business, so his career at Imperial is something of a mystery, especially since he always adopted a somewhat cavalier attitude toward employers. R. B. Bennett, who abominated alcohol, was a director of Imperial from 1925 to 1929. He sniffed the air suspiciously one morning and asked MacAdams sternly whether he had been drinking. "Hell, Mr. Bennett," MacAdams replied, "don't you know I'm the best damned drinking man Imperial has ever had?" Years later, during the Depression, when a superior was upbraiding him for some alleged failure in the performance of his duties—he was at that time described as "Field Superintendent, British Columbia"—MacAdams interrupted him with, "I suggest you tell that to my successor." Startled, the superior asked, "What do you mean, your successor?" Picking up his hat, MacAdams replied, "Whoever you appoint—I just quit." By then, a succession of outside business ventures had made him financially independent, a status he cheerfully signalled by asking his bank manager to henceforth please address his statements to "W. MacAdams, Capitalist".

In 1923, Bill MacAdams wrote a series of travel articles from South America for the *Imperial Oil Review* and was offered the post of editor. He turned it down and instead the company sent him to Calgary as a confidential land agent. In this capacity, he somehow became enthusiastic about the oil-producing potential of an area four miles south of the Royalite No. 4 well and tried to persuade the company to buy it. His enthusiasm was not shared by

Imperial's geological department, which believed the location was ruled out by a fault running through it: the rock beneath Turner Valley is full of faults and fractures and drilling there was always both difficult and chancy. To MacAdams' disgust, his recommended purchase was rejected.

No one seems to know where or when he met Jim Lowery. It might have been in Edmonton, because both were living there in 1912. Or they might have been introduced by another of Mac-Adams' sisters, a remarkable woman named Roberta who followed him out to the west in 1911. A graduate of the University of Chicago at a time when women did not normally pursue careers, Roberta taught school for a while, was then assigned by the Alberta government to establish Women's Institutes across the province, and when war broke out used her qualifications as a dietitian to become a lieutenant in the medical corps. Lowery certainly knew her overseas: he tried to date her once in England and she thought she was about to be propositioned, but it turned out he only wanted to borrow five dollars.

In the provincial election of 1917, Albertan servicemen overseas were given the right to elect three MLAS. Roberta was one of their choices and she and a well-known suffragette shared the distinction of being the first women to sit in the Alberta Legislature. While overseas, she had met Harvey S. Price, a Calgary lawyer serving as an officer in the engineers, whose background was similar to hers: he had emigrated to the west in 1911 from Ontario, where his father was publisher of the local newspaper at Gore Bay, on Manitoulin Island. Before Roberta's parliamentary career had really begun she abandoned it to marry Price and they tried their hand at farming in the Peace River district until 1921, when Price returned to Calgary and began to dabble in oil leases.

However they met, the friendship between MacAdams and Lowery soon became a close one—sufficiently so that when Lowery was visiting Calgary one day in 1924 MacAdams told him about the land Imperial had turned down, and his conviction that it would prove to hold oil. Lowery, of course, had no money to buy the land, let alone drill it for oil. But MacAdams put him in touch with his friend Fergus R. Macdonald in Vancouver, a consulting engineer and life-long promoter who was trying to get a toehold in the oil business and had already bought some leases in Alberta. Macdonald always had faith in his friend MacAdams' judgment and he was sufficiently impressed by Lowery's sales pitch to agree to help him form a company if they could get the rights to a likely-looking area. As an employee of Imperial Oil, of course, MacAdams could not associate himself with the project, but Price agreed to look around to see if any promising acreage was available, and Macdonald in Vancouver and Lowery in Alberta undertook to try to sell $500 "units" to finance its acquisition pending the incorporation of a company in which shares could be sold in the normal way. To get the ball rolling, Macdonald himself took the first five units, investing $2,500 in what was originally called the Price Oil Holding Syndicate.

By March 1925 Price had located two adjacent legal subdivisions,[1] a total of eighty acres, in the area suggested by MacAdams, the mineral rights to which were held by Alberta Pacific Consolidated Oils Ltd., one of the few companies formed in 1914 that survived and prospered. (Many years later, it became part of the present Norcen group of companies.) Officially the two parcels of land were described as LSDs 10 and 15, Section 20, Township 19, Range 2, West of the 5th Meridian, and Lowery checked them out with such experts as he could gain access to, including Stanley J. Davies, a British petroleum engineer who shortly afterward became the Dominion government's resident geologist in Alberta, and Dr. S. E. Slipper, a member of the Geological Survey who had done some early investigations in Turner Valley. Their verdicts were favourable and by June Price had negotiated a lease on the land for a down payment of $1,000 and an agreement to pay a further $5,000 later, plus an agreed percentage of shares in any company formed to drill them. He had already bought the surface and water rights to the western half of the acreage (for a payment that seems to have ultimately amounted to $5,800) from the estate of John Alexander Grant, a farmer who raised dairy cattle and Percheron horses and who had been killed in a traffic accident while driving a load of livestock into Calgary.

Also in June, Price drew up an agreement with British Petroleums Ltd.—a local company of that day, not the current British giant of similar name—covering the use of a heavy rotary drilling rig for a rental of $500 a month. This deal was negotiated by Robert L. Shaw, a Vancouver cigar manufacturer who was involved in the early days of the promotion but for some reason seems to have dropped out soon afterward.

The stage was thus set for the incorporation of the company, and no one was more eager to see it established than Jim Lowery. On June 15, 1925, he wrote to Fergie Macdonald and his brother and business partner, Bob: "I reached Calgary at 7:35 o'clock Saturday night and Bill [MacAdams] was out. He is the busiest man in Alberta today. He has Mr. McQueen [A. M. McQueen, then president of Royalite and a director of Imperial Oil from 1919 until his death in 1933] and others with him. However, I spent the big part of Sunday with him and we went over the whole situation. I was really surprised when he showed me what our location meant. It is plainly this, that without any qualifications we are the only ones outside of the Royalite who are on the structure [anticline] excepting the Spooner location up North where the Vulcan Oils are drilling but will never get down. . . ."

As the letter proceeds, Lowery's excitement mounts. After twenty years of seeking his fortune in the Golden West he clearly believes his moment has arrived: "If you had seen the map I saw, and had a talk with Bill you would understand as I do now that nothing in the World should stop us. We are made big if we go ahead. . . . My wildest hope was not that we were in so good. . . . You are aware that we can sell a fair amount of stock on the Prairies, but I think that you have a very good chance owing to your standing, and that we should raise $75,000 in your city. We must do it because we will never have this opportunity again. . . . I am endeavouring to raise some of the units here and am absolutely prepared to recommend to anyone in the World to put in their money even at the state it is in at the present time. We have to raise $5,000 and then we are an Oil Company and then we will not have to beg. . . ."

Thus inspired, Lowery was able to bring his latent promotional talents into play. If he had not yet made his fortune in the west, he *had* earned a reputation for absolute honesty and the men he now approached respected his shrewdness and realized he would not ask them to invest in any fly-by-night promotion. Six days later he wired Macdonald from Edmonton: "Have placed ten units with picked men here. . . ." Heading his list were the Hon. Vernon Smith, the province's Minister of Railways, and Senator P. E. "Pete" Lessard—in those days the participation of such public figures was considered not as a conflict of interest but an assurance that Lowery's scheme was a respectable one. E. T. Bishop, a lawyer, took two units; others went to a couple of doctors; Robert Jones, a consulting engineer; Mike Shaedy, a railroad contractor; and Joseph Van Wyck, manager of the Macdonald Hotel. At his end, Macdonald had started selling the units to a group of successful Vancouverites who shared a flutter with him from time to time, among them A. B. Palmer, another railroad contractor; several big lumber men, including R. P. Shannon; and A. R. "Sandy" Mann, owner of a large construction company.

As fast as the money came in Lowery, impatient to see his dreams come true, spent it. He hired a field superintendent, Kenneth Spence, and put him to work building a 122-foot derrick with lumber despatched from Vancouver by Macdonald, on a location selected by Stanley Davies. Lowery himself, still living in Edmonton but spending more and more time at the Palliser Hotel in Calgary, was desperately short of funds. George Cloakey, a veteran land man who spent a lifetime acquiring properties for oil companies, recalls driving him down to Section 20 with Davies because he lacked the money to rent a car.

The company upon whose behalf he was making all these exertions did not yet exist, but on July 10, 1925, the office of the Secretary of State in Ottawa issued letters patent sanctioning the incorporation of Home Oil Company Limited as a Dominion company, with an authorized capital of one million shares having a par value of $1 each.

It is not clear how the company's name was chosen. One version is that it was suggested by Roberta MacAdams. Another is that Bill MacAdams, Fergie Macdonald, and Lowery were considering the matter over drinks one evening and Lowery mused that when he was in the trenches the sweetest word of all to him was "Home". Whatever governed the choice, it can be assumed that none of the incorporators realized that no fewer than four Canadian oil companies, and at least one in the United States, had used the name before.

As early as 1873, a group of fifteen oil producers in Petrolia combined to open a refinery known as Home Oil Works, which was absorbed into Imperial Oil in 1881. Two companies calling themselves "Home Oil Company Limited" were formed later in Alberta, one in Calgary during the 1914 boom and the other in Medicine Hat in 1921. Yet another was incorporated in British Columbia in 1919. All had been struck off the register by 1924 without finding oil, and there is no evidence that any of their directors or shareholders were ever involved with the new claimant to the name. But many years later, when Jim Lowery's company had become the largest independent oil company in Canada, people cleaning out attics would occasionally come across "Home Oil" shares in an old trunk and for a short time—until Home's treasury department disillusioned them—would luxuriate in the mistaken belief that they had suddenly inherited a fortune.

With the derrick being built and a charter to hand, it was now time for the syndicate to recruit directors, get the company into business, and sell shares to raise the capital it would need—in those days it took about two years and cost a minimum of $50,000 to drill a well in Turner Valley. Lowery headed for Vancouver, where Macdonald introduced him to Stanley C. Burke, managing director of the investment and realty company Pemberton and Son. Burke, who was born in Cartwright, Manitoba, went to Vancouver in 1906 and rose to the summit of the city's business community. In his later years, as president of the Canadian branch of the Boeing Corporation during the Second World War, he supervised the building of Catalina flying boats in Vancouver and after the war went to Ottawa as one of "Minister of Everything" C. D. Howe's team of hotshot business leaders, his particular responsibility being to "oversee" the establishment of new industries in Canada.

In preparation for this important meeting, Lowery had written a four-page memorandum summarizing the history of the venture to that date, and after studying this and questioning Lowery personally, Burke took him along to see George S. Harrison, a banker who knew all there was to know about the financial standing of just about everybody in Vancouver. A dapper little man, never seen without his homburg, cane, and gloves, Harrison nevertheless had a deep, resonant voice that gave him a commanding air of authority. He had come to Vancouver from Manitoba to manage the local branch of the Winnipeg-based Union Bank of Canada and when the Union got into difficulties—through no fault of Harrison's —and was absorbed by the Royal Bank, he set up his own mortgage and insurance company, Guaranty Savings and Loan.

With a passion for tidiness of both mind and dress, Harrison was quite a contrast to Jim Lowery, whose mind tended to whirl from topic to topic with all the speed and unpredictability of a hummingbird and whose unruly red hair and rumpled suits often gave him the look of a small boy who has somehow had to dress himself for school without his mother's helping hand. But as a banker George Harrison had taken chances before on men who had good ideas but virtually no assets other than the energy and determination to make them pay off. Lowery's apparent sincerity and obvious conviction greatly impressed him, and he summoned some of the men he had backed and others among his wide circle of business acquaintances to an informal meeting in the august Vancouver Club. After Lowery had outlined Home Oil's brief history and limitless prospects, and Harrison had delivered his opinion that it was indeed a good speculative investment, the participants readily agreed that one of their number, W. C. Shelly, should visit Calgary to assess the situation in more detail.

William Curtis Shelly was the son of a baker at Jordan, Ontario, who had studied for the Baptist ministry in Missouri but then, disillusioned by what he considered to be too much carping among various religious sects, had gone to Vancouver and taken a job in his father's trade. Eventually he founded his own firm and with Harrison's backing prospered: Shelly's Four-X bread became a byword in the city and his immaculate vans drawn by prize horses were a feature of local parades and carnivals. When he undertook to visit Calgary he had plenty of money to invest, having recently sold his company to a national chain for $1.1 million. He reported the results of his investigation to Harrison on October 21 and his verdict was favourable. In fact he agreed to take 20,000 Home Oil shares himself and become the company's first president. Harrison agreed to become secretary-treasurer and Colonel Nelson Spencer, a lumber exporter, took on the vice-presidency. These three, with Lowery and Fergie Macdonald, were the original directors of Home Oil Co. Ltd. and they got together for their first board meeting in Vancouver on November 24, 1925.

By that time (in fact, before the formal incorporation of the company, which had taken place in Calgary on October 1) the leases obtained by Harvey Price had been signed over to Lowery, acting in trust for the Vancouver group. (There were rumours that Price and Lowery quarrelled, but if so the break was not permanent because they remained friends in later life. Another possible reason for Price's disappearance from the scene is that he was heavily involved at around the same time in a lease dispute that eventually led to litigation. He went on to form several other companies, one of them a predecessor to the present Western Decalta

Petroleum Ltd.) Lowery later assigned the leases to Home Oil in return for 75,000 shares, which seem to have been distributed among the original buyers of units to repay their investments—Lowery retained only a thousand shares for himself and a thousand for his wife, Ethel.

At their first meeting, the directors agreed to sell 200,000 shares to raise the capital needed for drilling. A further 120,000 shares were allotted to Alberta Pacific Consolidated to complete payment for the leases. The name of Bill MacAdams does not appear on any of the early lists of shareholders, though a notation on one of them might have referred to him: it shows Nelson Spencer as holding 9,000 shares "In trust, Bill". Certainly, while he never had any official connection with the company, MacAdams' advice was often sought subsequently and Lowery is reputed to have acknowledged his debt to him years later by giving him $100,000 out of his own pocket.

Stanley Burke, Macdonald, and a broker named Raymond S. Castle had been deputed to sell the 200,000 shares, at a commission of twenty-five per cent. Soon afterward, however, Castle surrendered his rights for a cash payment of $1,000 and was replaced on the selling group by Lowery. No public offering was made, perhaps because memories of the fleecing of the innocents in 1914 were still green in too many minds. But the members of the selling group were able to dispose of all the shares among their friends and business acquaintances. Lowery sold some, usually in 500 or 1,000 lots, to his old friends and partners like "Mike" Michaels in Edmonton, John Drew, who had worked in his store at Kitscoty, and Bill Cameron, a storekeeper in Lloydminster. But he also went after bigger game.

On January 5, 1926, he wrote to Macdonald from Calgary mentioning Pat Burns, the rancher who founded Burns Foods and became both a millionaire and a senator: "We arranged to meet in Vancouver on Monday next and he just wanted to give the money there and be one of the crowd. He knows all well and is pleased. It would have been bad for me to use the rush act on him here for his cheque but these are his words: 'Tell them you think Burns is coming in for $5,000.' . . . Burke wanted me to get Pat Burns so we will. . . . If I go on the train with him I can likely work out another five from his friends here or there. I saw him at his house and had a fine chat. Regarding R. B. Bennett, there were several good reasons why I did not approach him, which you will agree when I explain. . . . Am trying to get Fred Mannix, the big CPR contractor, but he lost a fortune last boom and has made a pile but working against his resolution not to play on anything whatever outside of his own line. [Mannix, founder of the nationally known construction firm that bears his name, now part of the huge family-owned Loram group of companies, did become a shareholder and director later.] We will get the $10,000 from Alberta and I will try for $15,000 by Saturday night. . . ." A later passage in the letter reflects Lowery's continuing financial plight. Explaining that he had drawn a $300 draft on Macdonald, he said: "I hope, Fergie, you will arrange this for me please as I had paid Kenny and the men and God knows where I would dig up three hundred easily. . . ."

Understandably, Macdonald and Burke were able to sell more shares in Vancouver than their hard-pressed partner could place on the Prairies, and the list of those who bought them reads like a guide to the city's establishment. To keep control of the infant company in their own hands, an inner circle grouped around the directors agreed to pool their shares in a voting-trust arrangement. Instead of receiving actual share certificates they received letters testifying that they owned so many shares, and the shares themselves were issued in the names of Nelson Spencer or George Harrison, as trustees, with the right to vote them. This arrangement achieved its aim of preventing any outsider from buying up enough stock to gain control of the company, but it led to some embarrassment within the inner circle a few years later.

The members of this circle were all interesting, hard-driving men, a surprising number of them entirely self-made, and they had at least two characteristics in common: enterprise and foresight. Fergie Macdonald, for instance, staked property in the area of the present Whistler Mountain resort in 1910, already confident it would one day be a skiing area. The son of a Lindsay, Ontario, railroad contractor who had worked in the west on the CPR, Fergie was taking engineering at the University of Toronto when he went to British Columbia on a survey crew in the summer of 1908. He was so impressed that he never went back to complete his course— an omission that does not seem to have hindered him in his life-long career as a consulting engineer and promoter of a long string of mining and lumber ventures. He always believed Vancouver would be "the New York of the west coast" and present-day Vancouverites might regret that one of his recommendations to the engineers who designed Lions Gate Bridge was ignored: he warned them it should be at least twice its present width.

Nelson Spencer was born in New Brunswick and worked in logging camps while still a boy. At the age of twenty-one he used his savings to put himself through business college and after working as a clerk for three years headed for Medicine Hat and opened a store. He was elected mayor of the city in 1911 and returned to the Alberta Legislature in the 1913 election that began Lowery's career as an MLA. After raising the 175th Battalion in 1915 he commanded it in France, where he was wounded and won the DSO for capturing an enemy machine-gun post. After the war, he pushed on further west and founded a company in Vancouver to export logs all over the world.

Other military men in the inner circle included General A. D. McRae, like Spencer a lumber man; General J. W. Stewart, a wealthy contractor; and Major-General Victor W. Odlum, who served in the Boer War and both world wars, was a newspaper publisher and diplomat at various times, and was destined to become a director of Home Oil in the thirties. Also destined to join the board later was William H. Malkin, a Staffordshire farm boy who emigrated to Saskatchewan at the age of sixteen, in 1884, and broke sod on the Prairies with a team of oxen. Eleven years later, after working for a while in a store, he arrived in Vancouver, bought a wagon and two horses, and founded a wholesale grocery business that eventually became one of the biggest in the city. As Mayor of Vancouver in 1929 and 1930, he sponsored a reorganization of the city's affairs that resulted in several municipal employees being jailed for graft. Interviewed on his eighty-first birthday, he said the second forty years of life were more fun than the first forty. And after surviving a downtown crash in his new Packard at the age of eighty-five, he died in 1959, aged ninety-one.

Among the other eminent and powerful Vancouverites who agreed to buy shares and join the pool were E. P. Davis, one of the city's leading solicitors; C. V. Cummings, a construction man; Chris Spencer, proprietor of a department-store chain and no relation to Nelson; A. L. Hager, who owned the Canadian Fishing Co. and worked so hard at it that he had two desks in his office; and Gordon Farrell, whose father had founded B.C. Telephones.

With the support of men like these, Burke, Macdonald, and Lowery were able to report to the board of directors on January 12, 1926, that they had now raised $127,400 and were willing themselves to underwrite the remaining shares, which would net the company $22,600 and bring its cash in hand up to the desired amount of $150,000—the proceeds of 200,000 shares sold for $1 each less 25 cents commission. Lowery could afford to join Burke and Macdonald in this underwriting, presumably, because he was about to receive his portion of the selling group's commission, which appears to have been 5,850 shares. Their offer having been accepted, the minutes of the meeting recorded that "the Board considers the company sufficiently financed to justify the company commencing business." After adding Cummings and Burke to the roster of directors the meeting adjourned until the next day, when James R. Lowery was named managing director of Home Oil Co. Ltd. at a salary of $400 per month.

CHAPTER FOUR

Home No. 1 Eclipses the "Wonder Well"

Soon after he invented tools early man probably began to use them to scrabble in the ground in search of a commodity even more vital to existence than petroleum is to the modern world. Water wells a thousand feet deep were dug by hand to provide irrigation in Mesopotamia 2,500 years ago. And the first attempts to bore into the ground with some form of drill were made in even earlier times: cylindrical holes up to twenty feet deep have been discovered in quarries used by the ancient Egyptians 3,000 years before Christ, and the remains of rock cores found nearby suggest that they were made by banging or rotating a hollow pipe into the stone—essentially the method used in drilling for oil today. Leonardo da Vinci sketched a well-boring apparatus incorporating an auger bit around 1500, and primitive tools based on his design used in Europe from the mid-1700s on led to the development of a diamond-coring drill in France in the 1860s which can be considered the true forerunner of the modern rotary drilling rig.

But Home Oil's No. 1 well—like most other oil wells in North America up to the 1920s—was drilled by a different system thought to have been used to bore for salt in China several centuries before Christ: the cable-tool rig.[1] The simplest way to describe the cable-tool drilling technique is to say that it involves repeatedly raising and dropping a heavy iron bit into the rock. A geologist named J. Ness apparently blessed with a whimsical cast of mind tried to explain the procedure to readers of the *Imperial Oil Review* in an article published in 1921:

"The initial proceeding in well drilling is to erect the rig or derrick. So much hangs on the derrick, metaphorically and actually, that we will . . . describe it in detail. . . . The derrick consists of four strong uprights or legs held in position by 'girts' and braces and resting on wooden sills which are levelled up and keyed together to form a sure foundation. The structure is generally of wood but latterly there has been a vogue for the all-steel derrick, which has the advantage of being more expensive. . . . Power is supplied through a portable locomotive boiler, the engine of 20–30 horse power being provided with reversing gears. The mechanism is so arranged that the driller controls the entire proceeding from the derrick, the boiler being placed at a safe distance to obviate danger of fire should gas or oil be struck.

"The lay mind may not grasp the intricacies of the proceeding but it is exceedingly simple, as the following will show. When drilling is going on, the band-wheel, which is in direct communication with the engine, confers motion to the walking-beam through a pitman, whilst the length of the stroke is adjusted by a crank having five holes to receive a moveable wrist-pin. While the tools are being raised the band-wheel transfers its influence to the bull-wheel, and if the sand pump is in use the efforts of a friction pulley divert its energy to that sphere. Should anything untoward happen to the walking-beam, it comes to rest on the headache post, whilst the driller probably does likewise.

"The drilling tools are suspended by a wire or untarred Manilla rope passing from the bull-wheel shaft over the crown pulley. The string of tools consists of two parts separated by jars, the lower part to give the downward blow and the upper part an upward blow which loosens the bit should it become jammed. . . . The experienced hand of the driller is ever on the wheel to control matters, his orders being conveyed to the engine by means of the 'telegraph', a wire attached to the throttle. He watches the 'jar' and his reputation as a driller hinges on his ability to read the signs supplied by the action of the walking-beam and the cable. By means of the temper-screw he keeps the bit in proper relation to the rock on which it is working, whilst all the time he nurses his crazy contraption along with an eerie certainty that would lead one to suspect that he actually saw what was transpiring at the bottom of the hole.

"The driller is not the type of a man to lead a dull and drab existence and fortunately his calling has provided him with a selection of accidents which add spice to his toil. The simplest method of raising the excitement is to lose the tools and go fishing. Not that he quits the job to follow Sir Izaak Walton; his fishing is done on the spot and consists of recovering the lost 'string'. For this there are special appliances which, strange to say, are never on the location. The driller, therefore, wires to headquarters for the necessary tackle and fills in the time of waiting by shooting craps, cleaning the boiler, or writing home to his mother. When the fishing tools do arrive they are usually unsuitable and are sent back, but eventually, under dire threats, he starts juggling with horn sockets, jar latches, boot jacks, spuds, mandrel sockets, rope-grabs, or other bait, and if the 'fish' proves willing, may finish the job in a month or a year or never. . . ."

It was into this stimulating, if bewildering, new environment that the managing director of Home Oil now plunged, and he revelled in it. As can be judged from Ness's account, cable-tool drillers, or "toolpushers", of the old school were tough, individualistic men of considerable accomplishment and resourcefulness, if a trifle unpolished by drawing-room standards. They directed the activities of a no less colourful and self-reliant group of rig workers, the "roughnecks", and were supported in their endeavours by a motley assortment of tool-sharpeners, blacksmiths, and "roustabouts", semi-skilled but inventive labourers who performed an infinite variety of more or less essential functions in the general vicinity of the rig.

In the 1920s, the normal work day in Turner Valley was twelve hours—longer when the frequent emergencies demanded. And since the standard wage hovered somewhere between $2 and $3 a day, the men lived in less than luxury, in camps at the well sites or as boarders on local farms. Later, they built two brawling shanty towns known, because of their free-and-easy lifestyles, as "Little Chicago" and "Little New York". (Little New York was on the site of the present village of Longview, some miles north of the EP Ranch, whose popular owner, the Prince of Wales, later became the Duke of Windsor; Little Chicago was later named "Royalties" and little now remains of either.) The custom was that as soon as a man found a job he would rent a small lot for perhaps $2 a month and hammer together an unlined wood or tarpaper shack often not much more than twelve feet square. For heating and cooking he would—unofficially, and usually surreptitiously—tap any nearby natural gas line, and the general lack of sophistication employed in making these connections led to more explosions and fires than would be tolerated by the most lax of modern municipal authorities. If a man prospered, he might then send for his wife, if he had one. If he hadn't, there were obliging souls around Little

Chicago and Little New York prepared to initiate other arrangements for him.

Having provided himself with knee-high field boots, riding breeches, and a stout work shirt, Jim Lowery now switched his energies from selling shares to supervising the multifarious activities at the well site. On February 4, 1926, he wrote to Macdonald from Calgary: "Came here with Harrison Thursday night and had the 'flu. Went to field Friday and kept going till Saturday night and then went to bed and have been there ever since. . . . Had bronchitis and nearly pneumonia but it's all broken now and feel fit. Kept busy all the time with the order and other work and had Kenny and all oil men coming day and night but got off the most complete and satisfactory order possible. . . ." The tools, rig irons, and casing (pipe sunk in the hole as it progresses) he had ordered were all assembled at the well site by the end of March, when the toolpusher he had hired arrived. He was an American named Sprague who had considerable experience in the oilfields of Wyoming and Montana, where the Kevin–Sunburst discovery in 1922, twenty miles or so south of the Canadian border, led to the drilling of more than a thousand wells during the next six years.

Home No. 1 was spudded in at the beginning of April 1926, and within a week an unexpected flow of water was struck at forty feet. Casing of twenty-four-inch diameter was cemented in the hole to cut off the flow and drilling resumed. By April 20 the well was down 115 feet and then on April 29, at 2 a.m., the drilling bit was lost. It was recovered by 10 a.m.—an efficient fishing job lasting only eight hours—but more trouble lay ahead. At 9 p.m. on Saturday, May 1, Sprague called Lowery in Calgary to tell him he had jumped a pin and lost the bit again, at about 178 feet. Lowery arrived at the well at 4 a.m.—Turner Valley was a long drive from town over treacherous roads in those days—and he seems to have stayed there for most of the following two weeks while the drilling crew struggled with a fishing job that ultimately lasted sixteen days.

Through the years, Jim Lowery learned a good deal about drilling for oil. But at that time he was still a tyro—and in the eyes of field superintendent Kenny Spence, at least, something of an unnecessary tyrant. Tempers around a drilling rig tend to become frayed during fishing jobs and at the height of an argument with Lowery around noon on May 12, Spence quit and stormed off the site. That evening he wired George Harrison in Vancouver saying: "With Lowery's continual interference I have no jurisdiction over operations stop Informed him this date I did not approve his methods and I was finished stop Mannix and Ferguson [Ira Ferguson, who ran an oil supply company] advised me wire you situation in field not satisfactory on account Lowery's attitude stop Parties mentioned as shareholders do not approve Lowery taking charge of outfit as he is entirely out of place stop Would suggest you confer with Fergus Macdonald who understands situation somewhat stop Wire me instructions here."

This was probably the first, but certainly not the last, occasion on which the Vancouver directors pondered with some nervous anxiety the activities of their self-assured managing director, who had nothing but impatient scorn for what are customarily referred to as normal channels. Harrison did talk to Macdonald, and next day Macdonald wired Bill MacAdams, who was in Toronto: "Rush wire are Jimmie and Spence essential to Home Oil stop They are at loggerheads and one or both must go." MacAdams' reply was succinct—and in the light of future events fortunate for the company with which he at no time appeared to have any official connection. "Circumstances regrettable," he wired back, "better keep Jimmie."

Drilling was resumed on May 19, but the rock formations through which Home No. 1 was penetrating were loose and unstable and the bit was soon lost again. Between then and June 10 the crew had to perform five more fishing jobs and the tension led to a dispute over procedure between Sprague and his assistant driller, Charles Nolan. Lowery consulted four geologists and some other drillers of his acquaintance and decided Nolan was right. Sprague had been in ill health anyway and so he was "given his time", in the terminology of the day. George Harrison and C. V. Cummings happened to be visiting Calgary at the time and they supported Lowery's suggestion that one of the best-known of the Turner Valley toolpushers, Chris Bennetsen, be hired to take over the job. Soon afterward, Bennetsen, a burly man whose chin frequently bore traces of the tobacco he chewed constantly on the job, came to the parting of the ways with Nolan, who was replaced by W. B. "Nick" Nicholson, an intense American whose practical accomplishments were such that the most ardently capitalistic oil men overlooked his regrettable predilection for Communism: during the Second World War his loquacity in support of the Soviet Union used to attract the scrutiny of the local constabulary and Jim Lowery several times interceded on his behalf, prompting Nicholson to remark, "If all employers were like you, Major, we wouldn't need Communism."

On June 12, the Major scrawled a hasty note in pencil to his friend Macdonald, apparently repaying a loan: "Enclosed please find draft for $205. The $5 is not interest but thought probably you might want to get a little Grant's Best on account of the fact that we were 535 feet deep at noon today." His letters to Macdonald around this time usually included information about other wells being drilled or projected in Turner Valley, assurances that various acreages held by Macdonald were "very, very valuable", and suggestions that Home Oil should pick up this or that lease.

On July 21, the board accepted one of these suggestions and took a half-interest in 4,700 acres in the Wainwright field, which had just been discovered 115 miles southeast of Edmonton. Nothing came of this deal—and indeed only five small wells had been brought into production in the area up to the outbreak of the Second World War, though the field was developed later and there are almost four hundred operating wells there now.

The first encouraging news came from Home No. 1 on August 19, when it struck "a very fine showing of amber-coloured oil" at a depth of 1,992 feet. (Oil as it comes from the ground can range across the spectrum from a light lemon colour, through deepening shades of green and brown, down to the black and sticky heavy oils.) Home Oil's president, Bill Shelly, and the immaculate Harrison promptly headed for the well and a conference with their managing director, and while they were there the crew bailed out oil at a rate that suggested a daily production of thirty-six barrels could be obtained.

Among others attracted to the scene were Dr. Oliver Hopkins, Imperial Oil's chief geologist for many years, and Charles Dingman, a nephew of the original Dingman who was at that time the Alberta government's petroleum engineer. The general verdict was that Home No. 1 was certain to become a commercial well, and Hopkins suggested it should enter the Mississippian limestone layer at about 3,700 feet. (The deepest well in the world at that time was the "Lake well" in West Virginia, 7,579 feet deep.) Shelly and Harrison supported Lowery in his desire to drill deeper, and a hundred feet further down another flow of oil was encountered, "a little greener in colour", which was described in a later report as "regular Pennsylvania crude oil". Bailing this time promised a production rate of only twenty-five barrels a day, so once again the drilling continued, heading for the limestone layer in which Royalite No. 4 had struck such a rich flow of gas.

Excited by these oil showings, which all took to confirm the prospects of the neighbourhood around Home's modest eighty acres, the board of directors readily acquiesced when Lowery suggested expanding. And on September 18 it sanctioned the purchase of LSD 14, the forty acres immediately west of its LSD 15, for $25,000 cash and 50,000 shares of Home Oil. LSD 14 was owned by the Advance Oil Co. Ltd., a company formed in 1925 which was never very successful and was finally dissolved in the early sixties; it came with two partly dug wells, the old Acme and the Advance No. 2. To finance the transaction, and provide more cash for operations, shareholders were offered the right to purchase one share at par for each five they held, and $55,000 was raised.

The Acme well, renamed Home No. 1A, had already been abandoned, but the Advance No. 2 (now renamed Home No. 2) was down almost to the level at which Home No. 1 had first struck oil, so it was decided to continue drilling. Oil was in fact encountered just below 2,000 feet, an encouraging sign, but since there was not enough of it to make its recovery commercially worth while drilling was suspended pending the satisfactory completion of Home No. 1, which by November was down 3,225 feet.

As the end of the first year of operations approached, George Hudson, the able and meticulous young man assigned by Harrison to keep Home Oil's books, was becoming desperate. For months now he had been sending funds to this Major Lowery in Calgary for "field expenditures", the nature of which were never entirely clear to him. Now it was time to prepare the company's annual financial statement and he had no idea what had happened to all the money, since Lowery had never bothered to account for it. Hudson appealed to Harrison, who summoned Lowery to Vancouver. He arrived early in December carrying a large cardboard box that bore the name of a Calgary tailoring establishment and apparently contained a suit. Instead, when the Major opened it triumphantly on Hudson's desk it proved to be crammed with scraps of paper: a jumble of almost illegible vouchers, receipts, invoices, and notes. Lowery was able to explain them all, and while it took Hudson and an auditor three weeks to sort out the mess, when they had finished the books balanced perfectly.

This was Hudson's first meeting with Lowery, but through the years he was to work closely with him, and like everyone else who knew him he would be constantly amazed that the possessor of such a quick mind and fertile imagination should be so evidently disorganized in so many ways. This peculiarity of Lowery's was most apparent in his speech, which sometimes lapsed into total incoherence. He seldom finished a sentence and even when he did he was given to jackrabbit leaps from one topic to another that left his hearers floundering in his wake. Even as a politician, his utterances had been considerably less than Churchillian. The story goes that once, asked to give a speech in a veterans' hall, he rose and said, "Boys, we've got to pull together. No hesitation. Well, I've got to be off now." The saying "No hesitation" was only one of his catch phrases. He often prefaced whatever he was about to say with, "Now, you take . . ." and then, after a thoughtful pause, tailed off into a series of incomprehensible non sequiturs. A group of directors amused by this inarticulateness once prevailed upon Hudson to make a verbatim note of the first thing Lowery said when he came into the office next morning. The result—"Now, George, you take . . . and . . . but . . . together with . . . and what we'll do . . ."

The general judgment was that Lowery's brain was always racing along formulating ideas faster than his tongue could enunciate them, and he was renowned for his ability to carry several topics in his head at one time. Once, talking on the long-distance telephone from his office in Calgary to a broker in Toronto, he was standing with his foot on the window-sill gazing outside when a dog darted out into the traffic. The broker, immersed in a discussion about oil wells, was startled to hear Lowery bellow, "Who the hell owns that damned dog?" and then go on talking as though nothing had happened.

On another occasion, in the lobby of the Palliser Hotel, Hudson overheard two men who had just left a business session with Lowery discussing their impressions. "I suppose it's a good deal," said one. "I'd trust Jim with my last penny. But I wish I knew what he was talking about." To an inveterate horse-trader, the idiosyncrasy probably was more of an asset than a handicap. Certainly

Lowery could be direct enough once he had made up his mind what he wanted to do—or when someone did something Lowery thought he shouldn't have done. But he was still a puzzle to many of his associates. Oliver Hopkins was once chairing a meeting of his subordinates at Imperial Oil when Lowery burst into the room and said, "Now Oliver, you take . . . and we'll . . . what do you say?" Hopkins turned to him blandly and said, "Okay, Jim, it's a deal." Lowery withdrew, beaming, and one of the men at the table asked Hopkins in wonderment, "What deal—how on earth could you understand what he was talking about?" Hopkins replied, "I couldn't—but I met Marsh Porter on the way up here and he explained it all to me."

Porter, a Calgary lawyer who later became a judge of the Alberta Court of Appeals, began to represent Home Oil in the thirties and eventually became one of its vice-presidents. He summed up Lowery in the Petroleum Club one day in a phrase that won wide acceptance among his friends. "Jim Lowery," he said, "has the worst-connected speech but the best-connected mind of anybody in the oil business."

During the early months of 1927 there was plenty to occupy that mind. When Lowery returned to Home No. 1 from his early December visit to Vancouver, he found the crew struggling against the elements—both above and below ground. As the heavy bit had crashed its way down past the 3,000-foot level an immense flow of gas had been encountered and there were signs that the sides of the open hole were beginning to cave in. It was decided it would have to be lined with ten-inch casing before drilling could continue and this job was proceeding at the rate of about one hundred feet of pipe a day when the weather turned nasty, as it often does in the Alberta foothills at that time of year.

Operations had to be shut down completely for two days when a blizzard blew powdery snow into the machinery, creating a grave risk that even with Bennetsen's experienced hand on the brakes a pulley belt might slip—a disastrous situation with seventy tons of steel pipe now dangling from the derrick. As a further complication, the flow of gas escaping from the hole was so strong that it twice lifted the tools ten feet up the well. On December 17, the crew lost the bailer and Bennetsen worked thirty-six hours straight on the fishing job—after which, to quote the well diary, "he was ready for the hospital". Some of the men wanted to return to their homes in Montana for the Christmas–New Year holiday anyway, so Lowery closed down the job on December 19.

It resumed on January 4 but a few days later, when the casing had been carried down to within seventeen feet of the bottom of the hole, Bennetsen suspected all was not well. With his driller's sixth sense he divined that the hole had broken through into an underground cave with a hard layer of rock as its floor. And whenever he dropped the bit it would bounce off sideways instead of penetrating the rock. One method of handling such situations was to fill up the bottom of the hole with rocks and any scrap metal that came to hand and re-drill the hole through that mixture to straighten it up. This was tried but after a few days it was clear it was not going to work. So Lowery agreed with Bennetsen's suggestion that the cave be filled with cement, which could be drilled through in the normal way once it had hardened. Forty bags of cement were required to fill six feet of hole, which would ordinarily have taken only ten bags. But the technique worked and by the beginning of March the cement had dried sufficiently for the drilling to be resumed.

There was another unpleasant shock in store, however. When the bit reached the 3,330-foot level Bennetsen recognized a change in the nature of the rock samples being brought to the surface. Lowery collected some of the samples and took them round to show to Stanley Davies and several geologists. Their verdict caused something close to panic and prompted Lowery to entrain for Vancouver and another conference with the directors. What had apparently happened, he explained, was that the well had crossed a fault at about 3,325 feet and was once again drilling through a layer of rock known as the Kootenay, which it had already passed through at about 2,700 feet. Hopkins had predicted that Home No. 1 would enter the limestone at 3,700 feet. Because of the fault, that estimate would have to be increased by perhaps 750 feet.

The company had by now spent almost $200,000 since its formation—a much more substantial sum fifty years ago than it sounds today. But if drilling was to continue, even more money was needed.

On such occasions in the early days it was customary for George Harrison to summon members of the inner circle to a dinner at the Georgia Hotel ("Canadian rules—each man to pay for himself") and sound out their willingness to become more deeply involved. Jim Lowery would often address these meetings himself, but the participants probably received more enlightenment from prominent oil experts he would invite along from time to time.

At one such meeting in April, the shareholders present supported the board's plan to make a new offering of shares—again to be taken up on the basis of one new share at par (one dollar) for each five shares held. As an inducement to subscribe to the issue, shareholders were offered a bonus in the form of an option to take up an equal amount of stock at par at any time during the succeeding year. As George Harrison's letter putting the offer to the shareholders said, "This option will be of very considerable value if our well comes in, as is confidently expected."

The issue raised $76,000 for the further drilling but for a while there seemed to be little happening to justify the confidence expressed by Harrison: at the end of May, Fergie Macdonald received a letter from a friend in Calgary saying, "There is no doubt in anyone's mind but that the Home is sitting on top of a large pool of oil and will reach it unless the Major and the crew die of old age." Throughout April and May, however, the drilling had been progressing at the steady, if unspectacular, rate of one hundred feet of new hole and one hundred feet of casing a week. By the beginning of June, the bit was 4,500 feet down in the earth.

It was now the middle of 1927, more than two years since Jim Lowery had been introduced to the oil business by Bill MacAdams; the company had been in existence for almost as long; and the drillers had been at work for more than fourteen months. All this patience was rewarded on June 9, at 4,565 feet, when in the words of the well diary: "The well blew in at 5:50 in the afternoon and at 6:10 it blew pieces of rock over the derrick, some falling at a distance of over 250 feet. . . ."

Ecstatic, Lowery telephoned Harrison immediately from the well site and fired off telegrams to the other directors. Harrison, Shelly, Stanley Burke, Nelson Spencer, General Stewart, Pat Burns—all headed for the well as fast as they could make it. C. V. Cummings even cut short a business trip to Quebec to be in on the excitement. By the time they arrived, the initial flow of almost ten million cubic feet of wet gas per day had tapered off somewhat but the well was yielding about thirty barrels of crude oil a day, which was being collected by an improvised drip apparatus.

After a week of celebration and mutual congratulation in Calgary, Lowery and his fellow directors took train for Vancouver and a meeting of shareholders called at the Georgia Hotel for June 27. Bill Shelly showed "moving pictures" he had taken at the well site and Lowery and Harrison brought the shareholders up to date on developments. And next day, the board allotted 2,000 shares of Home Oil to be divided among the crew as Lowery saw fit, and voted the Major himself a bonus of $500.

George Harrison returned to Calgary with Lowery at the beginning of July and for the rest of that month there were frequent visits to the well site by various directors, often accompanied by Hopkins or other officials of Imperial Oil. The reason for these visits became apparent in August, when it was decided that henceforth Imperial would take over the exploration of all Home's property and the drilling and operation of its wells. Under the agreement, Home retained all the revenue from the No. 1 well (which amounted to $14,568 by the end of the year, even though August was so wet that the oil trucks were often unable to negotiate the primitive roads to Okotoks). Imperial, it was agreed, would recover all its costs, plus ten per cent, from the gas, oil, or naphtha produced by any new wells it brought in. And Imperial agreed to buy all production from the Home wells "at the highest prices prevailing". Sam Coultis, of Royalite and Imperial, took over the operation of Home No. 1 on September 1 and a few days later drilling was resumed on the No. 2 well, inherited from the Advance, and preparations began for two new wells.

By now, Home owned two hundred acres of Section 20, having bought LSDS 2 and 7, immediately south of the Home No. 1 well, from Alberta Pacific Consolidated. The total payment for the four legal subdivisions bought by Home seems ultimately to have amounted to $200,000 and 150,000 Home Oil shares. In a letter to the shareholders explaining these deals, George Harrison wrote, "Dr Hopkins . . . estimates our 200 acres will carry from 10 to 20 wells—drilling only can determine. . . . If at all favourable results accrue to expert operations, our revenues should within a reasonable time be quite substantial, and we are in the happy position of having no more operating outlay. Might we outline a reasonable probability, without being charged with undue optimism? If we get half the number of wells contemplated by geologists, each half as good as Royalite No. 4, can you visualize what our revenues will be?"

Imperial negotiated similar contracts with a dozen or so smaller independent companies in Turner Valley between the wars, but the terms secured by Home were considered to be particularly favourable and in October the directors voted to reward with 50,000 shares the man credited with negotiating them, who, while not one of the original shareholders of Home, soon joined its inner circle.

Austin C. Taylor was born in Toronto in 1888 and went to work at the age of seventeen in a carriage factory owned by his father. At the beginning of the First World War, though still only twenty-six, he was general manager of Montreal Locomotive Works and sufficiently established to become a dollar-a-year man for Ottawa, at first supervising the production of artillery shells in eastern Canada and later organizing the supply of B.C. spruce needed to build British war planes. His prodigious success in this task created a substantial but short-lived industry in British Columbia: several thousand men were thrown out of work when the armistice cut off the market for the product of their labour.

Taylor liked the west and after the war he settled in Vancouver, where he devoted his energies to mining and other promotions. His most spectacular venture was probably Bralorne Mines Ltd., which he organized in 1931 to explore some unproved claims in the Bridge River area, about one hundred miles north of Vancouver, where he eventually developed the biggest gold mine in British Columbia. He was president of Bralorne until 1958, by which time the company had produced $64 million worth of gold. As a dollar-a-year man again during the Second World War, he organized the controversial removal of Japanese Canadians from the west coast and ran the wartime company that built Victory ships in five west-coast yards. He was well-known as a racehorse breeder and philanthropist and when he died in 1965 he left assets of more than $10 million.

Taylor does not seem to have played any role in the formation of Home Oil, so it is not clear how or why he was enlisted to conduct the negotiations with Imperial; probably it was because he had a major interest in an oil company called Sterling Pacific, whose wells south of the Home leases were also operated by Imperial. Home was obviously grateful for his help, though there were some who considered his allotment of 50,000 shares too generous, particularly since at one stage the negotiations seemed to be bogged down until Lowery, who had by now established a close relationship with the Imperial executives himself, entered the lists and had a session with

R. B. Bennett, Oliver Hopkins, and Jack McLeod, Imperial's manager in Alberta.

Company directors in those days lived by much more cosy rules than those considered ethical, and indeed enforced by law, today. At around this same time, the Home Oil directors voted themselves 18,000 shares as recompense for "the immense amount of work and responsibility assumed, undertaken and carried through by the directors in the interests of the company". (The only other remuneration the directors received was a ten-dollar gold piece set down by George Harrison at each place around the table before a board meeting; and if a tardy director arrived after the meeting had begun he would find Harrison had removed the ten-dollar piece and replaced it with a five-dollar piece.) A few months later, in April 1928, the Board set aside 7,500 shares to be offered to selected buyers at par "on account of services rendered to the company". First listed on the Curb market in Toronto in 1928, Home's one-dollar shares sold for a low of $2.25 and a high of $4 during the year. Among those thus presented with the opportunity to more than double their money overnight were Jack McLeod of Imperial, who was offered 1,000 shares at par, and Alberta premier John Brownlee, who headed a list of dignitaries offered 500 shares each.

While the services rendered in return for this offer were not detailed in the company's minute book, and such transactions would clearly be considered scandalous today, the members of the inner circle of Home Oil at the time were men of the highest reputation, at the summit of the Vancouver establishment, and they were merely following what was normal corporate practice in the years before the Great Crash of 1929, and for long afterward: current rules such as those governing "insider" trading in a company's stock are only a recent innovation.

At around the same time as he interceded with Imperial on Home's behalf, Austin Taylor and the Home directors co-operated in another venture which led to some confusion in western minds through the years: the establishment by Taylor of a refining and distributing company in Vancouver called Home Oil Distributors Ltd. Not unnaturally in view of its name, this was reported in the press at the time, and considered by the public for many years thereafter, to be a subsidiary of Home Oil Co. Ltd. But the connection between the two companies never seems to have amounted to much more than the similarity of their names and what appears to have been a token representation of Home Oil directors on the Distributors' board.

George Hudson, who had by this time become assistant secretary of Home, recalls that in 1927 Jim Lowery talked about forming a company to sell gasoline in Vancouver and discussed the idea with A. M. McQueen of Imperial. Perhaps, as on several later occasions, Lowery's fellow directors were unwilling to go along with their managing director's ambitious schemes. If such were the case, Austin Taylor certainly did not share their qualms. Hudson recalls that Taylor also went east to see McQueen, and in October 1927 the Home Oil minutes recorded the election of a committee consisting of Lowery, Harrison, and Cummings "to negotiate with Austin C. Taylor with regard to the participation of this Company in a plan for the formation of a distributing company". The board stipulated that the committee must not "on behalf of this Company incur any financial responsibility in respect of such distributing company", but it agreed that the proposed company might use "the name Home Oil Limited or other similar name".

When Taylor's company was incorporated in January 1928, Home Oil's "financial responsibility" was indeed limited: it paid fifty dollars for fifty special shares which entitled it to twenty-five per cent of Distributors' net profit and twenty-five per cent of any appreciation in the value of its assets. One theory for Home Oil's involvement in the venture is that Taylor wanted to exploit its name. If so, this seems an extremely generous payment for whatever "recognition value" attached to a fairly new company with only one small producing well. Another theory is that Distributors was originally intended to be the marketing arm of Home, but it seems improbable that at that early stage the company would have contemplated entering the refinery business and becoming an "integrated" company—especially since it had agreed to sell all its production to Imperial.

The reason for Home Oil's participation in the deal at all thus remains obscure, and in fact Lowery's personal connection with the new company appears to have been closer than Home's: he was named its secretary-treasurer. And when Distributors bought out Blue Star Oil Ltd., a company with a modest chain of service stations, Taylor and Lowery were both listed as directors of Blue Star.

Home Oil Distributors Ltd. opened quite literally with a bang:

it advertised its advent on the city's scene with a display of fireworks outside the Hotel Vancouver. And within a couple of years
its imaginative marketing program had made the name "Home" a
familiar one on the west coast: there were dance performances by
touring Alberta Indians in full feather; model-aeroplane giveaways
to children; the "Home Gas Hour of Music" in Stanley Park on
Sunday afternoons; and a series of radio concerts so popular that
when Distributors found their $1,100-a-month cost too much to
bear in the Depression year of 1930 and cancelled them there was
a storm of public protest. By 1930, Taylor's company was the third-
largest retailer of gasoline and home heating oil in British Columbia—after Imperial Oil and Shell—with a chain of several hundred
service stations on land and twenty marine stations between Vancouver and Prince Rupert.

Lowery's association with the company—at least formally—did
not last long: he resigned three months after its formation. And
while three of Home Oil's directors continued to sit on Distributors'
board for the next few years, the company received no revenue
from its fifty special shares—because Distributors paid no dividends. As Home Oil's annual report for 1931 said: "It must be
borne in mind that the past year has been a strenuous one for all
commercial enterprises, and the Home Oil Distributors Ltd. has
been called upon to bear its share of adverse conditions."

The question of securing an accounting from Distributors arose
several times at Home Oil board meetings during succeeding years
until on January 14, 1935, George Harrison reported that Taylor
had signified his willingness to buy out Home's interest in his company. After auditors appointed by both companies had assessed
the situation it was decided Home's $50 investment was now worth
$50,000. This was apparently a higher sum than Taylor had con-
templated: after a committee of Home's directors that included
R. H. B. "Bobby" Ker had bargained him up to $66,000—a sum
promptly accepted by the rest of the board—Taylor walked into
the Vancouver Club that evening, spotted Ker, and grumbled, "You
cost me $40,000 this afternoon."

The two companies were totally separate from then on. Distributors withstood both the payment to Home Oil and the Depression and continued to grow, though in 1937 Taylor sold his shares
to Imperial and it became a wholly owned Imperial subsidiary—
adding strength to the common belief within the industry that Im-

perial had backed it since the beginning. "Home" signs continued to shine above Distributors' service stations in British Columbia— sometimes right across the street from competitors advertising Imperial's "Esso" brand—until early 1976, when Imperial announced they would henceforth fly the "Esso" flag and Distributors would concentrate on the home-heating market.

Lowery's involvement with Distributors did not lessen his interest in the Turner Valley drilling and in June 1928 he reported to the board that the production of Home No. 1 was falling off. The well, he explained, had not yet reached the Mississippian limestone tapped by Royalite No. 4 and was producing, though modestly, from a layer of rock geologists had named the "Home sand". The directors accepted his recommendation that Imperial be asked to deepen it, and drilling resumed on August 11. The limestone was reached in November, at 5,106 feet, and a substantial quantity of gas rich in naphtha was struck about thirty feet deeper. This created a danger that the cable tools still being used might be frozen in the hole, so Imperial switched to a rotary diamond-drill rig. And the bonanza everyone had been waiting for came at midnight on Saturday, February 9, in that fateful year for the whole business world, 1929.

At 5,280 feet—more than 1,500 feet deeper than the level at which Royalite No. 4 had struck it rich—the drillers encountered a heavy gas flow. The crew worked on through the night to connect the well to separators designed to extract the naphtha from the gas, and at nine a.m. on Sunday the flow was measured at seventeen million cubic feet per day of wetter gas than any previously found in Turner Valley. Within days the well "drilled itself" further and the flow increased to twenty-two million cubic feet—a million more than the output that had earned Royalite No. 4 the nickname "Wonder Well". This huge flow yielded between 500 and 600 barrels of high-grade naphtha per day, worth from $3.50 to $4 per barrel at the Calgary refinery. Home Oil Co. Ltd. was now the proud possessor of the biggest well in Turner Valley.

By coincidence, the Calgary Stock Exchange held its annual banquet a few days later. Its menu celebrated the newest boom in Alberta oil by listing, along with the roast turkey, naphtha consommé, Turner Valley potatoes, and Home apple pie à la Royalite. More edifying still to Jim Lowery and his fellow directors was the performance of Home shares on the Calgary and other exchanges.

Having closed at $3.45 in Vancouver before the weekend of Home No. 1's strike, they had more than doubled, to $7.50, by the time the Toronto Exchange closed on Monday. By the end of the month they had reached $15. And even more spectacular things were in store.

CHAPTER FIVE

The Major Makes a
Million-Dollar Deal

The board of directors of Home Oil Co. Ltd. met in Vancouver on March 5, 1929, with feelings of both satisfaction and pleasurable anticipation. Home shares were still rising on the market—535 changed hands in Calgary that day at $18. Imperial Oil was in the process of moving its diamond drill to begin the deepening of Home No. 2—and since No. 2 had sold slightly more oil during 1928 than No. 1, who could tell what new thrills were in store when it, too, reached the lime? And now Nelson Spencer had just returned from Calgary and called this meeting to discuss what promised to be the most audacious proposition yet advanced by that man Lowery.

The meeting had been summoned so hastily that only four directors were on hand. Bill Shelly had been appointed Minister of Finance in British Columbia's Conservative government and so could seldom attend meetings. As vice-president, Spencer took his place in the chair. The others around the table were Stanley Burke, Bobby Ker, a young man with a flourishing real-estate and insurance business on Vancouver Island and interests in grain mills on the mainland inherited from his father, and J. W. de B. Farris, a prominent Vancouver lawyer who later became Chief Justice of the B.C. Supreme Court. They listened with interest as Colonel Spencer outlined Lowery's suggestion: he wanted to buy the four legal subdivisions adjoining Home's property on the east—a vertical strip of land a mile long by a quarter-mile wide—from United Oils Ltd., a company whose beginnings dated back to before the Dingman discovery well in Turner Valley. This seemed to make sense, in view of Home's success on Section 20, but Burke and the others exchanged incredulous glances when they heard what Lowery was prepared to pay: nothing less than a million dollars.

Home Oil, of course, did not have $1 million, or anything like it. But, Spencer explained, Lowery already had a firm offer of $1 million for 50,000 treasury shares of Home from a Montreal broker and promoter named I. W. C. Solloway, who had in the past couple of years made waves in Canadian financial circles by opening a string of busy brokerage offices right across the country. The minutes of the meeting do not record any discussion on this point, but the directors undoubtedly would have asked why Solloway was prepared to pay $20 for shares selling that day for $18. And Spencer presumably gave them the explanation that Lowery always gave for the deal in later years: that Solloway, following a custom that was widespread in those days and is not altogether unknown today, had gone "short" on Home shares. In other words, expecting the market to break after such a steep and sudden rise in prices, he had sold far more shares of Home than he had available, confident that when the time came to deliver them to their buyers he would be able to turn a quick profit by picking them up cheap on a falling market. Since the price had continued to rise—and would no doubt rise even more if he had to start buying shares in quantity on the open market—he faced a heavy loss if he was to meet his obligations.

A transaction such as this obviously needed the sanction of more than the four directors present at the meeting, so Burke and Ker were assigned to go to Victoria immediately to discuss it with Shelly, and George Harrison agreed to consult the chairman of the board, General Stewart, and W. H. Malkin, in Vancouver. All must have agreed to sell Solloway the shares, and Lowery must have been given the go-ahead by telephone, because two days later he closed the land deal at the agreed price. It was approved by the United board the same day, and by the Home board two days later, on March 9.

Through the years—thanks to that magic $1 million figure—this deal has become a legendary one in Alberta oil circles and several versions of "the story behind the story" have been given currency. Lowery negotiated it with Robert Arthur Brown, head of Calgary's "street railway" and a director of United Oils, whose eldest son, twenty-two years into the future, would take over the company Lowery had created and push it to new heights.

Probably the most commonly accepted version of the episode is that in a classic contest between masterly horse-traders Brown simply outmanoeuvred Lowery: that Lowery originally offered $500,000 for the land—far more than a surprised Fred Green, president of United, had expected; that Green would have closed the deal then and there but Brown asked him to step outside the room to discuss it; and that Brown told Green, "Leave it to me," went back in and bluffed Lowery up to the $1 million figure. That may have been so—but Lowery was a pretty shrewd bargainer himself: he already knew he had his million in the bag, so to speak; and thanks to the news from Home No. 1 choice land in Turner Valley was reported to be fetching $10,000 an acre, which made $1 million for 160 acres something of a bargain.

Another version of the story is that Brown and Lowery got together with Solloway and cooked up the deal to grab the headlines and give the shares of both companies a much-needed boost. There are several weaknesses to this version, perhaps the most telling being that when Lowery closed the deal Home's shares had already quintupled in value in less than a month, thanks to the genuine success of Home No. 1, and United was also rising on the crest of a wave of renewed enthusiasm for Turner Valley oil issues generally. On March 14, for instance, the Calgary Stock Exchange was closed to give brokers' offices time to catch up with a record-breaking surge of business sparked by a Regent Oil Company discovery the day before. Also, had Lowery's desire been merely to keep the pot bubbling he might have been expected to summon the reporters and give them the story right away. Instead he waited almost two weeks, until March 19, before making any public announcement, and even then he refused to confirm the magic $1 million purchase price he was supposedly trying to exploit. By that time the crest of the wave had broken: Home shares on March 15 had reached a high of $29 before sinking back to $26.50 at the close; in spite of Lowery's announcement four days later, neither figure was reached again for many years. Another weakness of this version of the story is that while Lowery undoubtedly did speculate in shares of companies he formed—at least until he was badly burned in 1929—this was not the way R. A. Brown, Sr., operated: in succeeding years he and his son founded more than thirty-five separate oil companies, and almost every one of them was financed privately, with no issue of shares to the public at all.

Yet another theory advanced to explain the "million-dollar deal" is that Solloway wanted the 50,000 shares to "make a market"—to force up the price by buying and selling to himself. But by this time there were more than 800,000 shares of Home Oil outstanding, widely dispersed among thousands of ordinary shareholders across the country, so it seems unlikely that a block of only 50,000 shares would have been large enough to enable Solloway to control the market. And while the Home directors might have agreed to sell him the 50,000 shares to rescue him from a "short" position, it is hardly likely that as respectable pillars of society with nothing to gain from the transaction they would have knowingly risked their reputations by participating in an illegal "wash-trading" operation.

Whatever the real reason for the deal, it benefited United more than Home: Solloway's million dollars was distributed to United's shareholders as a special dividend but the only well drilled by Home on the property, Home No. 7, was abandoned the following year without finding oil. At that, the Home directors probably considered themselves lucky: they undoubtedly heaved a collective sigh of relief that Home Oil was not involved in any way when Solloway and his partner Harvey Mills were arrested in January 1930 on fraud warrants issued by the Alberta attorney general.

A transplanted Englishman, Solloway had prospected in Northern Ontario before opening his brokerage business in the mid-twenties with money provided by Mills, the proprietor of a cigar store in Buffalo, New York, who liked to fish in Canada and had occasionally grub-staked prospectors he met in the bush. In a couple of books he had printed privately in the thirties, Solloway expounded a philosophy of Canadian business nationalism that sounds more familiar today than it did then, and the brokerage offices he opened across the country—in 1929 his Calgary office occupied four floors in a downtown building and employed 115 people—were ostensibly designed to permit ordinary Canadians to participate in the development of Canada's rich natural resources: it was Solloway's theme even then that too much of the profit therefrom was going to U.S. investors.

Before the universal disillusionment of the 1929 stock-market crash there was a rather fine line between normal brokerage practices and out-and-out "bucket-shop" operations: ten well-respected Toronto brokers were arrested soon after the Alberta authorities launched their proceedings against Solloway and Mills. Not that all the money so hopefully "invested" by ordinary citizens pursuing the mirage of instant riches went into the pockets of crooked promoters and fly-by-night market operators: some was used to develop mines and other ventures that still provide employment years later. Solloway himself, for instance, financed the first transportation system on the Mackenzie River and formed a company known as Commercial Airlines,which, with Canada's First World War flying ace Captain W. R. "Wop" May as its chief pilot, pioneered airmail flights in the Canadian north.

A remarkable blend of visionary and "operator", Solloway had an uncanny ability to "see down the road", as the saying has it: he begged his biggest accounts to sell out before the 1929 crash, but such is human nature that few of them heeded his warning. He was able to safeguard his own fortune—he lived in style in a Westmount mansion—and after serving his four-month jail sentence and paying the $225,000 fine imposed on him for conspiracy to defraud the public, he lived out his remaining years in comfort. He died in Vancouver in 1965. It is possible to feel a twinge of sympathy for the hapless Mills, who also went to jail: when the trouble began and Solloway was trying desperately to balance his books, he telephoned Mills in Calgary and asked him, "How much stock do we have on hand out there?" Mills replied, "About two truckloads."

Those who knew Jim Lowery best doubt that he was fully aware of all the ramifications of Solloway's *modus operandi*. Certainly he was not naive enough to think that everybody won on the stock market. But he referred to the money invested by purchasers of speculative shares as "mad money" and often said "mad money" was essential to develop Canada because the "pawnbroker types"—by which he meant bankers—didn't have the courage to take risks. He was not alone in this belief. Even before the 1929 crash it was difficult to persuade those who controlled large pools of capital in eastern Canada to invest some of it in western oil development—after the crash, and until long after the Second World War, it was almost impossible.

As a writer in *Maclean's* magazine said in May 1929: "Unfortunately, Canada lags behind in the oil industry. Each year more and more of this valuable commodity is brought into the country. Last year the imports were 680 million gallons of crude oil alone. This enormous trade puts millions of dollars annually into the pockets of foreign operators, while our own oil districts lie waiting for more intensive drilling. Western Canada is the greatest undeveloped oil region in North America, where, in the opinion of many authorities, the next great world movement in oil development will occur. A few fortunes have already been made in Turner Valley, but if instead of spending $50,000,000 annually for imported oil,[1] Canada would invest some of that money in the development of her own petroleum fields, many more fortunes would be made and the country would be enormously benefited by a developed oil industry which would follow upon the investment of Canadian funds in Canadian fields."

The article summed up Lowery's sentiments very well, and though there is no way of knowing whether he was one of the sources consulted by the author, he might well have been: for Major J. R. Lowery was now acknowledged as a leading figure in the oil business, as well-known and respected in the financial circles of Montreal and Toronto as he was in Calgary and Turner Valley. His suits still had a tendency to rumple and his eyes retained the boyish twinkle they had held when he was "going at the ball game" in Frankford, but he was widely considered to be a millionaire, and certainly lived like one. He loved big cars—though his driving style used to terrify all who travelled with him—and he enjoyed startling salesmen by fishing a huge roll of bills out of his pocket and paying for them in cash. He had a seven-passenger Cadillac in Vancouver, where he bought a house in 1928; in Calgary he drove a Packard (which was not simply ostentation: its high clearance often enabled him to negotiate the unpaved roads in Turner Valley when others couldn't); and he kept a Stutz Bearcat (with leather body by Fisher) at his parents' home in Frankford, for use on his frequent visits to the east, not minding in the least when his younger brother Harold—"Bid" Lowery, who later became Home's field manager in Turner Valley—borrowed it to go courting.

Jim Lowery loved to throw expensive parties, and once took a group of business acquaintances and their wives to New York, where he not only paid all their bills at the Roosevelt Hotel but escorted the ladies to Saks and genially insisted that they buy themselves presents, discreetly setting the upper limit for their purchases by presenting his wife with an ermine-trimmed black velvet coat. He favoured the King Edward Hotel in Toronto and the Windsor in Montreal and never checked out of either without bestowing ten-dollar bills on their head waiters and bell captains. At one of his parties, for which he took over the King Edward's opulently chandeliered ballroom and imported an orchestra from New York, his younger sister Thelma was enthralled to find herself being swept around the floor by Captain Plunkett, of the celebrated wartime concert party, the Dumbells.

Lowery's generosity was genuine and not deviously designed to purchase loyalty or favours. While his gifts were sometimes expensive prints or antique china, his friends were just as likely to receive a can of salmon in the mail: having run across a particular brand he liked Lowery would want everyone to sample it. And, always proud of his heritage, he would seldom visit the east without despatching a good Ontario cheese to some friend out west who might have betrayed an unwitting lack of understanding of its excellence.

Some time in 1928 or 1929, Lowery packed his wife and daughter, his sister Thelma, and "Bid" and his bride into the Cadillac and set off to tour North America, starting out from Campbell River, "the salmon-fishing capital of the world". Striking south from there down the coast of Vancouver Island, they came to a pretty little place Lowery had never heard of called Qualicum Beach—and got no further. Lowery checked them all into the local hotel and immediately began to make arrangements to build a large log house in the village he loved for the rest of his life: eventually he owned five houses there, which he crammed to the attics with antiques, his hedge against inflation after the unhappy events of 1929 convinced him that "things" were more reliably marketable than paper.

Little, if any, of the money that flowed in to finance this expansive lifestyle came from Home Oil: Lowery never at any time owned much stock in the company, often explaining to friends that if he did, it might impair his objectivity when, as managing director, he was trying to judge what was best for the shareholders. This unusual business philosophy did not extend to the affairs of several other oil companies he founded in the late twenties, from all of which he took shares in exchange for leases, selling them later at a gratifying profit on the crazily spiralling stock market.

Perhaps he felt he should have received a larger allotment of shares for himself from Home Oil, but at any rate once that company was financed and in business he lost no time in founding the first of his other companies: Associated Oil and Gas Ltd. was incorporated on April 7, 1926, just a few days after the newly appointed managing director of Home Oil had supervised the spudding-in of Home No. 1. Chris Spencer, the Vancouver department-store owner who was also a director of Home, agreed to serve as its president and Lowery was once again appointed managing director. Associated eventually brought in two wells on eighty acres of Section 20 adjoining the Home leases. In 1929 its shares were selling for $4.90 and it had more than 3,000 shareholders across the country.

Lowery's next company appears to have been Baltac Oils Ltd., incorporated in 1928, which brought in one well on Section 20 and had Fred Green of United Oils as president and Lowery as one of the directors. Finally, in March 1929—just after Home's "million-dollar deal" with United—he founded a company under his own name: Lowery Petroleums Ltd. This time, Lowery was president and general manager (and remained so until the company was sold to an Imperial subsidiary in 1939 for $300,000) and the list of his directors testified to the high-level contacts he had so quickly made in the east. As well as Pat Burns and the publisher George Melrose Bell from Calgary, and Cummings, Ker, General Stewart, and Nelson Spencer from Vancouver, it included a former prime minister, Arthur Meighen (who later became a director of Home Oil, also); two well-known Toronto stockbrokers, Manning W. Doherty and Thomas Roadhouse; and two millionaires from Montreal, Lorne Webster and Senator Donat Raymond.

Among those who shared an interest with Lowery in the acreages that went into all three companies were three of his friends: William Douglas Lundy and Ernest A. Freeman—who owned a large Chrysler dealership and repair business in downtown Calgary—and Bill MacAdams. All three companies had drilling and operating contracts with Imperial Oil, similar to the one negotiated by Home, and all were later absorbed by Imperial. And once having promoted them and sold their shares, Lowery left them to run themselves and continued to devote most of his time to Home Oil business, which during the summer of 1929 was mainly concerned with plans for a merger with the Winnipeg-based Calgary and Edmonton Corporation. C. & E., as it was known, was an outgrowth of a company formed with British capital in 1890 to build a railroad between Calgary and Edmonton, in return for which it received two large blocks of land: one running from the south end of Turner Valley to the U.S. border and the other north of Calgary. The company perspicaciously retained the mineral rights when it sold the land to settlers, so by the late 1920s, when the negotiations with Home began, it was sitting on 1,150,000 acres of potential oil property.

In anticipation of the merger, Home Oil applied for a new charter, under its own name but increasing its capitalization to ten million shares, which it planned to distribute in equal proportions to the shareholders of both companies. At around the same time, however, a Vancouver group entirely separate from the Home inner circle had also recognized the potential value of the c. & e. acreage and had begun to buy up its shares from Britons who perhaps had not heard of the developments in Turner Valley. Eventually, c. & e. was split into two: the old company, based in England, which received the surface rights to the c. & e. land and continued to collect the mortgage payments made by the farmers who had bought it,[2] and the new c. & e. Corporation, which retained the mineral rights and went into the oil business itself.

Probably because of this development, the merger negotiations collapsed at the last moment, but by that time Home had received its new charter. So while the present Home Oil Co. Ltd. dates officially from 1929, the only material change that took place was from the original capitalization of one million shares with a par value of one dollar to three million shares with no par value (the application for ten million shares having been scaled down after the merger fell through). The board of directors remained the same and Home shareholders merely received one share of the new company for each share held in the old. There were 880,000 shares outstanding at the time.

Whatever disappointment the Home directors may have felt at this miscarriage of their plans was soon utterly forgotten as the grim events of that autumn brought share prices tumbling down faster than leaves from the trees. October 24 was Black Thursday, first day of the great Wall Street crash. Next day, Home Oil shares lost 25 points, down to $12.65. They slumped to $10.45 on October 29, a day on which the Calgary exchange contemplated closing because of the prevailing panic. But on October 31, as other issues continued their slide into oblivion, they bounced back to $14. In fact, Home investors suffered less than most in the market disaster: with three wells producing and two more being drilled, the company's revenue for the year 1929 was $1,271,761, a staggering increase from the previous year's $55,633. And between June and

December the directors voted no fewer than four twenty-cent dividends. This successful performance cushioned the onset of the Depression, at least temporarily, for the whole of Turner Valley: drilling continued for quite some time after the flow of capital into other industries had dried up.

But the policy of unrestrained distribution of the profits from the naphtha sales as soon as they came in was not without its critics, among whom was E. Gerald Hanson, a peppery little First World War colonel and ultra-conservative Montreal broker who had been tipped off to Home Oil's potential by Bobby Ker soon after the company's formation. The well-connected Ker, whose grandfather had been auditor general of the Crown Colony of Vancouver Island before Confederation, was among the original shareholders of Home. One day in 1926 he found himself in Calgary on his father's business and sought out Jim Lowery, who had just returned from Home No. 1 in his leather field jacket and high boots—but was so pleased to meet an interested shareholder that he turned right round and drove back to show Ker the well. Ker was duly impressed by Lowery's enthusiasm and without even waiting until he returned home to Victoria wired Hanson—to whom he was related by marriage—saying: "If you want a good gamble, buy Home Oil." Hanson did, and he subsequently was so successful selling the shares to others that for a long time, out of Home's approximately 10,000 shareholders, more lived in Quebec than in any other province. This achievement gave Hanson a certain influence with the Home board—he joined it himself later—but in their euphoric state before the October crash the directors ignored his advice that they should be more conservative in their dividend policy and put more of the profits into a reserve fund.

Neither were they much inclined to sympathy when George Hudson, as assistant secretary, complained that the physical process of paying out such frequent dividends imposed a heavy strain on the staff of Harrison's company, which was still keeping Home's books, and furthermore was an unnecessary drain on Home's funds. Hudson was a busy man toward the end of 1929, since his boss, George Harrison, had gone off with his family for a year's cruise around the world aboard a Canadian Pacific liner—the board voted in December to send him Christmas greetings by cable to Tokyo. This trip may have contributed to Harrison's fall from grace later, and since he was away while all the paper work involved in setting up the new company was going on, the board asked Hudson to accept the post of secretary-treasurer of Home.

George Hudson had been brought to Canada as a boy by his father, who had left his native Dublin to manage the Hudson's Bay liquor department in Vancouver and had rapidly made himself indispensable to the city's upper crust by his devotion to the care and treatment of fine wines. Young George early evinced a good head for figures and his father encouraged him to enter a bank. He was working for George Harrison as head of the discount department of the Union Bank when it folded and instead of accepting an inspector's job with the Royal Bank he threw in his lot with Harrison. He felt a twinge of conscience about resigning his post as secretary of Harrison's company, but when his father agreed with him that the Home Oil position held more promise he accepted the board's offer.

The first meeting of the new company was held on January 22, 1930, and a few weeks later Home's fourth well was successfully completed. It proved, like its three predecessors, to be a good naphtha producer. But Home No. 5, which came in on August 31, was not a commercial proposition, producing only 84 barrels of naphtha between then and the end of the year. Home No. 6 was drilled to 4,689 feet and the directors then decided to take the modest crude oil production at that depth instead of deepening it into the limestone—because production from all wells on Section 20 had suddenly begun an alarming decline.

CHAPTER SIX

The Wells Dry Up–
and Home Goes Looking for Gold

When it created the Prairie provinces, the Dominion government in Ottawa retained control over their Crown lands and mineral resources. This left the new provincial governments severely limited fields of taxation from which to raise the funds they needed to provide the roads, hospitals, and other services demanded by their rapidly growing populations. Since Ontario and Quebec and the other original members of Confederation had been permitted to keep their own natural resources, Prairie politicians were able to make a good case for an end to this discrimination. It took years of agitation and the customary royal commission hearings, but in September 1930, the Dominion government relinquished its control over land and mineral rights on the Prairies.

The Alberta government was now free for the first time to enact legislation regulating the activities of the province's budding oil industry, and the first problem it tackled was one that had worried the oil men themselves for many years—the deplorable waste of Turner Valley's natural gas. The trouble was that there was no market for the vast quantities of gas remaining after its liquid content, or naphtha, had been extracted, so it was simply burned off in flare pits dug at a safe distance from each well. As the biggest producer in the field, Royalite was supplying Calgary's gas requirements through a pipeline built in 1925, but the city could use only a fraction of the gas Royalite processed through its extraction plant. The rest was burned off in a man-made inferno known far and wide as Hell's Half Acre. There was talk in 1930 that gas pipelines might be constructed all the way north to Edmonton and east into Saskatchewan, but the time for such ambitious projects was not yet ripe. In the meantime, 90 per cent of the gas produced by the field was wasted, at an estimated rate of 200 million cubic feet per day, and at night the glare from Hell's Half Acre and the other companies' flare pits could be seen from Calgary.

The government's response to this intractable problem—the first of many conservation measures passed through the years—was the Oil and Gas Wells Act of 1931, which restricted the flow from every Turner Valley well to forty per cent of its capacity. With this Act, the government built better than it knew, for no one at that time could have realized the worst side-effect of the gas wastage—an effect still being felt today: the primitive exploitation methods in vogue in Turner Valley in the early days siphoned off much of the gas cap pressing down on a billion and a half barrels of crude oil that no one had yet discovered. Partly because of this depletion of the underground pressure, when the crude *was* found, some years later, not much more than ten per cent of the field's reserves could be recovered by natural, or primary, methods. It is estimated that secondary recovery methods—the injection of water and/or gas into the rock to maintain the pressure—may eventually raise this figure to almost fifteen per cent of the reserves in place in the ground, but this technique, introduced to Turner Valley in the late 1950s, adds greatly to the expense of producing the oil.

The 1931 conservation restrictions, coming on the heels of the natural decline in Section 20's production, almost wiped out Home Oil. In retrospect, Gerry Hanson's warning against the 1929 dividend spree was a wise one, there being some very rainy days ahead. But the rest of the directors were still dazzled by the bounteous performance of Home No. 1 and as one after another the next three wells gave every promise of repeating its success they thought the bonanza was only just beginning. They may even have thought some display of confidence and optimism might help to dispel the fog of gloom that was enveloping the whole business community as the country slid into the Dirty Thirties. At any rate, in April 1930, before the wells began to peter out, they once again declared a dividend, this time of 25 cents—bringing the total dividend paid on each $1 share in less than a year to $1.05.

No sooner had this pay-out of $220,000 been made than the bad news began to filter back from the wells, and with the treasury virtually empty all hope of declaring further dividends vanished and the emphasis switched from enjoyment of the fruits of prosperity to bare survival. Thanks to increased production in the first half of 1930, as the new wells went on stream, the company's gross income for the whole year was not too disastrously down—it slipped to $969,465 from the previous year's $1,271,761—but the handwriting was clear on the wall. As the government's restrictions took hold, and with the price fetched by naphtha falling as general economic conditions worsened, gross income crashed to $187,890 in 1931 and only $83,079 in 1932. And Home shares, which had managed to remain above the ten-dollar level for many months after the stock market crash, slumped all the way down to fifteen cents, their lowest price ever, in 1932.

Most of Home's directors survived the shambles—if not unscathed, at least still solvent. But such disastrous collapses invariably leave casualties in their wake. This one provoked a rift in the Home inner circle that scandalized the Vancouver Club; ruined at least one of its members, the amiable Bill Shelly; and—unfairly but no less surely—disgraced another, George Harrison.

When Home shares began their downward slide, the members of the inner circle pledged themselves not to sell without warning each other. Those who could afford it even did some buying in an attempt to stave off the collapse. They included Shelly, who was reputed to have almost $2 million tied up in Home shares when they were selling for $18. Having noticed that some of the shares he was buying bore George Harrison's name, Shelly concluded he was being double-crossed. In fact, the shares had been among those held in trust by Harrison in the voting pool, which had been disbanded as no longer necessary in 1928, and they were clearly stamped on the back "Ex-Pool". (The misunderstanding would not have arisen if the directors had accepted George Hudson's suggestion back in 1928 that new share certificates be issued to the actual owners when the pool was broken up.)

Perhaps Harrison's long absence on that world cruise at the time when everything was beginning to crumble aroused suspicions that he had indeed been doing some profit-taking at the expense of his friends. At any rate, once the story began to circulate there was no stopping it. Shelly evidently realized he had been mistaken because he bore no grudge against Harrison in later life. But the punctilious Harrison found the opprobrium too much to bear and when his explanation of the episode failed to still the whispering campaign against him he never again set foot in the Vancouver Club.

Shelly was unable to stem the tide of disaster, of course, and he lost everything in the attempt. He resigned the presidency of Home Oil in 1931 and went to work for the bakery chain that had bought him out originally. But he was a resilient man—he once climbed into the ring with Jack Dempsey in a Rotary charity bout at the Hotel Vancouver—and within a few years he had re-established himself in business as a grain exporter. He died in 1951, after raising more than $20,000 for various Second World War charities with his magic shows—in addition to his other talents he was an amateur magician of near-professional skill.

Jim Lowery, too, lost his newly acquired affluence in the attempt to prevent the roof from falling in on Home Oil. He used much of the money he had made with his other promotions to buy Home shares, and watched it melt away as they continued their downward plunge. There were rumours, also, that he lost heavily on another speculation Arthur Meighen had recommended to him. At any rate, he told friends later he would never dabble in the stock market again. He still had his salary as managing director of Home, but the high living was now only a memory. There was a providential echo of it, though, one day in the depths of the Depression when he received a letter from the Roosevelt Hotel in New York reminding him that he had a credit balance there of $2,500: apparently he had provided that institution with an even bigger bankroll than was necessary to pay for his celebrated party and shopping expedition some years earlier. Lowery responded by return mail, asking the hotel to please send him its cheque for the balance right away, and told Marsh Porter, "That's the most money I've had for a long time."

Casting round for some way to improve Home Oil's own straitened circumstances, the directors examined several proposals for amalgamations with other companies. Under one of these, Lowery told the board in June 1931, the company would be "more of an industrial gas enterprise than an oil operating company". Nothing came of any of these proposals, however, and as the funds in the company's treasury continued to dwindle the directors tried to remedy the situation by taking another plunge: this time into gold-mining in British Columbia, which unlike other segments of the country's economy was enjoying a mini-boom in the early 1930s.

On April 15, 1932, the board voted to invest up to $5,000 in shares (then selling for 15 cents) of Placer Engineers Ltd., a mining property in the Cariboo about twenty miles south of the fabled Barkerville. As the minutes said that day: "All the directors present at the meeting were conversant with the set-up of Placer Engineers Ltd., and the majority of them had taken a monetary interest in it. . . ." Home later bought the controlling interest in Placer and George Harrison was installed as its president. There *was* some gold on the property—George Hudson's wife, Jo, once found some tiny nuggets in the creek that ran through it and the elegant Harrison had a tiepin made from a somewhat larger piece about the size of a peanut. But the Chinese miners who had worked the creek years before had apparently skimmed off the cream of the deposit and Placer Engineers never repaid Home's investment. Eventually, in 1940, the company's entire interest in the venture was sold—for $200.

Home had no better luck with its next gold-mining investment, the purchase of a controlling interest in P. E. Gold Mines Ltd., a company set up by Fergie Macdonald (who had by now resigned from the Home Oil board—perhaps to pave the way for this trans-action) and a group of his friends that may have included Jim Lowery and certainly did include Bill MacAdams. The company had mining claims on Cadwallader Creek, in the Bridge River dis-trict close to Austin Taylor's Bralorne mine, which was just getting into production, and the well-established Pioneer mine. The Home board voted initially—in June 1932—to invest $12,000 in 150,000 treasury shares of P. E. Gold (which works out to eight cents a share), "provided the above-mentioned expenditure does not de-plete the Home Oil treasury below $12,000". It later bought more shares and the following year a new company, Pacific Eastern Gold Ltd., was set up to take over P. E. Gold and two neighbouring companies, Dan Tucker Ltd. and Plutus Ltd. Jim Lowery became president of Pacific Eastern and several of the Home directors served on its board, together with Fergie Macdonald and Bill MacAdams. The company's claims extended for five miles along the creek but a program of diamond drilling over the next few years failed to find gold in commercial quantities. Home Oil relin-quished its interest in the company in 1937 and it was later taken over by Noranda Mines, which spent hundreds of thousands of dol-lars on further exploration before it, too, gave up on the area.

Before the gold fever abated, Home Oil put $215,000 into British Columbia mining stock[1] and some of that money came from a long-awaited windfall the company received in 1933. Almost from the start of the company's drilling and operating arrangement with Imperial Oil the Home directors had been dissatisfied with Im-perial's reporting of the expenditures made on Home's behalf. As early as September 27, 1928, the board authorized George Harrison "to specially press the Imperial Oil Limited officials to furnish the company with statements regarding expenditures made on our account". Whatever action Imperial took to rectify the situation was apparently inadequate, because the topic was still being discussed at Home board meetings during 1930. On May 16, for instance, there was a complaint that "no statements, etc., had yet been received from the Imperial Oil Ltd. covering receipts, expenditures and disbursements . . . during this year." And on December 18, the company's finance committee recommended to the full board that if Imperial's statements up to the end of November were not in Home's hands by December 31, "the directors bring the matter up with the Toronto office of the Imperial Oil Limited." George Harrison told a board meeting next day he had received a wire from Jack McLeod, Imperial's field manager in Calgary, promising that the required records, including "all adjustments for overcharges", would be in Home's hands before the end of the year, and the directors decided they didn't need to take the matter up with Toronto.

The records duly arrived—accompanied by a statement purporting to show that Home owed Imperial $270,295.01. The reticence of the prose favoured by compilers of company minute books is legendary, and had tape recorders been in style half a century ago it would have been interesting to read a transcript of the discussion that occasioned the following entry in the Home Oil minutes for January 16, 1931: "This statement was perused and discussed at some length by the directors present." Home's auditors were forthwith instructed to proceed to Calgary, there to "peruse" the records in further detail, and the examination dragged on for months, with the Home board becoming more and more convinced Imperial was overcharging for its services. Unfortunately, with Imperial handling the affairs of more than a dozen companies, the auditors could not clearly separate the expenditures made on the Home wells from those made on all the others. And naturally enough the Imperial office in Calgary was in no hurry to produce expenditure sheets or other documentary evidence that might substantiate Home's claims.

Eventually, Home enlisted the legal assistance of Marsh Porter, who had made some lucrative investments in Turner Valley properties on his own behalf and knew his way around the oil business. Porter examined the contract with Imperial and concluded that all the oil that had come out of all the wells belonged to Home, and that Imperial merely had the right to sell it and recover its costs, plus its agreed profit, from the proceeds. So he told Nelson Spencer, who had taken over as president when Bill Shelly resigned, "Sue them for the value of all the oil that has come from your holes since they were brought in, then they'll have to produce their expenditure sheets to prove their claim to the proceeds." Spencer was reluctant to sue, but Porter wrote to R. V. LeSueur, Imperial's legal counsel in Toronto, clearly hinting that legal action was a possibility. LeSueur immediately telephoned Calgary to find out how things had come to this pass and Porter told him he believed a court action was the only way to compel Imperial to disclose all the figures Home needed to prove its claim that it was being overcharged.

LeSueur said that would not be necessary—all the relevant details were in the basement of the Royalite office in Calgary and if Home would appoint an accountant to go over them with an Imperial accountant he was sure matters could be adjusted to everyone's satisfaction.

The laborious process of going over all the books and vouchers occupied more than a year, but in 1933 Imperial admitted Home had indeed been overcharged for the work on its wells: it seems that over-zealous field supervisors, anxious to make the performance of their own departments look better than it actually was, had been charging other work to the Home account, and there were such mix-ups as Home being debited with the whole cost of a drill sharpener used by Imperial to sharpen all the drills for miles around.

The records no longer exist to establish exactly how much Home was overcharged, but Imperial certainly repaid a substantial sum during 1933. Reminiscing about the episode with this writer in 1976, Marsh Porter recalled that it was $350,000. Porter recalled with a chuckle that he billed Home $3,500 for his services—one per cent of the amount repaid—and that he received a letter from Spencer complaining that this figure was considerably higher than the fee paid to a Vancouver firm which had also advised Home during the dispute with Imperial. Porter countered, "They were charging you for looking at your problem; I'm charging for seeing through it." Jim Lowery used to tell friends the overcharge was $400,000; and George Hudson told this writer he thought it might have been even more than that. Certainly it was at least $209,796.15, because that sum appears in a supplementary statement to Home's annual report for 1932 (dated September 1, 1933) as a repayment by Imperial "in respect of transactions prior to December 31, 1932". And it is quite possible that the settlement also included a forgiveness of at least part of the debt allegedly owed by Home to Imperial under the contract.

Whatever the exact sum was, it provided a welcome injection of funds into the company's treasury at a time when revenue from the wells had all but dried up. In gratitude for Lowery's role in the negotiations—he made frequent visits to Toronto to plead Home's case with the Imperial directors—the board voted him a $5,000 increase in salary for the period between June 1932 and September 1933. Typically, Lowery asked that $500 of that sum be paid as a bonus to Sammy Mains, a bookkeeper employed by Home Oil Distributors who had given him invaluable assistance "at a very nominal salary".

The Major was by now serving his apprenticeship in the gold-mining industry with the same enthusiastic disregard for conventional wisdom that he had brought to the oil business. Fergie Macdonald commented on his eagerness in an April 1933 letter to his friend Glen Hyatt, vice-president of Pacific Eastern Gold: "He is all ready to go on to the ground himself and do over again what he did in Turner Valley. And what is more, I guess he can do it." Lowery himself wrote to Bill MacAdams at around the same time: "I am convinced that there are no supermen among engineers and mine operators and that the mistakes that have been made in the past are that directors have delegated too much to these men and spent their own time playing golf."

There is no record of an excessive preoccupation with golf among the Home Oil directors during those grey years of the Depression, but by now they were certainly pinning all their hopes for the future prosperity of the company on its gold interests. So they were in a receptive frame of mind in 1934 when Royalite approached Jim Lowery with an offer to buy all the Home wells in Turner Valley. The wells produced fewer than 5,000 barrels of naphtha during the first nine months of 1934—in contrast to the 168,000 barrels produced by Home No. 1 alone in 1929—and the directors readily agreed to exchange all their leases and wells on Section 20 for 20,000 shares of Royalite stock. Home retained 18,333 of these shares, valued for the purposes of the transaction at $20 each (they rose considerably on the market in subsequent years). Imperial Oil received 1,000 shares in return for surrendering its production participation arrangement with Home, and United Oils received the remaining 667 shares in lieu of royalties it had enjoyed on the No. 2 and No. 4 wells. Soon afterward, Home bought more Royalite shares on the open market at an average price of $17.85, to bring its total holding up to 22,000 shares.

Home Oil Co. Ltd. was now an oil company in name only. In effect, the Royalite deal transformed it into a holding company, with its major assets approximately $550,000 in federal government bonds and oil and mining shares. The Section 20 wells had produced naphtha and crude oil which had been sold for $2.7 million, and Home had paid out $924,000 in dividends. Explaining the decision to sell out to Royalite, President Nelson Spencer told the shareholders the oil venture had been a disappointment because technical advice at the outset had been that one well could be placed on each ten acres of the company's property. This had proved to be a mistake, since so many wells had been sunk that Section 20 was quickly drained.

If the Home directors had showed a certain lack of prescience in this matter, they did not intend to make a similar mistake again: when the wells passed into Royalite's ownership on November 1, 1934, they instructed George Hudson to file the formal notification that the company was no longer in business in Alberta and its head office would henceforth be located in British Columbia. Thus, when an evangelist-turned-politician named William Aberhart wiped out the United Farmers of Alberta government and swept his Social Credit party into power in August 1935, the Home directors were able to congratulate themselves, from their vantage point on the other side of the Rockies, that the $25-a-month "dividends" he had promised to pay all Albertans would not be coming out of *their* pockets.

CHAPTER SEVEN

The Major Strikes Out
on His Own

Jim Lowery, as jaunty as ever, drove into Calgary early in June 1936, his daughter by his side in the big LaSalle convertible that he managed to hold on to throughout the Depression. Ostensibly he was taking a brief vacation from his gold-mining duties, looking up some of his old friends, and doing a spot of fishing. This last was true enough—but his quarry was not trout. Stanley Burke had told the Home board in February that the oil situation in Alberta was showing "definite signs of activity" and he thought the company should take steps to find out what was going on. After a good deal of discussion it was decided to ask Lowery to visit Calgary "to see if it would be advantageous for this company to again, in any way, become interested in oil development", a decision ratified by the shareholders at the annual general meeting in May.

Lowery poked around Calgary and Turner Valley for a few days investigating various prospects with his usual keen eye for an opportunity, then left on June 13 for the Bridge River district and the Pacific Eastern mine, for which the company still held high hopes. Uncharacteristically, he therefore missed the excitement when R. A. Brown, Sr., brought in his famous Turner Valley Royalties No. 1 well on June 16—the well that finally found Turner Valley's real buried treasure, its crude oil reservoir.

While Lowery was not there to see Brown's well blow crude oil all over the surrounding fields, the Home directors were well aware of its significance by the time they met on June 25 to hear their managing director's report on his mission to Calgary: the well, immediately hailed as the biggest in the British Empire, made headlines across the country and launched a new bull market in oil shares. Nevertheless, some members of the board were firmly set against any new venturing into Alberta: Aberhart's "funny money" policies were about as welcome in business circles as a rabid dog at a picnic. There was thus a great deal of nervous discussion when

Lowery outlined a proposition that had been put to him by Marsh Porter.

As Lowery explained it, a city engineer in Medicine Hat named Ashburner, who was an enthusiastic amateur geologist, had come across gas seeping from a hole several feet across in a wilderness area of the Alberta foothills known as the Brazeau, about 110 miles west of Red Deer and 140 miles northwest of Calgary. He had approached a lawyer named Stuart Blanchard and together they had taken out exploration permits covering 64,500 acres of still unsurveyed territory around the seep. Blanchard had then enlisted his friend Porter's assistance in an attempt to secure financing and set up a company to explore and develop the land. Judging from everything he had been able to discover, Lowery told the board, the Brazeau might well be another Turner Valley—and Home could own it all. After another long discussion, his persuasiveness won the day and the directors voted to spend $5,000 on a survey of the area, on the understanding Home would eventually have a half-interest in the acreage.

After an interval of almost two years, Home Oil—however tentatively—was now back in the oil business and Lowery returned to Calgary full of his old fire. To conduct the Brazeau survey, he engaged the services of a geologist named Dr. James O. G. Sanderson. "Pete" Sanderson, as he was universally known, had some Indian blood and as a boy he had been a ranch hand in Medicine Hat; renowned as one of the best horsemen in that part of the country, he had ridden in the Calgary Stampede in 1912. At one time he worked for Addison Perry Day, a showman who staged rodeos in New York and London, and Day, taking a liking to his intelligent young hand, had paid for his education, which included a sojourn at Yale.

Even before Sanderson rode off into the bush to begin his survey, Lowery was casting around for new properties in Turner Valley. The board sanctioned a few minor expenditures for small acreages he was able to find, but there was still a strong feeling against becoming too involved in Alberta and on August 17 Lowery wrote to Nelson Spencer asking to be relieved of his post as managing director. The resignation seems to have been amicable enough, since the motion proposing its acceptance was put to a board meeting by Lowery himself and seconded by Bobby Ker, who was usually Lowery's ally in his running battle with some of the stodgier directors. Lowery retained his seat on the board and the reason for his resignation would not emerge for some time.

The nervousness about Alberta's Social Credit policies persisted, and on October 2 Spencer tendered a written report to the Home board recommending against the investment of further funds in the province. Someone around the table mentioned that Charles C. Ross, Alberta's Minister of Lands and Mines, happened to be in Vancouver that day, and the meeting was adjourned long enough for Hudson to track him down and invite him to address the board. Ross accepted the invitation and tried to put the directors' fears to rest. He "spoke at some length", according to the minutes, and assured them that the province's natural resources would be "amply protected".

At least partly reassured, the directors continued to support the Brazeau venture: on November 6 they sanctioned the expenditure of $12,000 to keep the leases in good standing for a further year and approved several other minor deals proposed by Lowery. But on November 14 he was instructed by long-distance telephone not to acquire any additional acreage for the company.

Shortly thereafter, Bobby Ker was in Calgary and he learned the reason for Lowery's resignation: he had become convinced there was a large pool of crude oil waiting to be discovered in the north end of Turner Valley and, impatient with his fellow directors' reluctance to plunge back into Alberta, had wanted to be free to pick up leases there himself. After a quick trip east to raise funds from some of his old cronies on Bay Street, he had personally taken up CPR and Alberta government leases covering no less than 7,500 acres. He had received several offers for these leases which would bring him a handsome profit, but he wanted Home to have them and thought the directors should change their policy on investments in Alberta.

Ker knew that Gerry Hanson had been in Calgary that day to attend a meeting of the board of a local brewery and was leaving by train that evening. Unable to reach him at his hotel, he and Lowery rushed to the station and intercepted him as he was boarding the train. After Lowery had explained his position, Hanson agreed with Ker that Home should take over his leases—after all, oil was what the company had been formed to find; it had found it and profited thereby once; and this seemed like an excellent chance to do so again.

As the train steamed out, Hanson promised to make his views known to the Home board and he evidently did so with some conviction, for a few days later Spencer and Victor Odlum, vice-president of Home, arrived in Calgary to hear Lowery's story. He soon convinced them that this new area looked even more promising than Section 20 had in the beginning, and there and then they agreed that the company would buy his leases "on terms to be worked out in detail later". Multi-million-dollar deals have often been settled in the oil business on no more than a handshake, but as events were to show, Lowery would have been wiser to insist that those terms be spelled out on the spot.

The leases he had bought covered an area near the town of Millarville, where in days gone by exiled Englishmen sustained by contributions from their excellent connections in the Old Country used to stage polo matches that are still celebrated in local lore. One factor in his choice of this location was a paper presented to the western division of the Canadian Institute of Mining and Metallurgy in October that year by a couple of Winnipeggers employed in the petroleum and natural gas department of the Alberta government, J. Grant Spratt and Vernon Taylor. This suggested that as the wells on top of the Turner Valley anticline—including those on Section 20—had drained the gas cap and lowered its pressure, crude oil had begun to migrate upwards from deeper levels on the west flank of the structure. As evidence, the paper pointed out that even before Turner Valley Royalties No. 1 struck crude oil in quantity, the production from several of the deepest west-flank wells had begun to change from high-gravity naphtha to the heavier crude oil. "It would appear," the paper concluded, "that a crude oil reserve of major importance to this country exists along the Turner Valley west flank. . . ."

The area Lowery had leased was on the west flank of the structure, but it was much further north than anyone had ever drilled before—R. A. Brown, Sr., had brought in his well on the west flank but in the south end. And the man Lowery always credited with directing his footsteps to the north end of the valley was the government petroleum engineer Charlie Dingman. There was a theory in those days that the north end of the structure was cut off from the rest by a fault; and that even if oil did exist there it would be too deep underground to be reached by contemporary drilling methods. But Dingman knew—as did others—that most of the Turner Valley wells up to that time were crooked: deviation surveys, which enable the driller to keep the hole vertical, had not yet been introduced to Canada and after penetrating the ground for a few hundred feet the drill would often begin to slant off to one side. This, Dingman realized, meant that many of the wells' depth logs were misleading—that 5,000 feet of pipe would not actually penetrate 5,000 feet into the ground if it sloped off at an angle. Hence the estimates of the depths at which various rock strata would be encountered would also be misleading. So, working painstakingly at home, he plotted all the wells in the valley and by hanging strings of proportionate length perpendicularly from a wire framework assembled a picture of the underground structure which proved to his own satisfaction—and to Lowery's—that what had been thought to be inaccessibly deep was actually within reach.

When Spencer and Odlum returned to Vancouver to report to their fellow directors on their meeting with Lowery, the rosy expectations aroused by their explanation of Dingman's theory evidently outweighed the reservations about investing further funds in Alberta and the board readily approved their action in purchasing Lowery's leases. A committee was set up to negotiate with Lowery on the terms of the purchase—it consisted of Odlum, Ker, and Stanley Burke—but in the meantime, Odlum told the board, he and the president had promised Lowery that the $36,000 he had paid for the leases would be reimbursed immediately. The board formally approved that arrangement, too—but protests erupted a few weeks later when the committee disclosed the terms of the settlement it had arrived at with Lowery: he was to be granted an option to purchase 45,000 Home shares at $1.28 per share—the closing price on the day Spencer and Odlum had agreed to buy his leases—and permitted to buy a ten per cent interest in a subsidiary company Home was contemplating setting up to hold all its interests in Alberta.

A contract to this effect was drawn up but when it came before the board for approval in January 1937, doubts were expressed that the company could legally enter into it. At the very least, some of the directors maintained, the shareholders should be asked to approve it, and it was decided to call a special meeting for this purpose. W. H. Malkin, the millionaire grocer, went so far as to question the propriety of Lowery's acquiring acreage for himself while he was a director of the company. General Odlum gallantly sprang to Lowery's defence and pointed out that not only was he not in Home's employ at the time he bought the land, but he had been expressly instructed not to buy any more leases for the company.

The acrimony with which the subject was discussed probably disgusted Lowery, but it could not have surprised him: he had crossed swords with some of his more cautious fellow-directors many times before. He did, however, see the merit of one argument advanced against the proposed settlement: the company was at that time considering a plan to raise new financing by offering shareholders the right to buy one share at $2 for each share held. Giving Lowery an option to buy at $1.28 might well make it impossible to market such an issue, so at another board meeting next day he voluntarily renounced the company's offer. In a letter drawn up by his solicitor overnight he said he had acquired the leases personally, with his own funds, when he had not been working for the company or under its instructions. "However," the letter continued, "due either to a misapprehension or lack of knowledge of the facts, there have been, at times, suggestions that the leases were acquired by me on behalf of the company. In view of the embarrassment already caused to the Directors of the Company and to myself, I now prefer not to take from the Company any consideration whatsoever in this connection. . . ." As far as he was concerned, the letter said, the option offered him "is cancelled, void, and of no effect, as if it had never been granted to me or, in fact, considered. . . ."

Bobby Ker, in particular, was not content to let the matter rest there. He felt Lowery had been shabbily treated, and so did Spencer and Odlum, who after all had given their word that satisfactory terms would be worked out for the purchase of the leases. No recompense at all could hardly be called a satisfactory return to Lowery for his initiative in picking up the leases or his loyalty in turning down other offers for them until he could give Home the chance to buy them. Several months after he had given up the option, the Alberta Committee of Home (which had been set up to handle operations in the province pending the establishment of the new subsidiary) recommended to the board that Lowery should receive 25,000 shares of Home stock or $50,000 in cash in return for all his interests in acreages, permits, and leases in Alberta—not simply the CPR and government leases—and that he should be re-engaged as managing director at a salary of $600 a month.

But the inexplicably shabby treatment of Lowery had not yet ended. On July 22, 1937, when the board finally disposed of the matter, it rehired him at the recommended salary but halved the cash payment, to $25,000. Bobby Ker could hardly believe it, and he never ceased to campaign for a more generous settlement. Years later, in 1945, he managed to have himself elected chairman of a directors' committee to revive the issue. With Gerry Hanson and Marsh Porter, he combed the company's minute books all the way back to 1936 and reported, "From these it appears that the majority of the productive property of the company was acquired by Major Lowery for his own account after the company had elected to refrain from taking up acreage. . . ." The report said the $25,000 settlement he had received in return was "by any test at the time it was made wholly inadequate, and in the light of subsequent developments grossly unfair." The committee was therefore trying to find some way to compensate Lowery "in a manner appropriate to the value of the properties acquired and to an extent sufficient to enable him to continue to devote his talent to the Company's capital benefit rather than to make further acquisitions for his own account and profit." Strangely, there is nothing in any subsequent minute to indicate that any further payment was ever made.

The properties acquired by Home in 1936—either from Lowery personally or through his efforts—were listed in the company's annual report for that year. They included a total of 8,521 acres in the north end of Turner Valley; the half-interest in 64,500 acres in the Brazeau; and exploration permits covering 4,000 acres in the West Coutts area, along the U.S. border a few miles north of the proven Cut Bank oil field in Montana. To explore and develop these properties Home Oil set up two wholly owned subsidiary companies during 1937: Home Oil (Alberta) Ltd. and Home Oil (Brazeau) Ltd. (Home put up $200,000 for a controlling interest in the Brazeau company on its formation, and later bought out the original partners completely.) The directors were still wary of Aberhart's policies—they seriously feared he might confiscate any company funds held in Alberta—so the idea was to keep the subsidiaries' assets to a minimum and supply the funds needed for operations by means of loans from the parent company, based in Vancouver. The value of Home Oil's investment portfolio at the beginning of 1937 had mounted to $1.27 million and its total assets to $1.45 million. But to finance the new oil operations the company went ahead with the plan to offer each shareholder the right to buy one new share at two dollars for each share held. The 736,101 shares taken up raised $1.47 million, more than doubling the company's assets.

The stage was now set. Could "Hustling Jimmie Lowery" repeat his earlier success with Section 20? Certainly the outlook for Home Oil (Brazeau) Ltd. looked bright. Pete Sanderson had reported after his 1936 survey of the area that it contained a prospective gas and oil structure thirty-five miles long and that in some places the drill should enter the limestone at the extremely shallow depth of 3,200 feet. "The writer wishes to state his belief," Sanderson said in his report, "that your prospects of finding a very large deposit of valuable oil and gas appear to be unusually good." Before committing itself to the project completely, Home sought a second opinion from a noted oil authority, Professor Harold F. George, head of the department of petroleum engineering at the University of Pittsburgh, Pennsylvania. George reported that Sanderson's methods and conclusions were "of the highest order" and said that if the Brazeau structure had been known back in 1924, and had it been as accessible as Turner Valley, he would have developed it first, "based upon its more favourable geology".

The inaccessibility of the Brazeau area was certainly a formidable problem. Home's acreage lay in a thickly forested area and stretched across the valleys of four rivers and two creeks. Sanderson, who was now hired as Home's first staff geologist, chose a site on Chungo Creek for the first well. Since the area was penetrated only by pack trails, the company had to build a twenty-eight-mile road in to the site from the railroad town of Nordegg, and to do so it bought the first bulldozer seen in those parts. Construction began in June 1937, and the road, which snaked up and down steep hillsides and crossed several bridges, was completed by the end of October at a cost of $25,000. The trucks were now able to begin ferrying in the derrick and the tools—it was decided to use a cable-tool rig—200 tons of casing and 300 tons of coal to fire the boilers. Despite delays enforced by rain and snow storms, Home Brazeau No. 1 was spudded in on December 11, 1937.

Great hopes were also held for the West Coutts acreage, which lay between the small Red Coulee field, discovered in 1929, and another small field, Del Bonita, which had just been found. Home Coutts No. 1 was spudded in on July 23 but two months later it struck brackish water at 3,150 feet and was abandoned. It had cost $43,500 to drill and the company evidently decided that was enough and surrendered its West Coutts leases.

An even worse setback was soon to occur in the area for which Lowery had the highest hopes, his cherished north end of Turner Valley. Sanderson had advised that Home–Millarville No. 1, the first test well, should be sited on LSD 8 of Section 33, in Township 20, Range 3, West of the 5th Meridian—roughly in the centre of the company's holdings—and an Alberta company, Snyder and Head, was commissioned to do the drilling with a rotary rig. The well was spudded in on June 22, 1937, and for the first few thousand feet its progress seemed normal. But on September 24, at 6,130 feet, "sharp sand" was encountered which cut the cones in the Hughes bit and three were lost in the hole. It was necessary to drill these cones out before the drilling could continue, and in that process another set of cones was lost. On October 4, however, Lowery wired his fellow directors: "Well down sixty-one forty-four at eight o'clock this morning, being fourteen feet below where cones were lost so it looks as if the fishing job is over."

By the following month, though, it was obvious that something else was wrong. Even though the well was now down more than 7,000 feet, it was not encountering the rock layers Sanderson expected to find on the basis of previous drilling in the valley—Turner Valley Royalties No. 1, for instance, had struck its oil at 6,828 feet. One possible explanation for this was that the hole was not straight. The only instrument in Alberta capable of measuring a well's deviation from the perpendicular at that time was owned by a recent arrival from the United States, an experienced driller named Ralph Will. Will had graduated from the University of Oklahoma as a geologist in 1929 but had considered himself lucky, as the Depression got under way, to land a job as a roughneck. He had risen through the ranks, first to toolpush and then to drilling superintendent, on jobs all over Oklahoma, Texas, and Colorado, until an Alberta company, Anglo-Canadian Oil, had brought him to Turner Valley to take charge of its drilling and production.

One day in November, Lowery asked Will if he would drive over to Home–Millarville No. 1 and see if he could diagnose its trouble. When Will arrived at the well he found that the small engine used to turn the drill had been disconnected because it was not powerful enough to do the job. This surprised him, because he had used that same model himself and never had any trouble with it. The crew had switched to the hoisting engine normally used to handle the heavy strings of casing—and the anguished note of its exhaust told Will immediately that even this much larger engine was labouring hard to rotate the drill, a clear indication that the hole was crooked. He asked the crew to shut down the engine and disconnect the drill pipe—and his suspicion was confirmed: the pipe spun back three or four turns as the pressure was taken off it, showing that it had been badly twisted in the ground. "That hole is just as crooked as hell," Will told Lowery. And when Lowery asked if he could measure the deviation he replied that he couldn't —because his instrument would only register a departure from the vertical of up to eight degrees, and in his view Home–Millarville No. 1 was much further out of line than that.

When Lowery communicated this grim news to the board it accepted Will's suggestion that an American company with specialized measuring equipment be brought in to survey the well. Its report horrified everyone: the well had slanted off to the northeast as much as thirty degrees from the vertical, so instead of entering the productive limestone the bit had been sliding across the top of it. What was thought to be a 7,600-foot hole had actually penetrated the ground to a depth of only 4,830 feet, and the bottom of the hole was almost half a mile away from where it should have been, entirely off the company's lease. As one of the crew put it later, "We finished up underneath the tavern in Black Diamond."

By the end of the year the company had accepted expert advice that it would not be possible to redrill the well and after Snyder and Head had managed to salvage a few thousand feet of casing— the rest of it proved to be frozen in the hole—Home–Millarville No. 1 was abandoned. Some of the directors wanted to sue Snyder and Head for negligence and the company once again consulted Marsh Porter, who dryly pointed out that on a recent visit to the well General Odlum had told reporters what a magnificent job was being done there; worse still, he had repeated this sentiment in an official report to the company. This was hardly, as Porter pointed out, the kind of evidence that would support Home's case, so the threat of legal action was dropped. Snyder and Head refused to accept payment for its final month of work but another company, Newell and Chandler, received the contract to drill the second test well, which was spudded in 2,000 feet west of the crooked hole on April 9, 1938. (To keep the records tidy, the abandoned hole was later renumbered 1A, and a successful well brought in near by by Ralph Will on December 20, 1940, was henceforth known as Home–Millarville No. 1.)

By this time, Jim Lowery was once again out of a job. However unjustly, some of the directors blamed him for the crooked well and in January his sensitive antennae detected indications that his days as managing director of Home Oil were numbered. Beating the company to the punch, he resigned in a letter to Spencer disclosed to the board on February 11. The letter prompted a spirited debate and the directors were not unanimously in favour of accepting his resignation—perhaps because one of those present was Bobby Ker, who had always supported Lowery and had no great admiration for the executive qualities of the president and vice-president of Home, Spencer and Odlum. Well into the evening, it was resolved to adjourn the meeting until noon the next day, a Saturday. This time, Lowery himself turned up—which was fortunate, because without him the meeting would have lacked a quorum and could not have taken any action. Obligingly, the Major stayed on long enough to vote against the motion recommending acceptance of his resignation, but it was carried and the meeting agreed (Ker kept his forebodings to himself) that management of the company's operations should henceforth be in the hands of Colonel Nelson Spencer and Major-General Victor Odlum.

CHAPTER EIGHT

A New Bonanza Puts the Major
Back at the Helm

By the end of 1937 there were thirty-three wells producing crude oil in Turner Valley, even though Dingman's predictions for the north end had yet to be proved. Their total production during the year—1.9 million barrels—was enough to make Alberta virtually self-sufficient in oil for the first time and the producers began to look around for new markets. In September, the two largest oil companies in the country—Imperial and British American—announced that they would co-operate with the many small independent companies in seeking lower freight rates from the railroads, if necessary with government subsidies, to enable Turner Valley to compete with imported U.S. oil for the Saskatchewan and Manitoba markets.

Home Oil was not yet contributing to this production, but presenting the company's report for 1937 at the annual general meeting in April the following year, Nelson Spencer told the shareholders he expected a fifty per cent increase in Turner Valley's crude production during 1938. He hoped this would persuade the railroads to bring their shipping rates down to "a reasonable level". If not, he thought a pipeline to serve the growing west-coast market would be necessary, and he regarded the nine-hundred-mile route through the Yellowhead Pass to Vancouver as quite feasible.

In the event, Spencer's estimate of the increase in Turner Valley's production during 1938 was as conservative as his pipeline proposal was premature. Thirty-nine new wells were completed during the year, all but three of them crude-oil producers, and production more than tripled, to 6.02 million barrels. And while the campaign for lower freight rates did not succeed, by the end of the year Alberta was supplying not only its own oil requirements but those of eastern British Columbia, Saskatchewan, and western Manitoba.

It was a busy, exciting time for everyone connected with the industry and even though he was no longer employed by Home Oil an outbreak of the Black Death could not have kept Jim Lowery from the scene. Nor, it soon turned out, could Home Oil function for long without him: neither Spencer nor Odlum had his intuitive feel for the oil business or his easy rapport with everyone in it, from the rowdiest roughneck to the loftiest company executive. Nelson Spencer was a big, imposing man, and he could be intimidating: what he intended as joviality was sometimes interpreted by others as bluster. Victor Odlum, too, was a commanding figure, as befitted a much-decorated infantry officer credited with inventing the trench raid in the First World War. But he was also an austere man who neither smoked nor drank, and the men of his battalion in France dubbed him "Pea Soup" Odlum when he replaced their rum ration with what he considered to be a much more sensible refreshment, hot soup. The kind of discipline that came naturally to Odlum did not endear itself to the free spirits who ran the wells in Turner Valley, and there was some barely concealed amusement when, in the late stages of the drilling of Home–Millarville No. 2, he ignored a warning from Pete Sanderson and insisted on poking about the derrick—only to be knocked unconscious by the pall of gas surrounding it. George Hudson received a late-night call in Vancouver asking him to prepare Mrs. Odlum for the worst, but the old soldier recovered after a night in hospital.

Lowery had received $2,000 as a severance payment when he resigned his post but there is no record of how he supported himself and his family during 1938. He does not seem to have taken a job with any other company and his confidence in his own judgment remained unimpaired, as reflected in a letter he wrote to his daughter in October: "The oil business is shaping up well and your Lowery Pete should soon be worth $1 a share. . . . Within two months Turner Valley will be the largest producing oil structure in the world outside the East Texas structure. . . . I guessed right in 1924, again in 1928, again in 1936 and now in 1938 I am confident that six months later the public will waken up to that fact."

Since he had not resigned his directorship of Home, Lowery was continually called upon to solve problems that Spencer and Odlum were evidently unable to handle. On October 3, for instance, he was asked to go to Edmonton to intercede with the provincial government in the matter of drilling credits the company felt it should receive for its Brazeau expenditures, which were mounting steadily—the exploratory well on Chungo Creek had run into trouble with cave-ins and a string of casing had been lost in the hole, necessitating a difficult, and costly, fishing job. A few weeks later, Lowery's aid was enlisted again when negotiations for the purchase of a further 820 acres in Turner Valley bogged down.

Throughout that summer there had been growing dissension among members of the Home Oil board, which seemed to be falling apart, with director set against director as a stream of gossip first trickled through Turner Valley, then gathered momentum in Calgary and Vancouver, and finally reached all the way to Montreal, which was then still the heart of Canada's business world. There the fiery little colonel, Gerry Hanson, was not at all pleased by what he heard: that the management of Home Oil appeared to be collapsing into total disarray. Hanson wrote to his friend Bobby Ker saying that the eastern shareholders were becoming very anxious about the situation and suggesting it be thrashed out at a board meeting.

The letter reinforced what Ker had always privately thought and while it worried him he did not relish the idea of mounting an outright attack on the company's president and vice-president. But he did show the letter to W. H. Malkin, who suggested that Wendell Farris,[1] a no-nonsense lawyer who had just been elected to Home's board, could legitimately, as a newcomer, ask questions about the company's management. Hanson made a trip to Vancouver to discuss his concern with Farris, who then consulted other directors to get their views. All of these men, with the possible exception of Bobby Ker, had been irritated at one time or another by Lowery's maverick ways. But they agreed, some of them reluctantly, that the company seemed to run better with him at the helm than without him. So Farris sought out Lowery, asked his views about the company's operations and felt him out about resuming his post. The prospect delighted Lowery but he made one condition: on no account would he work under Nelson Spencer.

Farris opened his campaign by suggesting at the end of an otherwise routine board meeting on December 22 that the situation in Turner Valley, where progress on the second test well was reported by Sanderson to be encouraging, demanded the appointment of a full-time manager to take charge of the company's affairs. As Bobby Ker recalled shortly before his death in 1977, "He practically told Spencer his resignation was demanded." Predictably, this suggestion incensed Spencer and he fired off a letter to Farris next day in such terms that Farris complained about them at the next meeting, on December 29. After some embarrassed discussion by the other directors, Spencer apologized and Farris was asked to put his recommendations into writing.

Less than two weeks later, on January 8, 1939, the news everyone had been waiting for gave new urgency to the surgery that Farris was about to perform: Home–Millarville No. 2 blew in with a tremendous roar at 8,945 feet and Home Oil was sitting on 10,000 acres of leases surrounding what ultimately became the largest crude-producing well in the British Empire. Dingman's predictions for the north end and Lowery's foresight in picking up the CPR leases in defiance of the board were vindicated at last, and yet another boom was under way in Turner Valley. Ironically, Jim Lowery was not even working for the company he had founded when its biggest well came in, but Farris knew he was the only man who could move fast enough, and effectively enough, to exploit the new discovery.

On January 19, when he submitted his recommendations to the board, he pulled no punches. "The president of the company," his report said, "should be a comparatively young man with executive ability who is prepared to devote at least half his time to the company's interests." His nomination: Bobby Ker, who was then 43, considerably younger than any other member of the board. Even more important, though Farris did not mention it, was that Lowery had assured him he could work with Ker.

As to the choice of a managing director, Farris said, two considerations must enter the picture: his knowledge of the technical and other operations of the company and his willingness to give practically his entire time to the work. "There is no doubt," the report went on, "that . . . Major James Lowery is the only member of our board capable of meeting the required qualifications. . . ."

Newcomer to the company though he was, Farris had clearly been well-briefed on the foibles of its in-and-out managing director. The duties and powers of the president and the managing director, he said, should be clearly defined, and "the final responsibility of management must rest on the board as a whole." The president's responsibility should be to give leadership and act as a liaison officer between the managing director and the board; and the managing director, subject to the board's direction, should have general supervision of the field work. But "generally in all matters of policy and importance, the managing director should make definite recommendations in writing to the board before acting." They were brave words, but hardly likely, as those listening to them knew, to sway "hustling Jimmie Lowery". Recalling the episode years later, Bobby Ker told this writer, "When I was railroaded into the job, I said, 'I'm going to depend on Jim Lowery.' So Jim went ahead."

The policy he was to go ahead with was also defined in Farris's report. He recommended that the company should "proceed in an aggressive way to develop its Turner Valley acreage with a view to production rather than exploration"; that three wells should be drilled in the most favourable area "at the first practical moment"; that new wells should be drilled with money taken from the capital account, which should be restored from the production of each well as it came in; that new shares should be sold to permit the drilling of at least ten more wells—and here he noted that if ten wells were drilled each year, one well to each forty acres, it would take twenty-five years to fully develop the company's 10,000 acres.

Perhaps as a salve to his wounded pride, Spencer was also permitted to deliver a report to the meeting. His view was that the company could not get in one man what was required in the way of management in Calgary, so he suggested the appointment of an advisory committee of three. He did agree that Lowery should be on his proposed committee and elaborated magnanimously, "He is, in many respects, the foremost oil man in Alberta. His capacity to ferret out knowledge is in a class by itself. His knowledge how to go out and come in and keep the respect and goodwill of all with whom he comes in contact is unquestioned. He stands high with government, major oil companies, railway and all personnel of the industry."

After both reports had been read to the meeting, Spencer resigned as president and was appointed chairman of the board, replacing General Stewart, who had died not long before. Ker was elected president and Lowery appointed managing director with a satisfying increase in salary, to $10,000 a year. And at the company's annual meeting in April another of Farris's recommendations was carried out, which pleased Lowery and might well have been suggested by him: the board was broadened to include more Alberta members who, unlike the older Vancouver directors who resigned to make way for them, were conversant with conditions in the oil industry and the province, whose government was by now beginning to be seen not as a rabble of wild-eyed socialists but as one of the more conservative and business-like of provincial administrations. The new directors, some of them close friends of Lowery's, were: Ray Milner, an Edmonton lawyer who was also president of the utility companies supplying both Edmonton and Calgary with natural gas; Herbert Greenfield, a former premier of Alberta and president of the Alberta Petroleum Producers' Association; Colonel Lionel Baxter, president of the Calgary and Edmonton Corporation; Reuben Ward, head of a large bakery company in Edmonton; and Marsh Porter.

Once back in the saddle, Lowery immediately began negotiations with Ralph Will for the drilling of two more wells in the north end of Turner Valley, at an estimated cost of about $150,000 each, and they were spudded in that summer. Home–Millarville No. 2 at that time was producing at the rate of 514 barrels of crude per day, which made it the biggest producer in the valley. Its potential capacity at full flow was much higher than that, but in 1938 the Alberta government had initiated the policy it still applies of setting a maximum "allowable" production for every well in the province.

The province's first attempt to regulate the oil industry in the early thirties had been challenged in the courts by one of the independent companies affected by it, Spooner Oils, and while the government managed to make its restriction of the naphtha wells' flow to forty per cent of capacity stick, the Supreme Court of Canada disallowed other aspects of the legislation. So in 1938 the province passed new legislation setting up a Petroleum and Natural Gas Conservation Board, which immediately began to control the output of the new crude wells, too—partly to slow the rate at which the field was being depleted and partly to try to assure orderly marketing of the oil produced: by 1939 the Prairie market for Turner Valley oil was saturated and production was permitted to rise that year by only 750,000 barrels, in contrast to the previous year's massive increase of four million barrels. Even that small increase was made possible only by the appetite of farm machinery for fuel to harvest 1939's bumper crop of grain on the Prairies. As the need for more production became apparent that summer, Home–Millarville No. 2's daily allowable was increased to 999 barrels, which netted Home Oil about $1,000 a day.

One of the many ironies of the history of the Canadian oil industry is that for years—virtually until the oil-exporting countries quadrupled prices in 1973 and forced the term "energy crisis" into the consciousness of every citizen of the western world—Alberta companies found it easier to find and produce oil than to sell it. Soon after Jim Lowery resumed his direction of Home Oil's activities, the outbreak of the Second World War would provide a temporary solution to this problem, but earlier in 1939 it was compounded by decisions of the two largest buyers of oil. Imperial Oil decided to reduce the quantity of Turner Valley oil it had been refining in Manitoba by 2,850 barrels a day, replacing it with imports from Montana. And British American, a Canadian company founded in 1906 which had later developed production in the U.S., followed suit and began to import between 700 and 800 barrels of East Texas oil to Manitoba daily to replace supplies from Alberta.

Decisions such as these, whatever economic rationale there may have been for them, infuriated the smaller Alberta companies whose wells were being choked down for lack of markets. The Alberta producers' problem was not solely their distance from the main oil-consuming region of Canada, Ontario and Quebec; other factors entered the equation, such as the major international companies' pricing policies and their natural tendency to prefer to refine oil from their own wells, whether in the United States or elsewhere in the world. The smaller companies were not therefore as "independent" as that commonly used term implies: to a marked extent they depended for their prosperity on the actions of the major companies—particularly the prices those companies paid for crude oil, since a producing company like Home, without its own refinery, had no choice but to sell to one of the major "integrated" companies.

This situation led the Home board in 1939 to revive its consideration of a possible merger with a larger company. As Nelson Spencer's remarks at the 1937 annual meeting showed, the company had for some time cast envious glances at the Vancouver market, which was then largely supplied by California oil brought in by sea. Home Oil, of course, did not have the money to build the pipeline across the Rockies that Spencer and other oil men coveted, but a larger company might. One day, Lowery had lunch with John Galloway, an American geologist who had recently arrived in Calgary to set up shop for Standard Oil of California.

Galloway's company had a wholly owned subsidiary in Vancouver, Standard Oil Co. of British Columbia, which had a refinery and a marketing organization but—unless Galloway could find some—no oil of its own in Canada. Lowery's company had some oil—Home–Millarville No. 2 produced the impressive total of 221,082 barrels during 1939—and every prospect of finding more very soon, but it had no refinery. Why not, Lowery suggested, join forces?

The idea made good sense to Galloway, particularly after he conducted a personal appraisal of Home's reserves in the north end and decided they amounted to about thirty-five million barrels. So he and Lowery worked out an arrangement under which Standard would put up all the money needed to develop Home's property, with Home receiving ten per cent of the gross production from its wells until Standard had recouped its costs, after which Home would have a half-interest in the company—including any other wells Standard developed elsewhere in the province.

Nelson Spencer described the proposed deal to the press as "a partnership in engineering, production, and marketing", and said the idea was to attain independence from the Royalite domination of Turner Valley. "We feel that we have an important property, and one that will eventually be a big factor in Alberta oil production," he said, "but we cannot expect to develop the full extent of our resources alone."

Lowery went to San Francisco several times to discuss the proposed deal with Standard's directors. On one visit he took Galloway to a vaudeville house to see the notorious fan-dancer Sally Rand, and after the show guided him backstage to the star's dressing room, where Sally greeted him as a long-lost friend and willingly fell in with his suggestion that she present the astonished Galloway with an autographed photograph.

Eventually all the details seemed to be agreed. A date was set for the final drafting of the agreement in Vancouver, but on his way there from a business trip to Denver Galloway was injured in a train derailment. Lowery thus found himself discussing the deal all over again with a lawyer from San Francisco—he described him to Galloway later as "a bookkeeper type", using a phrase he reserved for those who earned his deepest scorn. In Lowery's view, the phraseology the lawyer wanted incorporated in the agreement completely changed the terms of the deal. He pointed this out and suggested the drafting session be postponed until Galloway was out of hospital and fit to attend. But the lawyer insisted that his version of the agreement, not Galloway's, was what head office intended and Lowery indignantly stalked out on him. Galloway agreed with Lowery's interpretation of their deal but did not yet feel well enough to take up the cudgels for it in San Francisco and the merger fell through.

The collapse of the negotiations deprived Home Oil of one opportunity for rapid growth, but the outbreak of the Second World War in September 1939 soon provided it with another. During the next few years, Alberta became a vast training ground for hundreds of thousands of Canadian and Commonwealth troops—in particular air crews. To provide them with gasoline for their tanks and planes, George R. Cottrelle, a Toronto bank executive who had been pressed into service as Dominion Oil Controller, urged the Alberta government to relax its restrictions on the production of Turner Valley wells. The province was reluctant to set such a precedent but it recognized the necessity for greater production and so asked the federal government to take it off the hook by *ordering* the increase, making clear it was an emergency measure. C. D. Howe, the minister in charge of war production, never shrank from issuing orders when the occasion demanded—even to people who had not signified their willingness to comply with them—and the Conservation Board was duly instructed to open the chokes on the wells. The daily "allowable" for Turner Valley, which was around 20,000 barrels at the beginning of the war, was raised in stages until in 1942 the Turner Valley wells recorded their peak production of more than 10 million barrels—approximately 28,000 barrels a day, almost a quarter of Canada's total oil consumption at that time.

Home Oil's share of this record production amounted to slightly over ten per cent. The company had entered the war with one producing well, Home–Millarville No. 2. Its second and third wells came into production at the beginning of 1940 and three new ones were spudded in immediately afterward. By the end of 1942 it had twelve wells, which produced 1.14 million barrels of crude that year. And on February 9, 1943—fourteen years to the day since the company's first naphtha well had blown in on Section 20—Home–Millarville No. 2 set a record by becoming the first well in Canada to produce a million barrels of crude. It went on setting records—and Home Oil went on sinking new wells, until at the end of the war it had nineteen of its own and varying interests in twelve more drilled by other companies on sub-leases granted by Home on outlying parts of its acreage. By 1945, the company's production income was approaching $2 million a year, dividends were being paid again for the first time since 1930, and Home Oil was the largest independent company in Canada.

An expansion such as this could not, of course, have been achieved by one man, even one with Jim Lowery's diverse talents, and Home's development from little more than a corporate framework into a working company with a recognizable identity really dates from the war years. Until then, its handful of employees had been not only overshadowed but actually outnumbered by the members of the board, some of whom had always been more interested in the movement of its share prices than its operations. For the first few months after his reappointment early in 1939, Lowery worked out of his apartment in Calgary, until he was able to rent an office in the Lougheed Building downtown. The first field office for his younger brother Harold, whose title was field superintendent, was built in the summer of that year near the boiler house of the No. 2 well; from it, "Bid" Lowery supervised the activities of perhaps four or five drivers and general handymen.

The expansion began in February 1940 when Jim Lowery hired the company's first production engineer, Gordon Webster, a University of Alberta graduate in chemical engineering who had worked at Imperial's refinery in Calgary and for an oil-well servicing company in Turner Valley. Webster then took over field operations and "Bid" Lowery moved into the Calgary office. In 1941, Charlie Dingman left the government and joined the staff as chief petroleum engineer, and by the time the directors sanctioned the establishment of the company's first pension scheme at the end of that year there were ten salaried employees. As their number, and the volume of their work, continued to grow throughout the war, Lowery asked George Hudson to move to Calgary, where the company officially re-established its head office in 1942, the "funny money" scare having now abated. Hudson did not want to leave Vancouver, so he assumed the newly created post of comptroller and continued to run virtually a one-man office on the coast—where Lowery still maintained his home—and James W. Hamilton replaced him as secretary-treasurer. Hamilton brought a wealth of experience as a "land man" to Home Oil: he had worked first for the Dominion Lands Office in Medicine Hat and later, after mineral rights had been ceded to the province, in the Alberta government's land department.

The company's growth was not achieved without some setbacks. The investment in the Brazeau, for instance, was a costly disappointment. The Chungo Creek well was down more than 6,000 feet at the beginning of the war. Sanderson had expected to strike the limestone long before that depth, but he remained optimistic and the company persevered with the drilling. There was a flurry of excitement in October 1939, when a strong flow of gas was encountered at 6,686 feet—powerful enough to blow the string of tools, fifty feet long and weighing more than two tons, right out of the hole and a hundred feet into the air above the derrick. Unfortunately, the flow was short-lived and soon afterward the directors approved a change from the cable-tool rig to a rotary rig, which could penetrate deeper into the ground, at an extra cost of $150,000. But in November 1940, at 8,728 feet, the well was abandoned when it became obvious it had encountered a major fault: the drill once again entered a rock formation of the same geological age as the one it had passed through just below the surface.

By now, the ill-fated well had cost Home Oil $600,000, but the company did not give up on the Brazeau altogether: it surrendered some of its leases but retained a block of more than 22,000 acres for possible future exploration and kept Home Oil (Brazeau) Ltd. alive. (Home later acquired leases on a further 150,000 acres in the Brazeau and in 1945 formed a syndicate with Anglo-Canadian Oil Company, the California Standard Company, Imperial Oil Company, Shell Oil Company of Canada, and Socony-Vacuum Exploration Company, which spudded in another well in March of that year. It was completed as a gas well at 11,689 feet in February 1946, and though there was no market for the gas at that time the area is now a substantial natural-gas producer.) Its other subsidiary, Home Oil (Alberta) Ltd., was absorbed back into the parent company when the head office was officially re-established in Alberta.

The production of oil, for Jim Lowery, had originally been a means to an end—that end being the making of lots of money, fast. But during the Second World War it became more than that, almost a personal crusade: the best contribution that he, so far from the scene of the action, could make to the welfare of the boys at the front. Early in 1940, Victor Odlum resigned from the Home board to take command of the 2nd Canadian Division in Europe. Lowery, in his mid-fifties, was now too old to lead infantrymen into battle, but he felt himself uniquely fitted to bolster the war effort by vastly increasing the supply of that vital commodity, oil. Given Lowery's missionary zeal and his life-long impatience with authority of any sort, it was probably inevitable that sooner or later he would have come into conflict with the Oil Controller, even if that man, George Cottrelle, had not been every bit as tough and combative as Lowery himself: his pre-war duties at the bank had been the liquidation of companies unfortunate enough to have defaulted on their obligations.

A feud between Lowery and Cottrelle, which enlivened the war years for those on the fringe of it, began early in 1941. The Alberta Conservation Board, still experimenting to find an equitable formula for allotting wartime production among the many companies active in Turner Valley, had asked Lowery for permission to conduct an efficiency test on Home–Millarville No. 2. Lowery agreed to the test but, knowing the well would produce far more than its allowable, sought an assurance that it would not be charged with any over-production registered while it was going on. For some reason, the well *was* penalized for over-production when a later order of the board increased most allowables in the valley but cut back Home–Millarville No. 2's output during the month of June from 846 barrels to 610 barrels a day. Lowery wrote to Cottrelle in protest, explaining the situation and adding, "In other words, we are forbidden to produce 7,075 barrels from our No. 2 well at the most critical time in the history of the world."

He made no attempt in his letter to hide his scorn for what he described as "the absentee Conservation Board"—its chairman, an American, had lately been drafted into the government service in Washington. In his reply, Cottrelle naturally supported the board, but he also went further—much too far, in Lowery's view. He hoped no one would take advantage of his efforts to secure more oil production "in the hope of gaining a point that they may have had in mind for some time"—a thinly veiled suggestion that Home had been clamouring for more than its share of the increased production. And he continued, "You are familiar with the fact that I asked for the oil as a war emergency. In doing so, I thought I could depend on all to co-operate together to gain the desired end. It would be unfortunate if, through old or new antagonism or lack of co-operation, our war effort should fail."

The tone of Cottrelle's letter, and the imputations it contained, angered the other members of the Home board as much as they did Lowery. At their next meeting they instructed him to write to Cottrelle "and inform him that any special effort of this Company to produce oil at the present time is prompted solely by a desire to assist in the war effort, as the Directors are aware that this Company is now producing oil under high development cost with increased taxes and low price structure which would not justify the production of this oil under such conditions in peace times. . . ." Lowery followed up this formal letter two days later with another, offering to meet Cottrelle to "discuss matters" and adding, "I know in your letter that you were under certain impressions regarding my likes or dislikes of certain individuals. All I can say is that most of these technocrats do not dazzle me any longer with their theories as they have cost both me and my company a lot of money in my lifetime. So I have no hesitation at any time in demanding that they toe the line the same as you and I have always had to do in our business."

The implication that he was less than sincere in his commitment to the war effort continued to rankle with Lowery, and indeed his dedication to the cause of victory was so whole-hearted that it sometimes amused his friends. For long periods during the war he abstained entirely from alcohol as a sort of long-distance gesture of solidarity with the troops. And when the Japanese invaded Pearl Harbor he turned up at Home's field office with three heavy Winchester sporting rifles and 500 rounds of ammunition, which he entrusted to the care of a bemused Gordon Webster.

Unable to perceive any immediate threat of invasion, Webster locked the rifles in a closet and hoped he would never have to use them. But the oil industry has its own hazards and in March 1943 a long gas line being used to flush out Home–Millarville No. 14 snapped and whipped back on itself like a wild fire hose. Webster, supervising the operation, was standing beside the line: he lost one leg above the knee and the other below it. Fortunately, an engineer working for the drilling contractor had some first-aid training and he immediately applied the tourniquets without which Webster would probably not have reached the hospital in Turner Valley alive. He was in the hospital for three months, and when he emerged, still unsteady on his new artificial legs, Lowery had a two-hundred-yard board sidewalk and handrail built between his house and the field office so that he could resume his duties, in the performance of which he quickly became known as "the Douglas Bader of the oilfields". Like many others hired by Lowery, Webster went on working for Home until his retirement in 1978.

The next clash between Lowery and Cottrelle arose out of their differing views on the oil potential of Lowery's cherished north end of Turner Valley. The cost of drilling a well had risen by 1942 to between $200,000 and $300,000, and since the price paid for oil was controlled (the average wellhead price rose from a low of $1.23 per barrel in 1940 to $1.68 per barrel in 1945; by 1948 it had risen to $3.67), along with other wartime prices, it took producers a long time to recover their costs. Investors were therefore hesitant to put up capital for drilling in marginal areas where both the chance of striking oil and the potential productivity of a successful well were smaller than in established producing areas. One such marginal area was the centre of Turner Valley, south of Home's successful wells but north of the main producers in the south end. Anxious to step up the supply of oil at whatever cost, the federal government created a company named Wartime Oils Ltd. to finance wells in this area, with the leaseholders' only responsibility being to repay the cost of drilling out of production if the well was successful.

Lowery opposed all forms of government "interference" with private enterprise, particularly the use of public funds in such a risky field as oil exploration. He believed the existing companies, with their knowledge and experience, could produce all the oil needed if only they were given the incentives of tax reductions and price increases to match the steeply rising costs of drilling. But if the government insisted on spending public money to drill for oil, at least he wanted it spent in the area that promised the highest returns—and that, as he tried in vain to persuade Cottrelle, was the north end, whose wells consistently out-produced those in the south. Lowery was convinced that the full extent of the north end's reserves had not yet been delineated and he wanted "wildcat" wells drilled several miles away from Home's successful producers to prove his point.

Whether or not Cottrelle had originated the policy of subsidizing only those wells close to existing production, he certainly opposed any wildcat-drilling program in the north end. Lowery went ahead anyway, and issued subleases to other companies on outlying areas of Home's property. Cottrelle did not try to hide his satisfaction when three wells drilled privately on the northern and eastern boundaries of Home's acreage, at a cost of more than $500,000, turned out to be dry. But six other wildcats soon bore out Lowery's theory—including one well north of Home's producers which extended the company's proven area by three miles.

In a letter to Home shareholders in December 1942, under Bobby Ker's signature as president, Lowery "went public" with his complaints about Cottrelle. The letter said "present administrative methods" were handicapping producers and curtailing the production of oil, and went on: "The production of oil is retarded by the fact that there is no person in the employ of any governing body possessed of the necessary knowledge or experience to intelligently assist in the many complex problems of the production of oil in Canada. . . ."

Perhaps because of this public attack, Marsh Porter was also drawn into the Lowery–Cottrelle skirmishing. He had been asked by the Home board back in 1941 to prepare a brief for the federal income tax authorities to support the company's complaint that the tax structure penalized oil companies. In essence, this put forward a case that oil companies have never ceased to propound, and governments have never ceased to challenge: that the pace of oil exploration and development would inevitably slow down, perhaps to a halt, if oil companies were not permitted a quicker return on their drilling costs, a larger depreciation on their equipment, and an increased "depletion" allowance. The concept of depletion has always been controversial and complicated, but it developed from the proposition that oil and natural gas in the ground are part of a petroleum company's capital assets, and that as they are marketed the company is depleting part of its capital assets every year, which should be considered as a return of capital rather than taxable income.

Similar objections to the tax structure were voiced by other companies and in its budget early in 1943 the government went some way to meeting their complaints. It increased the allowance for depreciation of equipment and permitted a quicker return of well costs. But for some reason it made a distinction between producing companies and "integrated" companies possessing their own refining and marketing organizations. For instance, if an integrated company drilled a dry well it was permitted a tax deduction of forty cents on each dollar of its loss. But a company engaged solely in the production of oil, such as Home and virtually every other Canadian-owned company, was permitted to deduct only twenty-six cents on the dollar. (At that time, these deductions were available only for wells drilled in proven areas; no tax relief was permitted for wildcat wells designed to test entirely new areas.) The budget also ignored the general request for an increase in the depletion allowance, which, as Porter and others had pointed out, was considerably less than that allowed in the United States.

Porter was therefore asked to prepare another memorandum for the government pointing out some of the new policy's omissions. As a courtesy, he sent a copy of it to Cottrelle—and provoked a reply that can at best be described as testy. Dripping with sarcasm—one of its first sentences began, "It is interesting to know that you have suddenly become concerned over Canadian oil production"—the letter attempted to justify the performance of Cottrelle's organization, which had been criticized by other companies as well as Home: "The obtaining of petroleum supplies to take care of our war effort and essential services has been one of the greatest problems we in this office have had to face, and I judge we know more about the problem than anyone. I am quite willing to stand on our record as to what we have done to meet it."

Porter, along with others in the industry, had complained about the composition of several advisory committees Cottrelle had set up, and his reply continued: "You overlook the fact that it was not representatives of companies I was looking for, it was men of experience who would bury their personal interests and give unprejudiced advice—they have done so. In the light of what happened a year ago when these north end wells were drilling, you could hardly expect me to select either you or Mr. Lowery for this committee. . . ." And in an apparent reference to Porter's repeated warning that if companies were not permitted a better return on their investment the supply of capital for new exploration would dry up, Cottrelle asked: "Am I now to understand that your Company does not intend to assist the allied cause . . .?"

Never one to shirk plain speaking himself, Porter fired back an acknowledgement in which he wrote: "Your letter is full of assumptions, innuendoes, and untruths which I will not stoop to answer. Frustrated by your inability to answer the facts in the memorandum you endeavour to use the weight of your office to get the author. I observe that you are prepared to stand on your record. So were the French in the Maginot Line. At an appropriate time I will place in the files of your office some facts that will clear up the misstatements in your letter, in order that the position may be clear when your conduct of office ultimately becomes the subject of review by some appropriate public body."

Since Lowery had been mentioned in the letter, Porter showed it to him, and he immediately sat down and rattled off a letter to Cottrelle in which his indignation clearly overcame his always tenuous command of syntax: "So far as I am concerned, it would have been a shock to people who know me if I had joined any committee which, as I told you in your office last November, you wished to set up simply as a smokescreen and to pull your coals out of the fire for you. . . . It seems pathetic that your only boast to a claim for glory as Controller of Production is because you endeavoured to prevent development on Home Oil property. Since this development is one of the few successful ventures in oil since war began, I think if you check your data, then you will speak less caustically, and I believe, more intelligently on oil development. Personally, I would be flattered to be credited with the development program of the Home Oil Company in Turner Valley, especially at a time, while you were blustering around and writing similar letters as Oil Controller, that Company has produced some 3,000,000 barrels of oil 'to assist the Allied Cause'. I would much rather stand condemned by you for aggressiveness to help the war effort by such development than to carry the responsibility for the curtailment of the search for oil in Canada by private enterprise to such an extent that public money is being substituted for such drilling, which public expenditures you so bombastically announced would never be done while you were Oil Controller. You seem to have a mania for writing these silly letters to decent people in Alberta whose sole desire is to produce more oil in the midst of war. . . . Even though, in my opinion, the greatest obstacle to increasing production of oil is the attitude of mind of one George R. Cottrelle, still I feel, even in spite of that, if you would get down to business and cut out your chatter, we could all do more work and produce more oil. Let's get on with the war—we want to get it over."

Later, in a stiffly formal letter on behalf of the Home board, Lowery demanded specific details of any complaints Cottrelle might have against the company. In a conciliatory reply, the Oil Controller disavowed any intent to make "charges or threats" against

Home, which he had always considered to be "a fine company" with "a very fine Board of Directors". He hoped Lowery would realize he had a duty to perform and "Certainly, I have no intention of doing otherwise than assisting you and your Board in the operations of your Company. . . ."

Henceforth there was an uneasy truce between these two truculent characters, though for the rest of the war Lowery could not resist including passages in his letters to shareholders and annual reports contrasting Home's successes in the north end with the government-subsidized drilling program. In the 1943 annual report, for instance, he compared Home's drilling on Township 21 with the government's drilling on Township 19, to the south: "During 1943, the average production of each well in Township 21 was 92,932 barrels, against 35,483 barrels in Township 19. During the same period, it cost nearly three times as much to produce a barrel of oil and used practically three times as much casing in Township 19 as in Township 21."

The next year he wrote that while no government funds had ever been used in Home's development, both the Canadian government, in Alberta, and the U.S. government, in the Northwest Territories, had spent millions of dollars drilling for oil; yet during the past year, the Home wells had produced more oil than all the government-subsidized wells put together. "During the past two years," the report said, "your Company drilled five wells at a cost of approximately $1,000,000, while some $4,000,000 of government funds were being expended through Wartime Oils in Turner Valley to complete twenty wells. These twenty wells have not produced as much oil during the past year as your five."

Evidently Cottrelle considered discretion to be the better part of valour: he was not provoked to reply to any of these sallies. After all, the government *did* secure some oil from its wells, and it broke even on the deal, the production being adequate to repay the money advanced for drilling.

On Lowery's side, the wildcat drilling carried out on Home's property was so encouraging that the company bought up neighbouring leases and ended the war with 25,000 acres in the productive north end. Porter's efforts to modify the tax structure also bore fruit when an amendment to the Income Tax Act in 1944 permitted oil-producing companies a tax deduction of fifty per cent on losses sustained in drilling a dry wildcat well.

CHAPTER NINE

Leduc:
A New Era Begins

Bobby Ker had realized long before he was "railroaded" into the presidency of Home that Jim Lowery, however prickly and unpredictable he might be, had always been the indispensable mainspring of the company's operations. Early in 1944 he persuaded his fellow directors it was long past time to give formal recognition to this reality and resigned the presidency in Lowery's favour. The end of the Second World War thus found "the Major" at last in full, acknowledged control of the company he had organized twenty years earlier. He was now sixty, but the greying of his carroty hair had not been accompanied by any lessening of either his energy or his fiery stubbornness, and the next five years—those years during which most men slow down in contemplation of their retirement—were to be among the busiest and most productive of his life.

After their peak production of more than ten million barrels in 1942, the Turner Valley wells began a steady decline until in 1946 the total output of the field was only a little over seven million barrels. But Home Oil, with all its wells in the prolific north end, was touched hardly at all by this natural decline in production. As Lowery told Home's shareholders in his annual report in April 1946, the decline was "largely accounted for by the fact that the gross production is now much less in the older, earlier-drilled and exhausted areas of the Valley, in which your Company has no holdings." The report pointed out that during January that year the average production from a Home well was 138 barrels a day, more than twice the average for the remaining wells in the field, which was 62 barrels. And over the previous year the Home wells' output had declined at a much slower rate than the rest of the wells in the field: at an average rate of four barrels a day, compared with fourteen barrels a day for the other wells.

Despite this slight loss of production, Home's revenue increased as wartime controls were removed and the price of oil rose. "Even since the war," Lowery's report to the shareholders continued, "the Company has had to sell its production at a price far below its value. The average price received by your Company during the past year was $1.69 per barrel. During that time, on like crude oil shipped from the United States to Saskatchewan, the Federal Government paid to the refiners in Saskatchewan a subsidy of $1.30 a barrel more than you received. Recently, this subsidy was decreased and the price of your oil was raised 45¢. a barrel. Nevertheless, with the remaining subsidy being paid on imported oil, your production still sells at more than 75¢. a barrel less than its competitive value.

"The effect of this subsidy policy is to compel you to sell this wasting asset at a loss which can never be recovered. There is considerable informed opinion in the industry which anticipates increased oil prices. The importance of oil in world affairs, together with the continued low rate of discovery, combined with the increased cost of drilling and producing at much greater depths, should justify higher prices for crude oil." A year later, he was able to report that this prediction had been borne out: "With the removal of subsidies and price ceiling, prices have already increased from $1.69 to $2.64 per barrel, and a further increase in price is expected."

In these circumstances, naturally enough, Lowery continued to focus Home's main efforts in the immediate postwar years on the north end of Turner Valley, where he ultimately drilled thirty-nine wells.[1] But the valley's dwindling production made it obvious that unless a major new field was found somewhere in the province the Alberta oil industry would wither on the vine—in 1945, the output from all the other wells in the province, those in comparatively small fields such as Vermilion, Conrad, and Taber, was only 633,000 barrels, the equivalent of about one month's production in Turner Valley.

While Lowery was sometimes criticized for being insufficiently adventurous in his allocation of company funds to exploration outside Turner Valley—his main priority was always the payment of regular dividends, which he seemed to regard as almost a religious duty to the shareholders—Home did undertake in those years what the company's annual report for 1945 described as "a conservative program of wildcat exploration". In that year, for instance, it entered a three-way partnership with Imperial Oil and the Anglo-

Canadian Oil Co. Ltd.[2] to drill a well in the Folding Mountain structure, near Jasper, to test the Devonian layer of limestone, laid down between 350 and 400 million years ago below the Mississippian which had proved so prolific in Turner Valley.

That venture proved unproductive but by then Home had also entered another partnership with Anglo-Canadian and the Calgary and Edmonton Corporation to drill a series of exploratory wells across Alberta from Elk Point, on the Saskatchewan border, westward toward Edmonton. The first wells at Elk Point discovered not only a small gas field but a large deposit of salt, but the others further west proved disappointing. For a while in 1946 there was talk of drilling another well near an unremarkable little town a few miles south of Edmonton, but the exploration budget for that year was exhausted so the plan was dropped. A few months later, that town would make headlines. Its name was Leduc.

The failure to find a new field to replace Turner Valley was frustrating and worrying to other companies besides Home. Imperial Oil, for instance, drilled its first wildcat in Alberta in 1917 and by 1946 it had spent $23 million on exploration all over the west. All it had to show for those millions was a string of 133 dry wells and one discovery made in 1919 at Norman Wells, in the Northwest Territories about sixty-five miles south of the Arctic Circle, large enough only to serve the local needs of the north. Imperial had production indirectly, of course, through its Turner Valley subsidiaries, but by 1945 it was ready to give up its wildcatting in other areas and was contemplating instead the manufacture of synthetic gasoline from natural gas.

In the hope of assuring itself an adequate supply of gas for this project—its engineers estimated it would take 11,000 cubic feet of gas to make one barrel of gasoline—it took up large land holdings in the Viking–Kinsella gas field, southeast of Edmonton. But before investing the $25 million it was estimated the plant would cost, Imperial's management decided to take one last look at the possibilities of the central belt of Alberta and picked a location near Leduc for yet another exploratory well. Among the factors that contributed to the selection of the site were that it was in line with the Viking gas field, so that if no oil was found at least there was a chance of finding gas to fuel the new plant; and it was near the North Saskatchewan River, which could provide the large supply of water needed to cool the plant.

Imperial Leduc No. 1 was spudded in on November 20, 1946. The prevailing theory at the time was that any oil that might be found on the western Canadian plains would be in the Mesozoic rocks, younger and shallower than the Mississippian. But the drill penetrated to the base of this layer with only a modest showing of oil and some gas, hardly enough to make the development of the well worth while. So Imperial decided to drill deeper, more in the hope of fitting into place another piece in the jigsaw puzzle of underground topography geologists are always trying to assemble than of actually finding oil.

At 5,085 feet, past the Mississippian and into the Devonian layer of rock which had always before proved disappointing, the drill bit into a porous limestone containing obvious oil stains. On February 3, 1947, a few feet further down, the well was tested again and a gush of oil shot into the air, catapulting Alberta into its great postwar boom. Gone was the need to produce synthetic gasoline. Henceforth, the Devonian reefs, built by countless generations of tiny coral-like organisms in those inland seas so long ago, would provide the province with billions of barrels of recoverable oil reserves, riches beyond even the wildest imaginings of the early Turner Valley hands.

To celebrate its long-awaited success, Imperial invited about five hundred guests to see N. Eldon Tanner, Alberta's Minister of Lands and Mines, open the valve that put Imperial Leduc No. 1 into production on February 13, 1947. Among the crowd shivering in farmer Mike Turta's wheat field that afternoon with the thermometer lodged at well below zero Fahrenheit were Jim Lowery and Marsh Porter—who had already swung into action in their practised way to make sure that Home Oil would not be on the outside looking in at the new play.

There is in the oil industry a mysterious brotherhood of men called scouts, who make it their business to find out all they possibly can about other people's business. Their *modus operandi* being somewhat akin to James Bond's, their daily round might find them circling a rival derrick in a light plane, lurking in the woods watching it through binoculars from behind a convenient tree, or investing their expense-account dollars wisely in beer parlours frequented by loquacious roughnecks.

Whether or not Jim Lowery's source of information on this occasion was a scout, he certainly knew long before any public announcement was made about the new well that Imperial was on to a good thing, and he immediately began looking for likely acreage around Leduc. Imperial had a large part of the area sewn up in government and other leases, but much of the country around Leduc had been settled by Ukrainian immigrants before the turn of the century, so some of the farmers there still owned the rights to any minerals lying beneath their soil. And by February 8 the first of these, a man named Sereda, had been gathered into the fold: on that day, he sold his quarter-section farm to a group consisting of Home, Anglo-Canadian, c. & e. Corporation, and the California Standard Company.

But Lowery, every bit as excited as he had been in 1925, had no difficulty lining up with those optimists who even at this early stage judged Leduc to be the new Turner Valley everyone had been waiting for, and he wanted Home to get into the action on its own. Having carried his board with him easily enough, he commissioned George Cloakey, the land man with a bloodhound's nose for a promising lease, to round up all the acreage he possibly could. The first of several farmers whose confidence Cloakey was able to win was William Sycz, who had raised five children on a quarter-section close to the discovery well and seemed willing to sell it. Marsh Porter, who was by now vice-president of Home, handled the negotiations for the purchase, aided by the fact that he had for years represented the Alberta Wheat Pool: Sycz, suspicious of all city slickers, recognized him when they met in Cloakey's Edmonton hotel room and seemed relieved. "I know you," he said. "We can do business."

After some preliminary hedging, Sycz said he wanted $58,000 for his property. Then he suddenly reconsidered and asked for $58,400. Puzzled, Porter asked, "Why the extra $400?" Sycz replied, "I don't know. But it's for something my wife wants—she won't tell me what it is." He got his price—and, as the freehold owner of the mineral rights, a 12.5 per cent royalty on any oil produced from the property. But he refused to sign any papers until they had been vetted by his lawyer, the former premier John Brownlee. Porter knew Brownlee well and called him, to discover he was in Ottawa and would not be back in Alberta for at least a week.

Knowing that dozens of oil men were criss-crossing the back roads around Leduc waving bankrolls in farmers' faces as news of the Imperial strike spread, Porter tried to persuade Sycz to sign at least a provisional agreement without waiting for Brownlee's return, but he could not budge him. During the following week, representatives of other companies offered Sycz far more for his farm than the figure he had quoted to Home, but having shaken hands on the deal with Porter he turned them all down. The lease was signed on February 19, as soon as Brownlee returned and only six days after the "coming-in" party for the Imperial well.

Before the end of that year, Home had completed the first of eight successful wells it ultimately drilled on Sycz's 160 acres— four in the upper Devonian horizon, the D2, and four in the richer lower zone, the D3, which had been discovered by Imperial's second Leduc well. Since Sycz's royalty amounted to one-eighth of the property's production, he found himself in the happy position, in effect, of owning his own oil well. At the height of the eight wells' production, he was receiving more than $300 a day in royalties. This brought him up against perplexities he had never before encountered when filling in his income tax forms and one day, while "Bid" Lowery was sitting at his kitchen table helping him with this unpleasant chore, he gave vent to the fulminations against Ottawa that few taxpayers can resist at such times. "Oh Dad," he was admonished by his daughter, a teacher, "don't talk like that. You're a 'bloated capitalist' yourself now."

Presumably out of a lingering affection for his homeland rather than from any deeply thought philosophical position, Sycz had always professed to be a communist and a portrait of Stalin hung in his living room. Visiting him one day after his royalties had made him rich, Jim Lowery pointed at it and asked, "Is he a good man?" Sycz thought briefly and replied, "For Russia, yes, but not for this country."

Home used the Sycz place as headquarters for all its operations in the Leduc field, where it drilled twenty-four producing wells during the next couple of years. But it actually occupied only 14 of his 160 acres with the eight wells, a field office, warehouse, garage, and bunkhouses, and Sycz was permitted to continue to work his fields in return for paying the farm taxes, which he went on doing quite happily long after his oil income had made him financially independent.

Few Alberta farmers were as fortunate, of course, and many of those who did not own their mineral rights saw wells producing on land which had brought them only a modest payment for the surface rights. Citing the example of Bill Sycz and several other Leduc farmers whose land Home had bought, Porter once suggested to Eldon Tanner that much of the resentment this aroused against the oil companies could be avoided if the government would permit farmers at least a two per cent royalty on any wells brought in on their land. Tanner, whose later career included a term as president of TransCanada PipeLines and his subsequent elevation to the post of president and first counsellor of the Mormon Church in Salt Lake City, turned down his proposal after some thought, with a curious application of egalitarian principles: it would, he said, be unfair to farmers who had only dry wells drilled on their land.

Lowery's quick move into Leduc was only the beginning of the tremendous expansion of Home's activities he initiated in the postwar years, but at first he was frustrated by the scarcity of land available for leasing. At that time, the regulations governing the oil industry in Alberta permitted a company or individual to take out the exclusive rights to explore and develop as many as three "reservations" of up to 200,000 acres each. This policy, introduced by Eldon Tanner in the early 1940s, was unpopular with some of the independent Canadian operators because it enabled large companies, particularly those with several subsidiaries, to tie up huge tracts of land. In its defence, the government contended that it fostered exploration and development by encouraging the activities of those companies—even if most of them were American—with sufficient resources to operate on a large scale. But after Leduc, in August 1947, the government modified the regulations and a company making a discovery was permitted to retain only four square miles (2,560 acres) of any one reservation. The rest had to be returned to the government, which then put it up for sale to the highest bidder at Crown lease auctions. Later changes in the regulations further reduced the area that could be retained and introduced progressively stricter limits on the length of time land could be held without being developed.

Soon after its success at Leduc, Imperial Oil discovered another field, Woodbend, which lies across the North Saskatchewan River from Leduc and was later recognized as an extension of that field. Under the government's new land regulations it had to surrender some of its Woodbend acreage and in August 1948 Home—in partnership with Anglo-Canadian and C. & E.—made its first successful bid at a government land auction, acquiring two quarter-sections at a total cost of $64,959.84. At subsequent sales, the partnership picked up a total of more than 5,000 acres of Woodbend leases, in most of which Home held a majority interest, at a total price of $799,240. By 1950, the partnership had drilled twenty-six successful wells at Woodbend and a further thirteen in North Woodbend.

But before the first of these wells could be spudded in Imperial made another rich discovery, the Redwater field, northeast of Edmonton, and Lowery moved swiftly again. In November 1948, this time in a fifty-fifty partnership with Anglo-Canadian, he successfully bid $302,039 and $351,025 for the two adjoining quarter-sections closest to the Redwater discovery well. By March 1949 eight producing wells had been drilled on the 320 acres and their production was such—an initial average of more than 4,000 barrels a day—that within a few months they had repaid not only the cost of the land but the expenses incurred in drilling and operating them.

Spurred by this success, Home and Anglo-Canadian bought another quarter-section in Redwater at the July 1949 auction for $626,000—the highest price paid for a quarter-section since the government auctions had begun, though it fell short of the $1 million Home had paid United Oils for 160 acres back in 1929. Four more prolific wells had been brought in on this property by the end of the year.

Throughout his career as president of Home, Jim Lowery took pride in the fact that the company paid regular dividends and had no bank debt. But the vast expansion program he had plunged into imposed a heavy burden on its resources: he spent more than $3.5 million in 1948 alone, almost $925,000 of it on leases and $1.9 million on drilling costs. Even though the company's gross income from its production during the year rose to $4.5 million—$2.1 million more than the year before—for once it had to go to the bank. It took out a demand loan of $1.3 million from the Royal Bank of Canada during the year to help to finance its operations. And to pay it back the directors invited shareholders in January 1949 to purchase one share of treasury stock at $9 for each eight shares they held. (Home shares, which had risen to $5.75 in 1947—their highest point since the Depression—boomed to a high of $14.50 during 1948.)

Even though there were now more than 8,000 shareholders, the offer followed the formula Home had used for every share issue since its formation: a private invitation to all shareholders to take up the new shares on a *pro rata* basis. To Lowery's great indignation, the Toronto Stock Exchange ruled that this contravened one of its by-laws, and that instead, the shareholders should be offered warrants, or rights, to the new shares, which they could sell on the open market if for some reason they did not want to take them up themselves. Technically, the Exchange was right—George Hudson recalls that he had overlooked the relevant by-law. But threatening Jim Lowery—as the Exchange did when it warned him it would de-list Home shares if the terms of the issue were not changed— was as perilous as putting yourself between a mother bear and her cubs. He called in the reporters and told them he would not submit to "dictation" by the Exchange and the issue would go ahead as planned. When the Exchange carried out its threat, halted trading in Home shares and de-listed them, Lowery dismissed its action as merely "one more blunder" and said he was glad it had finally acted "so that they'll stop pestering me and I can get on with the job I like—digging for oil."

The Toronto Exchange's action was not supported by the Montreal, Vancouver, and Calgary exchanges, where Home shares continued to trade at around $13 throughout the battle of words. Nor, apparently, were Home's shareholders concerned by the de-listing: almost all the issue was taken up, bolstering the treasury by $1.78 million.

In succeeding months, emissaries from the Exchange and Toronto brokerage houses, which were being denied commissions while the stock was off the board, pursued George Hudson with requests that he reason with Lowery and persuade him to apply for re-listing. Still outraged, Lowery would not hear of such a thing. Why, he told Hudson, that would be admitting Home, and not those damned easterners in Toronto, had been in the wrong! For a time he even contemplated suing the Exchange, and the Home minute books contain a legal opinion from Marsh Porter that grounds for court action existed. Eventually—though not until April 1950—the Exchange invited the company to re-list its shares without penalty or prejudice. Grudgingly, Lowery agreed that the matter should be put to the shareholders and at the annual meeting that month it was formally resolved to make the required application for reinstatement. The Exchange accepted it gratefully and the shares were re-listed on May 3.

In the same month that this dispute arose, January 1949, Lowery was also embroiled in an acrimonious exchange with his old ally, Imperial Oil, over the price paid for Home's production. In an attempt to reduce its dependence on Imperial as its sole customer, Home had by now purchased from Anglo-Canadian the controlling interest in a small refinery at Brandon, Manitoba. Originally, under Lowery's prodding, the company bought a one-third interest in the refinery for $325,000 in 1945. Then, after the discovery of salt at Elk Point, Home, Anglo-Canadian, and c. & e. combined to set up a company to market it under the trade name "Cascade". The venture eventually became a commercial success but Lowery considered it too far removed from Home's real business and so in 1948 he exchanged the company's interest in the salt company for the rest of Anglo-Canadian's shares in the refinery. Controlling two-thirds of the refinery's stock, he was able to ensure that it bought all its oil from Home. But its requirements amounted to only about 2,000 barrels a day, so that Imperial remained the company's sole outlet for the rest of its production.

When Imperial suddenly cut the price for Turner Valley oil by forty-three cents a barrel in December 1948 Lowery was furious. He bombarded Imperial executives with letters and phone calls and protested to Henry Hewetson, its president, that he could get a much better deal from British American, which at that time was importing higher-priced U.S. crude to supply its refineries in Calgary and Moose Jaw, whose capacities were 6,500 and 5,500 barrels a day respectively.

On January 27, 1949, Lowery wrote to Jack White, one of Imperial's vice-presidents, formally threatening to switch to British American if Imperial did not raise its prices. Even though Imperial had been buying Home's production for twenty-one years, the two companies had no written, long-term contract. So when Imperial refused to match British American's offer—its new discoveries were by now making it less dependent on outside supplies—Lowery picked up the phone and made two calls: one to tell Imperial their long association was over and the other to Bill Whiteford, president of British American, inviting him to have his trucks start picking up Home's production at 8 a.m. on February 1.

This arrangement did not last long, because soon afterward the Alberta government introduced the "pro-rationing" scheme which still operates, under which refining companies submit their estimated requirements each month and the government decides how much of the total demand each producing well may supply, and to whom it may be sold. With the introduction of this scheme, its possession of the Brandon refinery no longer gave Home any competitive advantage and it sold its interest in it to British American in 1950 for $563,000.

These transactions led to a friendship between Lowery and Bill Whiteford, a talented and popular American brought to Canada in 1942 by Albert Leroy Ellsworth, the Canadian accountant who founded British American in 1906 to sell kerosene in Toronto and built it into the country's second-biggest oil company. And Whiteford soon let it be known that British American might be interested in buying control of Home.

Bobby Ker was in Toronto on business one day when he learned that Lowery was there, too, staying at his favourite King Edward Hotel. He phoned and suggested they go over to see Whiteford and find out what he had in mind: Ker thought he might be prepared to offer Home shareholders one share of British American plus ten dollars for each two Home shares they held. Ker had already talked this over with Gerry Hanson and they had both agreed it would be a good deal for Home's shareholders. But Lowery, despite his friendship with Whiteford, would not even agree to call on him to discuss the contemplated deal, and no more was heard of it when Whiteford returned to the U.S. soon afterward to join the huge Gulf Oil Corporation, of which he eventually became president, and later chairman. (Gulf subsequently acquired control of British American and changed its name to Gulf Oil Canada Ltd.)

There were other offers for Home Oil during those years, but Lowery's attachment to the company he had founded resembled an anxious mother's for her child and he refused to entertain any of them. At the time of his dispute with the Toronto Exchange, there were rumours that Home was about to be merged with Royalite. Lowery told reporters they were "ridiculous" and they probably were, since Imperial soon afterward sold Royalite to the Bronfman interests of Montreal for $15 million. But Imperial for many years maintained a substantial holding in Home Oil: as early as 1929 George Hudson had alerted Lowery to heavy share purchases by an unidentified buyer using banks as nominees. Lowery was about to make one of his frequent visits to the east and when he returned he told Hudson the mysterious buyer was Imperial, whose executives considered Home's liberal dividend pay-outs that year might land the company in difficulties and make it easy prey for a take-over bid—in which case, Imperial wanted to have one foot in the door to fend off its acquisition by a major competitor.

From time to time, Sam Bronfman, who had made his fortune with that other great lubricant of the twentieth century, liquor, put out feelers through Gerry Hanson to see if Home was for sale, and on one occasion the Singer sewing-machine empire in the United States expressed interest. "They want to shower us with money, George," Lowery told Hudson, "but we don't need 'em."

His refusal to consider any of these offers for Home was curious, since his own financial position was far from assured. He was now nearing retirement age and most of the money he had made through the years had slipped through his fingers like sand. Apart from his salary and the assurance of a modest pension, he still owned only a thousand shares of his own company's stock, his houses in Vancouver and at Qualicum Beach, and his attics full of "things", which, in the opinion of most of his friends, scarcely qualified as precious antiques. Any one of the potential purchasers of Home would willingly have provided him with a more secure financial future, but he apparently preferred to retain his freedom of action— even at the cost of a more or less permanent bank overdraft.

He was never happier than when he was entertaining in the rambling log house he had built at Qualicum, where he fancied himself as a barbecue chef before that black art of the backyard had attained its present ubiquity. Among the friends who sometimes donned aprons and joined him in the cloud of smoke was the Premier of Alberta, Ernest Manning. Now a Senator in Ottawa, Manning recalls that he once admired a cast-iron grill Lowery was using to barbecue steaks. Lowery told him it was an exclusive design manufactured only by a firm in Montreal, and when Manning found himself in that city a few weeks later he went in and asked if the company had a distributor in the west. The sales clerk rummaged through a file and came up with Lowery's address in Qualicum: he had ordered so many of the grills for his friends that the company had him listed as a distributor.

Salmon-fishing was a popular pastime with the guests at Qualicum. One day when Manning was out with him, Lowery boated a particularly large catch. "Let's go in early today," he said with his mischievous grin, "so we'll have more time to brag." Other regular visitors to the log house were Nick Grandmaison, the Alberta artist celebrated for his portraits of Indians, which Lowery often bought as gifts for friends; fellow-directors of Home such as Marsh Porter and Mervyn "Red" Dutton, who used his earnings as a hockey star and manager to follow in his father's footsteps and establish a substantial contracting business; and sometimes a particularly favoured member of Home's staff.

Lowery's approach to recruiting staff was often just as impulsive as his behaviour in other areas, but many of the men he hired remained with Home for life. One of his idiosyncrasies on his perpetual travels was to make several bookings on different trains or planes and then use the one that proved most convenient to him. A young Trans-Canada Air Lines booking agent in Calgary named Jack Balfour, recently returned from wartime service in Europe, proved so forbearing in the face of this practice that Lowery hired him for unspecified duties at Home. Balfour, who happened to be a nephew of Lowery's old friend Fergie Macdonald, was at various times assistant secretary, personnel manager, and until his retirement in 1977 manager of public relations for Home. Maurice Paulson, hired away from Imperial, where Lowery had first noticed him as a young engineer on Imperial Leduc No. 1, rose through a variety of executive positions until he became executive vice-president and general manager of the company. Ed Swiffen, hired as a clerk in head office in 1947, went on to become the company's purchasing agent until his retirement in 1977.

Lowery could be equally impulsive in dismissing men whose aims diverged from his own. In 1950, aware that he must gradually shed some of the load of running the company, he appointed Ted Trafford, a brilliant young English engineer with experience in the oil fields of the Middle East, to the newly created post of Manager of Home Oil. When Trafford assumed that his title carried some responsibility and opposed Lowery's plan to drill yet another well in the north end of Turner Valley, he suddenly found himself free to pursue a career as a consultant, which he did with considerable later success.

While Lowery was for the most part popular with his staff, who were endlessly amused by his eccentricities, he could also be a demanding taskmaster. Home Oil, for instance, was one of the last companies in Calgary to adopt the five-day week, and even though Lowery did not turn up at the office himself on Saturday mornings he would invariably telephone from his Palliser Hotel suite a few minutes before noon, presumably to make sure the staff was still on the job. One day he asked Rowan Coleman, whom he had hired as "general secretary" but treated as his personal assistant, to bring his car round to the Palliser at noon. Coleman, the much-decorated son of a former president of the Canadian Pacific, had commanded the Loyal Edmonton Regiment—Lowery's old unit—during the Second World War fighting in Europe. This, he figured, was why Lowery had hired him in 1947 to fill what was obviously an invented position, since Jimmy Hamilton was still ably carrying out the duties of secretary-treasurer.

When Coleman, who had no time to get lunch, arrived at the Palliser, Lowery climbed into the car and said, "I want to go out to the field." So they headed north to Leduc, then about a four-hour drive. When they arrived, Lowery did not even bother to get out of the car at the Home staff house but directed Coleman on a tour of the field, and for several hours they meandered around the back roads. They stopped nowhere and Lowery spoke to no one, merely gazing out of the window at the forest of wells. It was as if an aging warrior was revisiting the battlefields of his youth, with sad thoughts of "what might have been" running through his head. Eventually he broke his silence: "Okay, let's go back to Calgary."

Coleman's stomach was groaning when they reached the Palliser at about 11 p.m., but after dropping Lowery off he ate his supper content in the knowledge that he could sleep late next morning. Instead, at 6 a.m. on Sunday his phone rang and Lowery once again demanded the car. This time, he wanted to be driven to Turner Valley where—again without even talking to anyone—he lay down on a couch in the staff house and went to sleep. At noon he emerged, had Coleman return him to the Palliser, and said as he got out of the car, "I'm sorry to have disturbed your weekend, but I just wanted to keep moving and thinking."

It seems safe to assume that the source of his concern was the future—his own, and that of the company he had founded a quarter of a century before. Both were matters that were soon to be taken out of his own hands. On August 3, 1950, George Hudson wrote to him from Vancouver saying that he had noticed "persistent buy-ing" of Home stock on all markets, at prices up to $16. "During the first three days of this week," Hudson's letter said, "15,000 went over in Toronto, with about 6,000 each in Montreal and Vancouver, and buying is continuing today. Nearly all of the local buying is being done through Jack Lamprey's company—Yorkshire Securities Ltd.—but I do not know for whom."

It was some time before Lowery returned to Vancouver and Hudson was able to ask him if he knew who was buying up the shares and why. Lowery seemed surprisingly unconcerned. "Oh, don't worry about that," he replied off-handedly. "That's Bob Brown."

Part Two

Chapter Ten

A Wildcatter
Is Born

Bob Brown—Robert Arthur Brown, Jr.—was a treasure-seeker by inheritance. His father, the R. A. Brown who has been called the father of the oil industry in Alberta, was born in Lévis, across the St. Lawrence River from Quebec City, the eldest son of one of five brothers who owned a sailing ship and plied the river salvaging wrecks with the aid of one of the first diving suits seen in those parts. The brothers had all been born in Quebec, sons of an Irish Protestant army captain who had fled the perennial troubles of his native land for New York, where he married a Scots girl descended, according to family tradition, from the head of the Clan Campbell.

Shortly before the turn of the century one of the brothers drowned and the tragedy broke up the partnership. R. A. Brown's father—Bob's grandfather—moved to Montreal and found work as an electrician to provide for his growing family: young R. A. was eventually followed by four brothers and seven sisters and in 1900, at the age of fourteen, he had to leave school to help to support them. He followed his father into the electrical trade and proved an assiduous apprentice, cramming his bedroom with books and all the paraphernalia of electrical experiment and hoarding his pennies to pay for tutoring by McGill University instructors. While still in his teens, he went to Pittsburgh to work for the Westinghouse Electric Corporation, and for a while was an assistant to Charles Steinmetz, the German-born American scientist who pioneered in many fields of electrical research.

A brilliant student, Robert Arthur soon returned to Canada and after helping to install a water-power plant in Winnipeg turned up in Calgary in 1906, having been appointed—while still only twenty —superintendent of the North West Electric Company. A year later, he married Christina McLaughlin, a young woman who was every bit his match in sturdiness and self-reliance. Christina's father, a farmer from Priceville, Ontario, had taken her to Alberta in 1890, as a child of three, and in her teens she enrolled in Calgary's first business college and graduated as one of the first women bookkeepers in the province. That same year, 1907, Brown was hired as electrical superintendent by the city of Nelson, B.C., where he designed and supervised the building of a dam and generating station at Bonnington Falls. He returned to Calgary in 1911 as superintendent of the municipal electric light department and a few years later was put in charge of the city's streetcar system as well. A burly man with an immaculate thatch of wavy hair, R. A. Brown was hearty and gregarious, popular alike with his staff—who took naturally to calling him "the Chief"—and with the city's leading businessmen. Energetic and enterprising, he was soon fascinated by the fledgling oil industry: he can be seen as a presumably thoughtful spectator in a photograph taken to mark the coming in of the Dingman well in May 1914. His second son, Robert Arthur, Jr., was then two months old. (The elder son would die from a heart ailment a few years later, at the age of sixteen.)

The Chief had the gift of leadership and as soon as he had his city departments running smoothly he began to branch out into other ventures, seemingly without objections from the city fathers. He built up a network of small electrical utility companies—buying existing plants or establishing new ones—to supply nearby towns such as Strathmore, Gleichen, Bassano, and Okotoks, and invested the money he made from them in oil shares. He became a director of several companies, one of which rejoiced in the name Moose Dome, and at one time was president of the Bell Refining Company, which had a small refinery in Calgary. So he was well-known in oil circles when he joined the board of United Oils in 1925, the same year in which his neophyte contemporary, Jim Lowery, founded Home Oil. And, as can be judged from his handling of the million-dollar deal with Lowery in 1929, he soon became its dominant member.

R. A. Brown was as thorough in his approach to the oil business as he was in everything else he touched. He read all the books he could find that dealt with its technicalities, haunted the Turner Valley wells in search of practical information, and courted leading geologists and engineers for their expertise. And by the early thirties he was a firm adherent, if not the leader, of the small and not at all influential school of opinion which held that somewhere beneath all that gas in the Mississippian lime of Turner Valley there must be a substantial pool of crude oil.

Most oil men scoffed at this theory, accepting the prevailing view that only water lay beneath the gas. Brown was more impressed by the scattered pieces of evidence that had been accumulating to support the presence of oil long before the Spratt–Taylor paper and the advocacy of Charlie Dingman captured Jim Lowery's enthusiasm in 1936. As early as 1927, for instance, the noted New York geologist Joseph H. Sinclair predicted that crude oil would be found deep on the valley's west flank, held there under pressure from the Rockies. In 1930, when he published the first structure contour map of the valley, Dr. J. A. Goodman recommended that its west flank be tested for crude. And in that same year, Sam Coultis, the Royalite man in charge of so many wells in the valley, noticed that Model No. 1's production of naphtha was gradually becoming discoloured by what he told anyone who cared to listen was obviously crude; few listened, and ironically the Model well's product sold for less than other naphtha because of what was considered to be its "adulteration".

R. A. Brown did listen—and he was prepared to gamble his own money to prove his faith in what he heard. Eventually he found a partner willing to join him: George Melrose Bell, proprietor of *The Albertan* newspaper and, coincidentally, a director of Home Oil, though Home was at that time in the process of getting out of the oil business. In January 1934 Brown and Bell subleased sixty acres on the west slope of Turner Valley from Robert Williamson Brown, a baker in Gleichen and no relation to R. A., though they must have shared the same quality of boundless optimism: he had filed on the land seventeen years earlier and paid the lease rentals faithfully every year even though he had never been able to persuade anyone to drill on it. His perseverance was well rewarded, for before many more years had elapsed he was able to sell his bakery and retire in prosperity.

At that stage in the Dirty Thirties, with even the handful of wells that had resulted from the hundreds of sure-fire promotions of the past now apparently drying up, there was clearly no chance of selling shares in a new wildcat venture to the public. So Brown and Bell adopted a new method of financing. They formed a private company, Turner Valley Royalties Ltd., taking 9,500 shares each in return for their lease and some drilling equipment, tools, and casing they owned. John W. Moyer, a lawyer and staunch Baptist who hailed from Niagara Falls, became secretary-treasurer and took 998 shares. And instead of trying to sell common stock to the public, the new company committed seventy per cent of the production of its projected well to the payment of royalties. The price of a royalty unit, entitling its holder to one per cent of the well's production in perpetuity, was set at $1,500.

This was a safer form of investment than buying ordinary shares in an oil company, because if the well did strike oil the royalty holders were assured of a certain return on their money. In contrast, there was no guarantee that even a successful oil strike would benefit the holders of common shares in a new oil company: the directors might decide, for instance, to withhold payment of dividends, invest the profits from the well in drilling others, and go broke if they turned out to be dry.

The first company to invest was the New McDougall–Segur Oil Company, one of the earliest in Turner Valley—it had sunk a dry well two years before the Dingman well came in—which subscribed $15,000 for ten royalty units. This provided funds to build the derrick and with the help of private subscribers who clubbed together to buy a few more royalty units the well was spudded in on April 16, 1934. But in those dark days even royalties were hard to sell to a public whose lack of faith in the oil business was matched by its lack of money. On July 18, with Turner Valley Royalties No. 1 down 3,050 feet and still not encountering the expected markers, and with the company's treasury almost bare, Brown and Bell reluctantly suspended drilling and appointed a watchman to take care of the company's property until they could raise more funds.

This would take them almost a year. Legend has it that Brown mortgaged his house and car and borrowed on his insurance policies to raise enough money to continue the drilling. While this author could not confirm that, Brown certainly does seem to have thrown into the pot money he had previously settled on his family— with their willing acquiescence. His daughter Lois recalls, "I think he took back some money he had given to Mother—well, he wouldn't have to take it back, really; we were always a very close family." However the money was obtained, it was enough for only a brief resumption of drilling, which began on June 2, 1935, and was suspended again after two weeks.

Five months later, Brown's persistence as a promoter brought the final breakthrough. In return for the right to purchase all the well's production—if any—the British American Oil Company lent

Turner Valley Royalties Ltd. $30,000, secured by royalty units. For a 7.5 per cent royalty, the North West Company, a subsidiary of Imperial Oil, supplied drilling equipment worth $22,500, which enabled Brown and Bell to switch from the cable-tool rig which had begun the well to a rotary rig. Two other companies, Spooner Oils and Calmont Oils, subscribed $7,500 each for five per cent royalties.

With this long-awaited injection of capital, the drilling resumed, and on the sunny afternoon of June 16, 1936, R. A. Brown drove down to Turner Valley with his son Bob and John Moyer to see how it was progressing. Just outside the village of Black Diamond they met the toolpusher in charge of the rig, Henry "Woodrow" Wilson, and stopped to chat. "There's not much point in going any further, Chief," said Wilson. "There's nothing happening at the rig today." Having driven that far, Brown decided to carry on—he always enjoyed the camaraderie of the wellhead.

When he arrived, he saw what he took to be flecks of oil in the drilling "mud", a fluid of complex chemical composition forced down the well during rotary drilling to cool the bit and bring the rock chips cut by its action to the surface. He told the driller to bail out the well—to bring up some of the mud in the hole. As he did so, and the weight of the column of mud was reduced, the pressure of the oil in the reservoir suddenly became greater than the downward pressure of the mud and the well blew, showering crude oil over the field around the rig. (The outrage of the farmer who owned the land was assuaged when the company soon afterward paid him $2,000 for title to the five acres around the well.)

The oil was struck at 6,828 feet, much deeper than any other Turner Valley well had penetrated up to that time, and its initial flow was almost one thousand barrels a day. By eleven o'clock next morning the well had been hooked up to a hastily purchased 5,000-gallon storage tank and trucks were rolling into Calgary with the oil—which, as the *Western Oil Examiner* commented, "is not losing much time in getting the royalty holders back some of their investment." This was true enough—Brown's backers recovered their investment within a few months and went on to reap handsome profits from the deal, though George Bell's share went to his estate: he had died three months before the well came in.

The strike was the best news the province had had since the start of the Depression and it was proclaimed in banner headlines in the Calgary newspapers; on a day when the mayor announced that the city was so broke it would have to default on its monthly payment of the interest on municipal bonds, it was a welcome promise that better times might yet lie ahead.

The press reports of the find said oil men believed it proved the existence of a huge crude oil reservoir in Turner Valley, and the new wave of drilling it inspired soon substantiated their predictions.

More fanciful by far was a remark attributed to R. A. Brown, Jr., in one of the many accounts of that June day published during the years since: he is supposed to have turned to his father when the well blew in and asked, "What does it mean, Dad?" While it is possible to credit his father's alleged reply—"It means we get out of debt"—it is simply not possible to imagine Bob Brown, Jr., posing such a naive question, even during his school days. And by the time Turner Valley Royalties No. 1 came in, Bob Brown was twenty-two and already well embarked on his own remarkable career as a promoter and business prodigy.

There seems never to have been a time when the younger Brown was not fascinated by, and alert to, the opportunities afforded by business. No sooner had he acquired his first newspaper route, with his father's encouragement, than it dawned on him that it would be not only more instructive but more profitable to organize and direct the activities of a group of less enterprising carrier boys. During the three years he spent at University School in Victoria, B.C., he used to hide in the washroom reading financial newspapers. His friends from those days remember him as a serious, rather intense boy, but neither particularly studious nor outstanding academically. He was almost compulsively tidy, and while shorter than his father he had inherited the older Brown's stocky strength and curly black hair, which he hated to have mussed: only when he had suffered this indignity would he enter wholeheartedly into the games the school insisted all its students play.

At the University of Alberta, where he enrolled in the commerce course, Bob Brown was known as "Rabjer, the He-bear"— a nickname inspired by his initials and the unbreakable bear-hug he would clamp on more unruly fellow-members of the Delta Kappa Epsilon fraternity when scuffles broke out in their residence. The editor of the student newspaper, *The Gateway*, was a law student named Doug McDermid—now Mr. Justice McDermid of the Alberta Court of Appeal. He recalls that in his final year as editor Brown took over as *The Gateway*'s business manager, making it very clear that he would handle *all* business matters and would brook no interference in his department. The paper, which had been going broke, had its most successful year ever.

The Gateway was not Brown's only extra-curricular activity at the university. Just as wrapped up as his father in the affairs of Turner Valley Royalties Ltd., he spent hours cultivating a professor in a department in which he was not even enrolled, the geologist Dr. Ralph L. Rutherford, and writing surprisingly knowledgeable and mature letters to his father passing on the information he gleaned. Brown, Sr., in fact—unlike Jim Lowery, whose wife Ethel led her own life in Vancouver, entirely divorced from her husband's operations in Calgary—always enrolled his whole family in his enterprises. His wife Christina kept the books for his chain of electrical utilities, and as a teenager his daughter Lois was pressed into service to draw neat coloured maps of various Turner Valley properties. When Turner Valley Royalties No. 1 came in, Lois was on a liner bound for a holiday in Hawaii; she received a telegram giving her the glad news of the strike and offering her a job, and for a while on her return she kept the books for the newly prosperous company in the basement of the family home.

The time eventually came when Bob Brown was absent from his classes so often on company business that his accountancy professor took him aside and warned him that if his attendance record did not improve he would fail his course—with, as the professor gloomily predicted, dire consequences for his future career. "Don't worry, professor," Brown told him. "I'm going to hire your best two students to look after things for me." And in due course he did: at different times his classmates John Polomark and John Ewing both worked for him as his chief accountant. (Polomark was later killed in action in the Second World War; Ewing went on to become an executive with Imperial Oil.)

Unhappily, some of the young Bob Brown's absences on company business were marred by a regrettable failing of his father's: from time to time the Chief would lock himself away in a hotel room with a large supply of liquor—perhaps to brood or think, perhaps to blot out all thought for a while, but hell-bent to stay there until every last bottle was drained. He was never obstreperous or offensive during these bouts, and afterward he would always courteously return any bottles he had borrowed from friends during the days his bouts sometimes lasted. But his lapses were an embarrassment and sorrow to his family, and in time they told on his health: in addition to heart trouble he suffered from pernicious anemia and when he was drinking he would neglect to take the regular injections he needed.

His friends and employees all knew of his weakness but because of their admiration for his other qualities their attitude toward him was more protective than censorious. The Chief had an easy informality that inspired affection in all who worked for him, and his generosity was legendary: after the success of the Turner Valley Royalties well had established his own financial security he tore up IOUs from friends totalling about $15,000.

The coming in of the new well ended Bob Brown's formal education. He immediately became so busy exercising his inborn promotional talents in the setting up of new companies that he never bothered to return to the university to complete his studies. In a variation of the old bromide, nothing succeeds in opening up an investor's purse-strings as much as success, and those who had ridiculed the elder Brown's theories now lined up to board the bandwagon. Within weeks he and his son had formed three new companies to drill on leases close to Turner Valley Royalties No. 1, the precursors of a bewildering proliferation of interlocking ventures usually financed by the issue of royalties but with their control always safely lodged in the hands of the two Browns and their invaluable legal lieutenant, John Moyer. R. A. Brown, Jr., serenely uninhibited by his lack of a commerce degree, was president of the first of these, B. and B. Royalties; vice-president of the next, Westside Royalties; and treasurer of the third, Newfold Royalties.

By the end of 1936, Brown, Sr., was able to quit his job with the city and move in to the office from which his son was operating in Calgary's Lancaster Building. And even before the B. and B. well came in early in 1937—with twice the flow of Turner Valley Royalties No. 1—their activities had attracted the attention of a group of Toronto money men headed by Dr. R. J. Manion, a former federal railways minister, and General Garnet B. Hughes. In the biggest oil financing since the heyday of Lowery and Solloway, the Toronto group put up $420,000 to form the Brown Oil Corporation, to drill on three subleases obtained from Okalta Oils and the C. & E. Corporation. Brown Oil eventually drilled six successful wells but most of the other Brown-controlled companies, because of the royalty method of financing, were single-well operations, owning no more than forty acres of land, and if a well turned out to be dry that was the end of that particular company. Ultimately there were more than thirty of them, with names like Inter-Cities Royalties, Royal Crest Petroleums, Four Star, Three Point, and Vulcan-Brown, whose No. 1 well was for a time the biggest producer in Turner Valley after Home–Millarville No. 2.

Within a year of their first Turner Valley strike, the Browns had so many companies and so many wells drilling that their operation had become almost impossibly unwieldy. Field crews would work perhaps four hours for one company, eight hours for another, and so on, ending the week with four or five pay cheques for small amounts from several different companies. This created an enormous amount of paper work; so in October 1937 the firm of Brown, Moyer & Brown Ltd. was set up as an operating company for all the Brown interests. Henceforth, in return for a monthly operating fee from each company, Brown, Moyer & Brown purchased all the equipment and supplies for all the companies in the group, employed and paid their workers, handled all their administration and tax returns. And as the company's in-house lawyer, Bob Brown persuaded his father to hire his old colleague on *The Gateway*, Doug McDermid, who as time went on became one of his closest friends and his most trusted confidant and adviser.

The list of companies in which the Browns had an interest, or outright control, continued to grow during 1938, and to begin the process of consolidating them under one umbrella—and to provide a vehicle by which they might attract investment from the share-buying public—they set up Brown Consolidated Petroleums Ltd. in August of that year, with John Moyer their one-third partner, as always.

R. A. Brown, Jr., thus spent his early twenties, years when other young men of his background devoted much of their time to sports and girl-chasing, immersed in the formalities of directors' meetings, the intricacies of profit-and-loss statements, and the heady give-and-take of corporate financing. Other young men might possess his energy and enthusiasm, and his capacity for concentrating on business to the exclusion of everything else, but the clarity of his vision, his ability to see further down the road than even his much older and more experienced associates, had already begun to set him apart. Though short, he was handsome in a brooding, baby-faced way, and he was always soberly and immaculately dressed. He displayed a confidence far beyond his years, and whatever inward reservations he may have harboured about his place in the scheme of things never erupted to the surface in outbursts of boyish petulance or arrogance. His manners could best be described as courtly, as though he had been born into an earlier, more formal, age. Years later, an associate who had watched him negotiate multi-million-dollar deals marvelled at his ability to be deferential without sacrificing any of his obvious authority: "He was the only man I have ever seen who could bow from the waist without seeming either ridiculous or obsequious."

If this recital of his qualities makes the young Bob Brown sound almost prissy, his serious demeanour and his unfailing grasp of the business at hand inspired confidence in older men, and his father never failed to take him along on his often frustrating journeys to the east in search of capital. With the same objective, early in 1939, they travelled to London, where so many British money men wanted to see a movie they had made of their Turner Valley operations that they had to rent a theatre. Despite this promising beginning, the trip turned out to be disappointing and they were able to raise only $80,000, even though the press back in Canada in those prewar years was predicting that Alberta oil might find a ready-made customer in the shape of the Royal Navy.

As good promoters, the Browns managed to put a brave face on things when they returned to Canada in February. British financial interests, they told reporters, were "intensely interested" in finding new areas for investment offering political and economic security. "Recent months have seen a great change in British opinion in this regard," Brown, Sr., was quoted as saying, "and Canada is rapidly becoming, in their eyes, the country in the world offering the most security with the best investment opportunities."

The Browns were not the only Canadians trying to attract British investment at that time. Several groups had journeyed to London during the previous year seeking British capital for pipelines to open new markets for Alberta oil, most envisaging a line between Calgary and Vancouver[1] but one group proposing a more ambitious project—a line all the way east across the Prairies to the head of the Great Lakes. Brown, Sr., told the reporters he doubted the time was ripe for such a long pipeline and described as "bunkum" talk that the British government might build it. "This is a sober business of dollars and cents," he said, "and until Alberta oil production and oil reserves make a pipeline a good business proposition no one should expect it to be built. The time for a pipeline may come in 1939, but no one can tell, until more wells are down and a new field is brought in, just when it will be justified." In the meantime, Alberta had a small but good market on its own doorstep, and the future looked bright because "oil in the ground is just like money in the bank, and it keeps better there than in tanks above the ground."

The Chief concluded the interview by saying that with the money raised in Britain—he avoided specifying the sum but his expansiveness clearly suggested it was substantial—the Browns planned to drill three new wells, and at least one of them would be "on a structure other than Turner Valley". This was a reference to the young Bob Brown's pet project at that time—his first wildcat venture. In 1937, he had persuaded his father that B. and B. Royalties should buy from the CPR the prospecting rights on almost 17,000 acres of land in the Jumping Pound area, west of Calgary and about twenty-five miles north of Turner Valley. The next year, for some reason, he set up another company, Baroils Ltd., to hold this lease, and after he and his father returned from London in 1939 B. and B. Royalties sold its control of Baroils to the parent company, Brown Consolidated.

These transactions, like most others within the Brown network, involved the exchange of shares rather than cash, the twin problems always being to raise outside financing while retaining control in the family's hands. From the tortuous nature of many of those early deals, one might almost suspect that some of them, at least, were designed to further young Bob Brown's financial education as much as anything else, rather as five-finger exercises prepare a budding pianist for the concert stage. If that was so, they certainly succeeded, for R. A. Brown, Jr., became a true virtuoso in the field of corporate financing. His first wildcat venture, however, was a flop—at least initially. Brown Consolidated spudded in a well at Jumping Pound in May 1939, but was forced to abandon it the following December when it encountered a fault almost 7,000 feet beneath the surface.

There was no money for further drilling, but resilience is one of the trademarks of the wildcatter and Bob Brown set about finding another company with the resources to carry on the Jumping Pound exploration. He had by now virtually taken over direction of their companies' affairs from his father, and he himself handled the negotiations which resulted in the sale of the Jumping Pound venture to Shell Oil in 1942. Brown retained a 4.5 per cent gross royalty on the property for the Brown interests, the value of which became apparent when Shell struck what eventually became a major gas field at Jumping Pound in 1944.

The young Brown tried his hand at several other wildcat ventures, taking up leases in the Sarcee Indian Reserve and the Priddis area, southwest of Calgary, and while nothing came of them his capable direction of the Brown interests did enable him to establish a reputation of his own in the oil business. He was now no longer merely Bob Brown's up-and-coming youngster, and early in the war he was appointed, with the much more experienced John Galloway, of California Standard, and Ed Hunt, of Texaco, to one of the advisory committees established by Jim Lowery's adversary, the oil controller George Cottrelle.

In this capacity he could probably have remained a civilian through the war but in May 1943 he returned the direction of the family's interests to his father and joined the navy. After his basic training at Deep Brook, Nova Scotia, where he found barracks life altogether too spartan and confining for his taste, he was commissioned and posted to Ottawa in a staff appointment concerned with the supply of fuel to his comrades-in-arms.

This was long before the heyday of the oil sheikhs whose conspicuous consumption is today the marvel of Europe but Bob Brown —whose youthful appearance won him the nickname "Oil Baby"— was no more disposed to austerity than they. His service pay being only a supplement to his private income, he installed himself in a suite in the Château Laurier, which in wartime Ottawa was even more of an "in" spot than it is today. One of his few non-military contacts in the capital was a young lawyer working for the federal government, J. Ross Tolmie, whom he had met when Tolmie had represented the government in a tax case against B. and B. Royalties. The government had sought to levy corporation tax on B. and B. but the Browns argued that this would amount to double taxation, since the company had been so structured—entirely in accordance with the law—that it made no profits itself: all its income after meeting expenses was paid out directly to the royalty holders, who then paid taxes on it in the normal way. The company won its case, but this inauspicious beginning to their acquaintanceship did not prevent Brown and Tolmie from becoming close friends.

Never one to let the grass grow under his feet, Brown viewed his sojourn in Ottawa as a chance to broaden his understanding of the political and economic workings of the country. Liquor was hard to come by during the war, even in Ottawa, but Brown's resources, and his ingenuity at finding unofficial sources of supply, enabled him to play host on the generous scale he always favoured and his Château Laurier suite became a popular meeting-place for a varied circle ranging downwards from admirals to budding mandarins: Tolmie introduced him to several of his young civil-service colleagues, such as Robert Bryce, who would go on to positions of great influence in Ottawa and beyond.

Brown had not yet developed the drinking problem that would eventually prove more tragically self-destructive to him than it had to his father. For him in those days parties afforded an opportunity to meet new people, which he always enjoyed doing, and to benefit from their knowledge and experience: even in a crowded room he had a way of focusing his attention on a new acquaintance that encouraged friendship and confidences. He would supply the hospitality and in return his guests might be able to give him what he always craved—the knowledge of how things happened, or could be made to happen. In view of his unhappy experiences at the hands of various governments in later years, his guests probably benefited more from the exchange than he did: he was as generous with his inside information about the business world as he was with his liquor, and some of his wartime friends found their incomes satisfyingly augmented by his market tips.

When the war ended and he was about to return to civilian life, Brown took careful stock of his future. He was certain of only one thing: whatever he did he must be his own boss. But all the wildcatting back home, including his own, had so far failed to find the new oil field everyone realized was needed to replace the dwindling resources of Turner Valley. The oil business in Alberta, he concluded, was something of a dead end.[2] However, with the prescience that served him well in later years, he foresaw that the end of wartime austerity and the return of thousands of troops anxious to settle down with their brides and make a new start in life would create an enormous demand for consumer goods of all kinds, most of which would probably have to be imported from the United States. As soon as he was demobilized he started making the rounds of American cities seeking franchises to import, in particular, radios and household appliances. He was told by the U.S. manufacturers he approached that they could not export their goods to Canada because the Canadian manufacturers already established in their fields were operating a sort of closed shop by pooling their existing patents and thus preventing the licensing of competitive foreign imports. Brown returned to Ottawa and made some inquiries among his wartime friends, from whom he learned that the "patent pool" was indeed a fact of life, though its operation was unofficial and unadmitted by its participants.

Ross Tolmie had by now left the government and entered a law firm headed by Bill Herridge, a former Canadian ambassador in Washington and a brother-in-law of the prewar prime minister, R. B. Bennett. Brown enlisted their support to challenge the patent pool—Herridge was one of the country's leading patent counsel—and the Canadian manufacturers, when he threatened to launch an anti-combines action against them, permitted him to join the club. He was then able to obtain the franchises to distribute Bendix washing machines and home appliances across Canada and Emerson radios throughout the west.

To staff the three companies he set up—Northland Automatic Appliances, Northland Radio Industries, and Prairie Coastal Sales —he recruited a sales team that included several of his ex-service colleagues: John Scrymgeour, whom he had met during his basic training at Deep Brook, was a Maritimer who had had a summer job in the oil refinery at Dartmouth while studying commerce at Dalhousie University; Arthur M. "Scotty" Shoults was a Winnipegger and fellow naval lieutenant who went on to make a fortune in advertising and television and remained one of Brown's best friends; Rowan Coleman—who worked for Jim Lowery later— had served in the army rather than the navy but he had been at school with Brown and he readily agreed to join him when they met by chance on a train from Montreal to Ottawa; Egan Chambers, who headed operations in Montreal, was also ex-army (and later a Conservative MP). Ross Tolmie was engaged as the companies' solicitor and to the end of his days Brown retained him as his representative in Ottawa. And among the corps of young women hired to demonstrate the appliances was Genevieve Sulpher, a strikingly beautiful girl from Renfrew, Ontario, who had been a secretary in Brown's naval office in Ottawa.

The old Chief is reputed to have put up $100,000 to launch his son in the import business, but Northland was always plagued by a lack of capital and, some said, Brown's blithe disregard of costs. At least once, a carload of appliances sat in a railroad siding in Calgary for days while Brown chased round the banks trying to raise enough money to pay the freight charges and get them off. Also, in the postwar era of shortages of goods of all kinds, Brown did not have enough lines to generate the volume of business that might have made his enterprise profitable and supported him in the luxury to which he aspired.

Rowan Coleman had borrowed $16,000 on his CPR-President father's signature to invest in Northland, but with Brown apparently placing more and more reliance on his buddies Scrymgeour and Shoults he did not feel at all like a partner in the business and the time came when he wanted out. Hard-pressed as he was financially, Brown not only assumed Coleman's loan at the bank but gave him $1,500 as a severance payment and they remained friends.

The end came with a 1947 federal budget termed the "Vinegar Budget", since the only tax it lifted was that on vinegar; among its other provisions, because the value of the Canadian dollar was sinking fast, were currency restrictions prohibiting the import of "luxury goods"—such as radios and washing machines. Bob Brown's hopes of founding a commercial empire collapsed overnight. He told Scrymgeour and Tolmie to do whatever was necessary to wind up Northland and its allied companies. And to earn the money to pay off their debts he went back to the business he knew best.

CHAPTER ELEVEN

The Young Turk
Takes Over

After his son left for the navy, Bob Brown, Sr., was content to let their network of companies coast along under its own steam. He had established his own financial security and provided well for his family,[1] and it seemed he no longer felt the need to branch out and take risks. He did not, for instance, emulate Jim Lowery by jumping into Leduc after Imperial's discovery there—though young Bob, who had retained his directorships and kept a watchful eye on the oil business even while he was trying to build up Northland, once headed north with Doug McDermid when he heard that an old farmer might be willing to sell his land in a likely looking part of the field. Apparently thinking to dazzle the old man, Brown provided himself with a leather suitcase containing $80,000 in new hundred-dollar bills—and gave McDermid a bad moment when he came down to breakfast in the hotel and admitted he had left it in his room. But the farmer was less than overwhelmed by the sight of all those packages of crisp bills. He had already been offered twice that much, he told Brown; he figured he could get much more, and he was quite prepared to accept it in the form of a cheque.

The Brown family's main company when young Bob rejoined the business around the beginning of 1948 was Federated Petroleums Ltd. (When Brown Consolidated had applied for a listing on the Toronto Stock Exchange in 1940 the Exchange officials had objected that its name could be too easily confused with the earlier Brown Oil Corporation, which was already on the board, and Brown Consolidated therefore changed its name to Federated.) Probably because of the dislocation caused by the war and Bob Brown's absence in the navy, not much had yet been done to incorporate the various single-well Brown companies into their parent. Federated's largest subsidiary was Coastal Oils Ltd., which had been formed in 1944 to take over Brown Oil Corporation and had then absorbed Baroils and another Brown company, Chinook Oils, which had drilled a couple of unspectacular wells with the assistance of the government's Wartime Oils. Baroils had not yet begun to receive any royalties from its stake in the Jumping Pound field, partly because after its initial discovery Shell's second well struck water and partly because there was not yet a market for the gas. And most of the fifteen Turner Valley oil wells Federated controlled through its subsidiaries were now about ten years old and their production was declining.

Bob Brown knew the company must grow or, as its wells petered out, it would die. There are two ways to grow in the oil business: to expand your production and reserves by buying wells from other companies, or to go out exploring and find your own wells. Brown's immediate prospects of doing either, with Federated's limited resources, did not seem too bright. It was too late, for instance, to get into Leduc. But he *knew* more oil fields would turn up—it is one of the mysterious characteristics of the wildcatter that he *knows* what other mortals merely suspect or hope for—and when the next field arrived Bob Brown was going to be there.

Around the time he rejoined Federated, his father bought a King Charles spaniel pup from a breeder in Turner Valley. Unfortunately, no one had taught the pup how to behave around the house and Christina insisted it should be taken back. The breeder's farm seemed deserted when the Chief arrived so he stepped into the kitchen to call upstairs and see if anyone was home. In the kitchen was a trapdoor to the cellar—and it was wide open. Dazzled by the sun coming through one of the windows, the Chief fell through the hole into the cellar, with the pup still in his arms. A doctor called in by the breeder diagnosed several broken ribs and an ambulance was summoned to take him to hospital in Calgary. With his usual stubbornness, the Chief spurned the ambulance and insisted on Jack Hamilton driving him back to town in his own car. But it was a serious accident for a man of his age and it may have contributed to his death from a heart attack at the age of sixty-two in May 1948.

His father's death left Bob Brown in firm control of Federated Petroleums. Only 1.47 million of the company's authorized 5 million shares had been issued, and of that total only 185,024 shares were in the hands of the public. Brown Senior had left his shares to his wife, so Bob Brown and his immediate family, along with their ally John Moyer, owned more than a million of the shares outstanding. And a further 240,000 shares were owned by United Oils, which R. A. Brown, Sr., had always dominated if not controlled.

As President of Federated, Bob Brown had the full support of his board of directors, which, along with his younger brother Ronnie, consisted of three of his father's oldest and closest associates, all of whom had come to respect the heir-apparent's judgment and drive. After his father's death, Brown seemed to regard John Moyer as his mentor and the older man perhaps at times laid a restraining hand on his shoulder as his father might have done, though no one could restrain Bob Brown for long. The other two older directors were both long-standing members of the board of United Oils: Fred Green, an American who had owned a grocery store before emigrating to Calgary in the early 1900s and entering first the real-estate and then the oil business, and F. M. Compton, a contemporary whose occupation was always given simply as "Gentleman" on the lists of companies of which he was a director, usually in association with R. A. Brown, Sr.

As his right-hand man, Brown brought in the bright and eager John Scrymgeour, as soon as he had finished winding up the affairs of Northland. And at Scrymgeour's suggestion he hired as Comptroller of Brown, Moyer & Brown another ex-navy man who is remembered by his former colleagues as a financial genius. W. H. Atkinson was born in Regina in 1921 with, it would seem, rows of figures already neatly arranged in his head. At the age of thirteen he used to wend his way to and from school with his nose stuck in a copy of the *Financial Post* and before he was twenty he had graduated from the University of Saskatchewan, put in two years articling, and acquired all the qualifications he needed to take his final examinations as a chartered accountant. Since the prevailing red tape would not permit him to do this until he was twenty-one, he joined the navy, where his weak eyes confined him to shore duty, first as a pay lieutenant and later as secretary to the captain of HMCS *Protector* II, the naval base at Sydney, Nova Scotia. His astute investment of his service pay enabled him to take his time re-entering civilian life after the war—he bought a Studebaker and toured the U.S. before writing his final CA examinations, and he was working for a Regina auditing firm when his friend Scrymgeour summoned him to Calgary. During the next few years, the triumvirate of Brown, Scrymgeour, and Atkinson would preside over one of the most remarkable corporate expansions in Canadian business history.

The rudimentary organizational chart of Brown, Moyer & Brown Ltd.—not that such a thing even existed in those days—did not yet extend to the services of a geologist. But in October 1948 Brown engaged an eminent consultant, Theodore A. "Ted" Link, who during his years as Imperial's chief geologist had lived across the street from the Browns and had sustained the Chief with advice and encouragement as he struggled to bring in Turner Valley Royalties No. 1.

Imperial had just discovered the Redwater field and Link held high hopes for an area north of Redwater toward the Athabasca tar sands. So Brown allocated $64,000 from Federated's treasury to take out several government reservations covering more than half a million acres there, and set up yet another company to hold them, Redwater Petroleums Ltd. He then negotiated an agreement under which Barnsdall Oil Ltd. and two other companies—Honolulu and Seaboard—would carry out seismic exploration and test drilling on the reservations in return for part-interests in the holdings. But the success he hoped for did not come—while several gas wells were found in the area much later, they had to be capped because there was no market for their gas. Nor did Redwater Petroleums have any success with two wells it drilled near Redwater itself: both were abandoned when they turned out to be off the field to the south.

Brown's determination to find oil was in no way extinguished by these early failures, but as always his problem was to find the capital he needed to go on exploring. One of the influential friends he had made during his wartime days in the east was Brigadier James Buchanan Weir, a prominent Montreal stockbroker. Brown complained to Weir one day that Canadian banks and financial houses were cautious to the point of cowardice when it came to investing in the Alberta oil industry. Weir sympathized with him and mentioned that he had a brother-in-law, David Lovell, who was a partner in a Wall Street banking firm. Perhaps, Weir said, Lovell could open some doors for him in New York, where the financial institutions had much more experience with the risks—but potentially rich rewards—of the oil business.

Brown had now changed Redwater Petroleums' name to Time Oils Ltd., which he intended to be Federated's exploration arm. He went to New York, where Lovell introduced him to two leading investment houses, Blyth and Co. and Salomon Bros. Brown exercised his formidable charm in an effort to persuade either or both of these eminent houses to back his new company with a major financing, but neither Time, nor the time itself, was ripe: he came away empty-handed, with the realization that he, Bob Brown, and the unknown quantity, Federated Petroleums, must establish a more substantial track record before he could attract investment on the scale he needed. Then, in 1949, he saw an opportunity for expansion closer to home.

After its big discoveries at Leduc and Redwater, Imperial Oil decided to sell its subsidiary companies in Turner Valley, for two reasons: first, it needed large amounts of capital to exploit and develop the new discoveries; and second, its Turner Valley properties were not wholly owned—a minority of their shares were in the hands of ordinary members of the public—and Imperial began to feel itself vulnerable to conflict-of-interest charges. For instance, if one subsidiary, say Royalite, were to file on a lease which turned out to sustain some good producing wells, the shareholders of another subsidiary, say Foothills Oil and Gas, could legitimately ask why Imperial, as the controlling shareholder, had not put them, also, into such a profitable play. Though the taking up of leases is determined by many factors, involving technical and financial considerations and pure individual judgment, Mike Haider, an American who was president of Imperial at the time and went on to head its U.S. parent, Exxon, did not want to be put into the position of having no plain and simple answer to the question: whose shareholding are you really acting for?

So early in 1949 Imperial sold its majority shareholding in Royalite to Dominion Securities, acting for the Bronfman interests in Montreal (who later sold it to Gulf Oil). The purchase price, $15 million, was obviously far beyond the most wistful dreams of Bob Brown. But Imperial still held several smaller companies in Turner Valley—including the aforesaid Foothills—and Brown conceived the audacious idea of purchasing those. As John Scrymgeour recalled in later years, it was like a mouse trying to swallow an elephant: the companies he went after had more than three times as much production as Federated and about ten times as much working capital.

But wildcatters need to be lucky as well as bold, or they go broke and no one ever hears of them. And Brown, whether he realized it or not, had two aces in his hand: after the sale of Royalite, Mike Haider had decided it would be good public relations to sell Imperial's other properties to a local Alberta oil company rather than one of the majors, and for this reason he turned down an offer from a syndicate of Toronto financiers; and Brown's earlier ventures had brought him to the admiring attention of another young man in Toronto who was destined to become the most powerful, and possibly the most enterprising, Canadian banker of his generation.

Born in the Northern Ontario mining town of Cobalt, Neil John McKinnon joined the Canadian Bank of Commerce in 1925 as a boy of fourteen and worked his way up through the ranks. As an assistant manager of the Toronto branch, he distinguished himself in Ottawa by his presentation during the 1944 revision of the Bank Act and by the time he met Bob Brown he had been elevated to the post of assistant general manager at head office—in effect the bank's number-two man. It was in 1945, and one of the promotions Bob Brown had recommended to a group of his wartime friends had gone sour. His friends, collectively, had lost thousands of dollars he knew they could ill afford; Brown felt a responsibility to pay them back but did not have enough ready cash at the time to do so. His manner when he approached the Bank of Commerce for a loan, and his reason for wanting it, impressed McKinnon. He advanced the loan and watched Brown's later career with interest. Brown chose the Commerce as his banker for his Northland operation, and the way he paid off his debts when the business collapsed further established his reputation as a young "comer" who could be relied on to meet his obligations.

By 1949, McKinnon—virtually alone among the staid Canadian bankers of that day—could see that the western oil industry was going to be important not just to Alberta but to the Canadian economy as a whole, and he had decided the Bank of Commerce had better be involved in it. Horse-players have a choice: to back the mount or the jockey. And when Bob Brown approached him with his plan to buy the Imperial properties McKinnon did not dismiss it as an idle dream, as most other bankers considering Federated's balance sheet would certainly have done. To him, Bob Brown, Jr., seemed a jockey likely to get the best out of any ride he was offered, and he agreed to back him.

Brown, who was now thirty-five but still looked years younger, was then able to journey to Imperial Oil's head office in Toronto to do what he had wanted to do all his life: to sit at a boardroom table with captains of industry, savouring the exhilaration of negotiating a multi-million-dollar deal. In November 1949 Federated bought Imperial's majority holdings in three companies: Foothills Oil and Gas Ltd.; Lowery Petroleums Ltd. (one of Jim Lowery's early creations which had expanded considerably since it had passed into Imperial's hands in the early thirties); and Southwest Petroleums Ltd., a subsidiary of Foothills.

The deal was a triumph for Brown and an early demonstration of his skill as a negotiator. Imperial Oil's minute books reveal that Ford, Bacon and Davis, a U.S. consulting firm engaged to evaluate the three companies, had set a price of $4.8 million on Foothills and $759,000 on Lowery Petroleums. Brown picked up all three companies for a total price of $3.15 million. McKinnon arranged for the Bank of Commerce to lend Federated $2.65 million of this sum, a huge amount for a Canadian bank to lend a virtually unknown Alberta company headed by an untried entrepreneur—"that cowboy from Calgary" as Brown was sometimes called on Bay Street—even though the loan was secured by the shares of the purchased companies. But McKinnon thereafter had no reason to regret his plunge on Bob Brown as a jockey or the bank's entry into the oil industry. To nurture what eventually became a lucrative part of the bank's business he sent out a trusted lieutenant, Page Wadsworth, to become "superintendent" of the bank's Calgary branch.

(This was in an era when the head of a Canadian bank held the title of general manager, rather than president, and regional managers were known as superintendents. This archaic title was something of an embarrassment to Wadsworth when he travelled to the United States in furtherance of the bank's business. One oil man in the Midwest, having studied his business card, asked him politely but with considerable puzzlement, "Do you look after *all* the bank's buildings or just head office?")

In anticipation of the deal, Federated had raised some cash by selling $65,000 worth of bonds and several thousand shares of other companies from its investment portfolio. Even after this, its resources fell far short of filling the $500,000 gap between the bank loan and the purchase price of the properties. So the Browns' privately owned family company, Calta Assets, put up half the sum required by buying 250,000 shares from the Federated treasury at one dollar each, in return for an option to purchase a further 150,000 shares at the same price within eighteen months. At the time of this transaction, Federated's shares—which had sold for twenty-seven cents around the time Brown re-entered the business —were selling on the open market at ninety cents. With the announcement of the Foothills deal they shot up to $2.25 almost overnight. They continued to rise as Brown put Federated into one shrewd deal after another. And by early 1951, when Calta Assets exercised its option and bought 150,000 shares for $1 each, they were selling at $7.35.

Money was beginning to come to Bob Brown in the satisfying quantities he had always envisaged it would. By now he could probably have retired, still well short of his fortieth birthday, and lived in comfort for the rest of his life. But the desire to accumulate a fortune is only part of the complex drive of the wildcatter: the game is played for its own sake, and Brown's consuming ambition was to find oil and build an empire. This was the real significance of the Foothills deal: the sudden multiplication of Federated's assets and cash flow gave him the base he wanted for further expansion. Before the deal, Federated's production was 14,500 barrels a month from fifteen wells; it rose immediately to 61,000 barrels a month from fifty-three wells. And before the end of 1950, Brown had bought the rest of Imperial's Turner Valley producing companies, for $700,000, and all the wells owned by Pacific Petroleums in the valley, for $500,000. Federated now owned outright or had a major interest in 102 producing wells. John Scrymgeour estimated in a memorandum prepared for Brown in August 1950, before the purchase of the Pacific Petroleums production, that the deal with Imperial had increased the company's reserves by 2.7 million barrels, at a cost (taking into account $2.1 million in working capital inherited from the treasuries of the acquired companies) of 60 cents a barrel—for oil of a quality that was then fetching around $3.60 a barrel.

The cowboy from Calgary was now a man of some substance. But Federated was still obtaining all its production from the declining Turner Valley field—unlike its more established rival Home Oil, for instance, whose 108 wells at the end of 1949 were mostly outside the valley: 31 at Leduc, 19 at Woodbend, and 12 at Redwater. So Brown determined to use his new revenue, and his new-found credit, to expand into other areas. With a variety of partners, he picked up leases and reservations in widely scattered places such as Pincher Creek, Brochu, Buffalo Lake, and Golden Spike, another field discovered by Imperial. He also took out reservations covering 300,000 acres in the Brazeau, but even though he negotiated an arrangement under which British American would do the exploration in return for a half-interest in the property he had no more luck there than Jim Lowery had had before the war.

His first successful find came when he persuaded a group of partners to join Federated in putting up a total of $3.6 million to bid at a Crown sale for some of the acreage Imperial had had to surrender after its Redwater discovery. Federated was the largest contributor to this syndicate, with $1.28 million. Next biggest participant, with $900,000, was a group of partners in the leading Canadian financial house, Wood, Gundy and Company, Ltd., an association that came about through Brown's friendship with Alan H. Williamson, Wood Gundy's west-coast representative.

A tall and austere man with a coolly calculating financial mind, Alan Williamson joined the original Gundy company as a clerk soon after leaving high school and rose to become one of its earliest partners. He represented the firm in Vancouver and London, England, before joining C. D. Howe's wartime cadre in Ottawa. Back in Vancouver after the war, he rapidly established himself as one of the city's most influential financial figures and became the federal Liberal party's fund-raiser on the west coast. Brown, who greatly valued his advice, invited him to join the Federated board in 1952 and their close association lasted until Williamson died in 1961, his health wrecked, some said, by the strain of the controversy-plagued negotiations leading to the establishment of TransCanada PipeLines.

Three other companies—General Petroleums Ltd., New Superior Oils Ltd., and Devonian Ltd.—put $1.31 million into the syndicate between them and Brown, who had joined the board of United Oils when his father died in 1948, persuaded that almost dormant company to take a minority interest by subscribing a modest $180,000, which it had to borrow from the bank. And on May 11, 1950, the syndicate successfully bid what was then the record sum of $1.61 million—almost $10,000 an acre—for a quarter-section of land in the Simmons sector of the Redwater field, and $1.58 million for the quarter-section adjoining it to the north. Within two months, the company set up to develop this 320 acres, Highland Leaseholds Ltd., had drilled eight prolific wells. Spurred by this success, the same partners recruited several others—Leduc-West Oil Co. Ltd., Spooner Oils Ltd., Scurry Petroleums Ltd., Jupiter Oils Ltd., Calta Assets, and C. R. Spencer—to form a second company, Riverside Leaseholds Ltd., which on June 28 successfully bid $1.85 million for another quarter-section near by, on which four more productive wells were soon drilled.

Initial testing of the eight Highland Leaseholds wells showed they were capable of producing an average of 2,000 barrels of oil a day each, but the government allowable for a Redwater well at the time was only 225 barrels. And such was the glut of oil after the rash of discoveries following Leduc that the refining companies had had to impose their own rationing system: they were accepting only sixty barrels a day from each Redwater well pending completion of the pipeline to take Alberta oil to eastern Canada which had been talked about since before the war. Brown's timing, as usual, was impeccable: the line, from Edmonton to the head of the Great Lakes at Superior, Wisconsin, was built by Imperial Oil that summer and its opening early in October provided the industry with its long-awaited new market and the assurance that the post-Leduc boom would not be snuffed out for lack of customers.

Not that Bob Brown needed any reassurance about the future of the oil industry, or about the role he was resolved to play in it. The wildcatter's indestructible optimism and free-ranging imagination he always possessed were matched in those early years by a capacity for working as many hours as there are in a day. Until he married, in February 1950, at the age of thirty-five, he lived at home with his mother, whose maternal solicitude overcame whatever misgivings she might have had about his erratic hours—punctuality not being one of his virtues. Often he would telephone her in the morning and ask if he could bring three or four friends to dinner; then he would arrive home late in the evening with perhaps a dozen people—the original group of friends, people he had discussed deals with during the day, and sometimes just hangers-on who had adhered to the group somewhere along the way. Christina never reproved him on these occasions—even when the parties became noisy, as they frequently did—except to point out mildly that she could have prepared a better dinner if she had only known how many guests there would be, and when they would be arriving. Brown's marriage came as something of a surprise to his family. He had introduced his father and mother to Genny Sulpher in Ottawa during the war, and his mother was aware of his continuing friendship with her and her employment by Northland. But he did not announce his decision to marry her until the last minute, presumably because Genny was a Roman Catholic and Christina a staunch Scots Presbyterian who used to say she could "tell a Catholic just by looking at them". Once she realized that Bob had made up his mind to marry—and in the family home rather than in a Roman Catholic church—his mother accepted the situation gracefully, but it almost seemed to Brown's friends that he was too busy to get married at all. One story has it that he sent someone else to meet Genny at the train when she arrived in Calgary for the wedding, because he had to attend an important business meeting. Certainly he made no great splash of the honeymoon: he took his bride to nearby Banff for the weekend—and invited his friend "Scotty" Shoults to drive out and see them on the Sunday.

Brown's restless mind, always dreaming up ideas for expansion, would not permit him to fritter away time on relaxation. The bank's "superintendent", Page Wadsworth, once met him in the street in Calgary and told him he looked tired and should get away for a holiday. Brown confessed others had told him the same thing and he was off to the mountain resort of Jasper for a couple of weeks' rest. Wadsworth was surprised when he bumped into him again a few days later, and asked why he had not gone to Jasper. "Oh I did," said Brown, "but the telephone system there is lousy—it takes hours to get through to New York or Montreal."

The telephone was indispensable to Bob Brown's working style. Throughout his career he would spend hours at a time making calls to his continent-wide network of friends, sounding them out on his latest scheme, enlisting their help, or—just as often—alerting them to opportunities he thought they might be interested in; and sometimes just keeping in touch with developments in the oil business generally: he was always well-informed and his up-to-date knowledge often enabled him to take advantage of a new situation before his competitors were aware of what was happening.

He would never be in more need of the telephone, or be any busier, than he was during 1950, the year in which he completed his purchase of the Imperial and Pacific Petroleums production in

Turner Valley and formed the successful Highland and Riverside Leaseholds. In July, for instance, he substantially completed the buying out minority shareholders in seven of his subsidiary companies (Foothills Oil and Gas, Coastal Oils, Lowery Petroleums, Royal Crest Petroleums, Vulcan-Brown Petroleums, Three Point Petroleums, and Four Star Petroleums) and brought them into the Federated fold. And at the same time he was masterminding the behind-the-scenes operation that prompted George Hudson's warning to Jim Lowery in August that someone was buying up Home Oil's stock.

Brown had conceived this latest venture, his boldest to date, early in 1950. Federated's growing staff was by now housed in offices on the same floor of the Lougheed Building as Home Oil's, and Brown and his lieutenants, Scrymgeour and Atkinson, would sometimes sit around in the evening contemplating their future, evaluating the prospects of other companies, wondering if any were for sale and if so, whether they would fit into their ambitious plans for Federated. Building scenarios, the process might be called today. The only survivor of this triumvirate, John Scrymgeour, no longer recalls how Brown broached the idea of taking over their neighbour down the corridor, Home Oil, but obviously it was another case of the mouse trying to swallow the elephant. Home, with an annual revenue of more than $5 million and virtually no debt, was clearly a desirable property, and its 1.96 million outstanding shares were widely dispersed among more than 8,400 shareholders across the country, with no one person or group owning enough of them to constitute control of the company. But there was one big snag that it did not take Bill Atkinson's financial ingenuity to figure out: Jim Lowery ran Home, even though he held only one thousand shares; its performance was such that its shareholders were quite content to let him go on doing so; and Lowery had made it clear Home was not for sale. To take over, therefore, Brown would have to buy hundreds of thousands of shares on the open market; and with Home shares selling at more than ten dollars this operation, if it could be pulled off at all, would require millions of dollars.

The bigger the challenge, however, the more eager Brown always was to accept it. He set off for Toronto and explained what he had in mind to Neil McKinnon, who by now had become his friend as well as his banker. In his own field, McKinnon was as much of a builder as Brown himself. No doubt he recognized the plan as an audacious one—perhaps that was what appealed to him about it. At any rate, he agreed to lend Brown the millions he would need if he was to bring off his coup.

Brown then headed for Montreal, let his friend Jim Weir in on the secret, and told him to start buying Home shares—taking care, of course, not to reveal the identity of the purchaser or establish a buying pattern that would alert the market to the impending take-over and drive the price of the shares he needed up through the roof. Weir began buying in June, and some time toward the end of the summer, as the number of shares in his hands mounted, Brown told Scrymgeour he supposed it was time he let Major Lowery know what was afoot.

While relations between Jim Lowery and R. A. Brown, Sr., had been cordial enough, the two had never been close friends; perhaps, as rival promoters for so long, they were too wary of each other. But Lowery had always seemed to like young Bob and admire his ability. What passed between the old warrior and the young Turk when Brown set off down the corridor for the Home Oil office and dropped his bombshell in Lowery's lap is now lost to history: neither ever seems to have recorded what was said in that private session, or even to have spoken to others about it.

Lowery was too much the individualist, and too irascibly autocratic, to have followed a cardinal principle of the business world and groomed a younger man to succeed him. But he must have realized he would soon have to relinquish control of Home—at sixty-six, he was now a year past the normal retirement age. And it would have been well within the persuasive powers of Bob Brown to present his takeover as the best thing that could happen to Home, and to Lowery himself: Home would remain an Alberta company, run by an Alberta boy, and he, Bob Brown, would guarantee to look after Lowery. The specific arrangements he would make for Lowery's future were probably not spelled out at that meeting, but Bob Brown's word was evidently good enough for Lowery. When much later the Home directors learned that Brown was about to take over the company, George Hudson and others urged Lowery to fight, assuring him he could easily get enough shareholders' proxies to ward off Brown's bid for control. Lowery made no effort to do so.

On Brown's behalf, Jim Weir bought 481,579 shares of Home

Oil stock during the second half of 1950 and the first half of 1951, at an average price of $16. This gave Brown almost twenty-five per cent of the company's outstanding shares, acquired at a total cost—courtesy of the Bank of Commerce—of almost $8 million.[2]

The annual general meeting of Home shareholders at which Jim Lowery would report on the company's progress during 1950 and its plans for the future had been called for Saturday, April 28, 1951. By then, Brown had already assembled about 400,000 shares, giving him approximately twenty per cent of the total outstanding, and well before the date set for the meeting he let Lowery know he expected to be given some representation on the board of directors. The Home board met on the Thursday and Friday before the annual meeting and Lowery's relaying of this request kindled some spirited opposition. Bobby Ker, in particular, found Brown too rich for his conservative blood; if Brown was taking over, he told his fellow directors, he would sell his 10,000 shares and resign from the board. Marsh Porter, Lowery's long-standing legal ally, also objected to Brown's sudden advent on the scene and was disappointed with Lowery when he seemed unwilling to do anything to resist it.

That Saturday morning, as impeccably groomed as ever, R. A. Brown, Jr., walked unassumingly into the Home annual general meeting in the Palliser Hotel at the head of a group that included his brother Ronnie, John Moyer, Jim Weir, Fred Green of United Oils, the lawyer Doug McDermid, John Scrymgeour, Bill Atkinson, and W. A. Rockefeller, a collateral member of the famous U.S. family who had been introduced to Brown by Jim Weir and had agreed to lend his illustrious name to Federated by joining its board of directors.

As president of Home, Jim Lowery was chairman of the meeting and it can only be assumed that he was less than usually comfortable in that capacity. But there were no unseemly fireworks and the meeting ended with John Moyer and Jim Weir elected to the Board of Home Oil Co. Ltd. Two men retired to make way for them: Bobby Ker and Ernest Buckerfield, the last of Home's old Vancouver directors.

CHAPTER TWELVE

The Team
Is Formed

Bob Brown might have been expected now to rest on his laurels
for a while and consolidate his gains. In a little over three years
he had expanded Federated's annual revenue from $75,000 to an
astonishing $1.79 million; he had founded two other companies
which had brought in twelve good wells in the Redwater field;
and he had acquired control of the fourth-largest oil-producing
company in the country.

But if Brown had been a general he would have been a Patton
rather than an Eisenhower, content to let someone else handle the
routine staff work of consolidation and administration while he
raced ahead seeking new ground to conquer: he devoted much of
his energy during 1951 to assembling leases covering more than
400,000 acres in the Williston Basin, a newly discovered oil-
bearing structure running through the states of Montana, North
Dakota, and South Dakota.

The fact that he had taken over control of Home Oil went largely
unnoticed by its employees, to whom Jim Lowery still seemed to
be running the ship. Home continued to bring in new wells—including Home–Millarville No. 39, its last well in Turner Valley—
and to suffer its share of "dusters": it participated in the drilling
of four wildcat wells during the year, all of which turned out to be
dry. Even when Lowery resigned his presidency of Home in September 1951, few of his employees realized that his successor,
Robert B. Curran, was not his own choice. He announced the
change himself and appeared to be beaming with satisfaction as he
posed with the new president for the newspaper photographers.

But Curran, in fact, had been chosen by Bob Brown, who wanted
an executive with an acknowledged reputation as an administrator
to supervise Home's operations while he concentrated on his sortie
into the Williston Basin. Curran, an American, had been the
$25,000-a-year western manager for production and exploration

for Imperial Oil, and as such might have been expected to view his elevation to the presidency of Home Oil as sufficient reward in itself. But Brown, perhaps because he had never worked for any organization other than his own—and inexplicably, in view of his own unaided achievements as an entrepreneur—always seemed to hold in respectful awe those who had reached the senior-executive ranks of large, established companies. To secure Curran's services, he not only offered him a directorship of Home and an option on 25,000 of its shares, but dug into the pocket of his family company, Calta Assets, to provide him with a $250,000 signing bonus.[1] Curran assumed the seat on the board vacated by Marsh Porter, who had resigned when he was unable to reconcile himself to Brown's takeover of Home. Jim Lowery stepped upstairs to become chairman of the board, an honorary position, and accepted a ten-year contract as "consultant" at $25,000 a year.

The Williston Basin was the Prudhoe Bay or North Sea of its day, one of those periodic oil discoveries that seem so important they make news outside the industry itself and cause a fever of speculation on the stock market. One after the other, Shell Oil, The Texas Company, and several other operators brought in prolific wells miles apart and all producing from the same oil horizon. There were estimates that the field held reserves of 2.5 billion barrels—considerably more than the proven reserves of the rich oil states of Oklahoma or Louisiana. Using a string of local brokers, Brown moved in quickly and bought up parcels of land all over the area, spending a total of $1.76 million in Federated funds.

During this buying spree, which was complicated by the Canadian currency exchange restrictions still in force, he found himself in need of a quarter of a million dollars in U.S. currency at short notice. He asked one of his directors, Red Dutton, if he knew anyone in the U.S. who might lend it to him. Dutton took him to Great Falls, Montana, and introduced him to a friend of his, Jay McLaughlin, a contractor who hailed originally from Glengarry County, Ontario. On Dutton's recommendation, and having sized up Brown at one meeting, McLaughlin lent him the money on a mere handshake and his verbal promise to pay it back—an act of faith not unusual among western oil men.

But Brown needed far more money than that, of course, to drill his 400,000 acres, and he knew even his good friend Neil Mc-Kinnon could not advance him any more until he had arranged some means of paying back the millions he had already borrowed from the Bank of Commerce. So he set out to find a partner for the Williston Oil and Gas Company, which he set up in the U.S. in November 1951 to hold the properties he had acquired.

Ross Tolmie in those days represented several mining companies in Ottawa which were facing grave difficulties: gold-mining companies, in particular, were bedevilled by rising costs and an inability to increase their revenue since the price of gold was still pegged. Until the federal government introduced emergency legislation to subsidize the industry and save some of the mining communities, mines were being forced to close down by the dozen. So Tolmie had been urging his clients to diversify their interests by entering other fields, particularly the oil business. One of these clients was an American, Thayer Lindsley, who had founded a company named Ventures Limited to hold his Canadian mining empire, which included Sherritt-Gordon, Falconbridge Nickel, and Giant Yellowknife Gold Mine; and toward the end of 1951 Tolmie took Brown to see Lindsley in New York.

Tall, gaunt, and abstemious, a food faddist, and something of a mystic, Thayer Lindsley was one of the most colourful—and brilliantly successful—eccentrics ever to grace the Canadian business scene. The son of an American businessman in Japan, he was born in Yokohama in 1882 and did not set foot in the United States until he was twelve. After graduating from Harvard as an engineer he studied geology on the side without bothering to take a degree. This did not prevent him, after his arrival in Canada in 1924, from picking up mining properties no one else seemed to want with a prescience that amounted to genius.

By the time Brown went to see him he had expanded his empire by opening successful mines all over the world and had amassed great wealth, but he continued to live with the frugality of a Buddhist monk. During his years in Toronto he would rise at 5 a.m. to practise his yoga exercises; study his maps until 8, at which time, after a breakfast of corn flakes sprinkled with water, he would leave for the office with a neat pile of notes and correspondence ready for his secretary's attention; at noon he would break for lunch—two apples, two hard-tack biscuits, and a bottle of mineral water, which he would fish from the capacious duck pocket of the old jacket he always wore; then more work until 6 or 6:30, when he would return home to dine on a heaped plate of five different vegetables—though he would serve steaks to the assistants he often managed to inveigle home with him for a spell of unpaid overtime. Once, having flown in to Calgary for a conference at the Federated office, he reached into his pocket and discovered he had forgotten to bring along the banana he had intended to have for lunch. So he picked up the phone and called New York, to tell his secretary to rescue the banana from his desk drawer and lodge it safely in the fridge to await his return.

No man could have been more unlike the sybaritic Bob Brown. But Lindsley took to the younger man at once, perhaps seeing in him a reflection of his own single-minded dedication to the art of the entrepreneur. He promised to consider his proposition and after Brown had left discussed it with Dr. W. F. "Bill" James, the doyen of Canadian mining engineers and geologists who was at that time vice-president of Ventures. Brown, he told James, wanted him to put $7 million into Williston Oil and Gas. That, James protested, would be far too much, but perhaps it might be worth gambling $3 million. James then left for a sojourn in Florida and on his return Lindsley told him, "I've decided to put that $7 million into Williston." James gasped and asked why. "Well," said Lindsley, "seven million sounds so much better than three."

In the event, Brown promoted his cause so skilfully that Lindsley went further: in March 1952 Frobisher Ltd., Ventures' exploration subsidiary, agreed to buy a half-interest in Williston Oil and Gas for $8.25 million, payable in three yearly instalments. As his share of the deal, Brown put up the U.S. acreage he had already bought plus 232,000 acres of the basin extending northward into Saskatchewan which he had acquired later, and committed Federated to contribute a further $1.75 million to Williston in 1954, when Frobisher was due to make its final payment.

Williston's headquarters were established in Casper, Wyoming, and as his vice-president in charge of exploration Brown wooed away Shell Oil's chief geologist in the Rocky Mountain area, Alexander Clark. Born and raised on a Montana ranch, Clark was a tough, stubborn little man who had distinguished himself in his studies at the elite California Institute of Technology and found a lot of oil for Shell through the years. Brown had first met him before the war, when he had been sent north by Shell to investigate prospects in Alberta and had recommended that the company acquire acreage in the north end of Turner Valley and the Jumping

Pound area. For some reason, Shell turned down his recommendations. Jim Lowery then snapped up the Turner Valley acreage and Brown took over the Jumping Pound leases he sold to Shell many years later. Clark brought with him a lawyer from Shell's land department, Robert W. Campbell, who had taken a commerce degree at Creighton, a Jesuit university in his home state of Nebraska, before joining the paratroops during the Second World War. As a captain in the crack 101st Airborne Division, Campbell had been so seriously wounded at the Battle of the Bulge that he had to spend two and a half years in military hospitals. He had then returned to university to study law, and Brown was to find his blend of business and legal acumen invaluable in the years ahead.

With Clark exploring his 600,000 acres and Bob Campbell efficiently handling the complicated processing of his dozens of leases, Brown looked forward confidently to the success that seemed to be just around the corner: he had land all over the basin, in some places only a stone's throw from producing wells. As John Scrymgeour recalled to this author, "We couldn't conceive that we wouldn't end up big rich."

During the next three years, Williston Oil and Gas drilled or shared in the drilling of twenty-five wells. And all but three of them were dry.

A distinguishing feature of the wildcatter is his ability to take losses stoically and without discouragement: the gamble is accepted for its own sake and the thrill lies in the prospect of overcoming the probability of its failure as much as it does in the chance to make a million. So Brown was more surprised than dismayed by the disappointing outcome of his Williston adventure. But as one dry well followed another he became more and more embarrassed in the presence of Thayer Lindsley, whose eccentricities did not include a liking for losing money. Also, quite apart from his personal discomfiture, Brown knew that to stick Lindsley with a heavy loss at this stage of his career would not bode well for his ability to raise further financing for his future activities.

So in 1954 he offered Lindsley a chance to recoup his losses, and Federated and Frobisher became fifty-fifty partners in a new company, Trans-Border Oils Ltd., which took over Williston's Canadian assets (including a couple of not particularly productive wells in Saskatchewan) and participated with Federated and Home in some successful plays in Alberta. What was left of the Williston[2] company was sold in 1957 to an American company, the Midwest Oil Corporation, for $500,000, which was divided equally between Federated and Frobisher.

An incident during the negotiations for this sale demonstrated Brown's ability to take a loss with style. There had been a court case in the U.S. which suggested that the buyer of an unsuccessful company such as Williston might not be permitted to claim its losses for tax purposes; so Williston might be worthless, or it might be worth $1.5 million as a tax loss. The lawyers and accountants for one potential buyer had been despatched to negotiate with Brown and they were having difficulty arriving at a satisfactory price. Brown eventually told them, "Either there's nothing there or it's worth a million and a half. Let's toss for it." The spokesman for the group paled and protested they were not empowered to "negotiate" on that basis, and the deal fell through.

Many times during Brown's career one of his schemes that appeared on the surface to have gone awry would be found on closer examination to have contained some feature that enabled him to salvage at least a secondary benefit from the wreckage. Some of his associates attributed these occasions to gambler's luck; others, perhaps more perspicaciously, considered them proof of his genius for weighing all the angles before making a move and thinking through a deal more thoroughly than most men were able to do. So it was with his apparently ill-fated plunge into the Williston Basin. Far from being a complete loss to Brown, it paved the way for some more investments in his ventures by other mining companies and at the beginning, when the bloom was still on the rose, it helped him to bring off his first large public financing and repay the loans from the Bank of Commerce that had launched him on his way.

In 1951, when he was assembling his Williston leases, Brown raised some of the cash he always so badly needed by private placements of Federated shares. Jim Weir's company, Drinkwater, Weir in Montreal, took 200,000 shares for $1.34 million and Wood Gundy took 50,000 for $375,000. For a while, Wood Gundy also contemplated raising more money with a public issue of Home Oil shares and one of its partners, Jack McCausland, went to New York, where he was assured of the support of the investment bankers Dillon, Read. Nothing came of this plan, however—probably because Brown could not have used Home funds to repay loans made to Federated, and it was presumably considered inadvisable to attempt to float simultaneous public issues in both Home and Federated.

Dillon, Read refused to underwrite a share issue by Federated at that time on the grounds that the company was too speculative. But in 1952, with the Williston Basin fever at its height, Brown's large land holdings in the area were considered to give Federated enough "sex appeal" to ensure the success of a public issue in the United States. Wood Gundy enlisted the aid of two other Wall Street firms, Kidder, Peabody & Co. and Dominick & Dominick, and in June a million Federated common shares were sold at $10 each—half in the U.S. and half in Canada.

After deduction of the underwriting expenses, this bolstered Federated's treasury by $9.03 million—$6.87 million of which was immediately used to pay off the amount still owed to the Bank of Commerce. The remaining $2.16 million was available for the "general purposes" of Federated—which to Bob Brown meant exploring for oil. And soon after the stock issue, Federated scored its first wildcat success, a gas discovery on 5,000 acres of land it owned jointly with United Oils (which Brown had talked into taking a twenty-five per cent interest) about forty miles east of Red Deer. The well brought Federated no immediate return—it had to be capped awaiting a market—but it ushered in the important Nevis gas field.

With his huge initial bank loan paid off and both Federated and the newly formed Williston Oil and Gas assured of enough capital to meet their immediate exploration needs, Brown was now free to turn his attention to Home Oil, which during the first part of 1952 he had seemed content to leave in the hands of Bob Curran. That the old order was still changing had been made clear at Home's annual general meeting in April, when to his astonishment Jim Lowery's Montreal stockbroker friend Gerry Hanson discovered as the nominations for re-election to the board of directors were being read out that he was being dropped. Despite Lowery's embarrassed attempts from the chair to cut him off—it would seem he either had forgotten to warn Hanson what was in the wind or, more likely, had ducked that unpleasant task—the peppery little colonel insisted on having a statement expressing his indignation recorded in the minutes. After the meeting, a contrite Lowery asked George Hudson to deliver a bottle of whisky to Hanson's hotel room with his compliments. Hudson agreed to do so only with great reluctance—and as he had feared Hanson angrily spurned the peace offering.

Under Curran's direction during 1952 Home Oil seemed to be merely ticking over. It drilled four unsuccessful test wells itself during the year and participated with other companies in the drilling of four more. Through no fault of Curran's, but because the price of oil fell during the year, its revenue declined by $234,000. And its slight increase in production—from 1,463,782 to 1,530,673 barrels—was accounted for largely by Brown's decision to have Home buy the companies he had founded a couple of years earlier, Highland Leaseholds and Riverside Leaseholds. Since Highland and Riverside had completed the maximum number of wells permitted on their properties by the government's well-spacing regulations, it was realized they would in future have no exploratory expenses to set against their liability for tax. Brown therefore arranged for Home—whose exploration losses gave it more room for manoeuvre in the tax field—to buy both companies by an exchange of shares: one share of Home for each two shares of Highland and Riverside. George Hudson recalls that Jim Lowery was not unduly enthusiastic about this transaction, even though it doubled the number of Home's wells in the productive Redwater field. But by now it was more than ever clear to Lowery that while Brown had big plans for Home Oil he, as chairman of the board, did not figure very largely in them. In January 1953 he resigned the chairmanship (though retaining his $25,000-a-year position as "consultant") and Brown assumed the title.

Lowery's successor as president of Home had by now departed the scene also. Home's performance under Bob Curran had not satisfied Brown, and in November 1952, just fourteen months after he had been paid $250,000 as an inducement to leave Imperial, Curran cleaned out his desk and returned to the United States, to be replaced as president by John Moyer.

Home and Federated at this time were still operating as entirely separate companies, Brown not yet having found a way of amalgamating them—of having the mouse swallow the elephant—without endangering his control of the much larger organization that would result. But soon after he took over active direction of Home's affairs he evolved a scheme for pooling the two companies' resources, and staffs, which, as such reorganizations sometimes will, created a whole that was greater than the sum of its two parts.

Home had a dormant company, Oilwell Operators Ltd., which had been formed during the war to operate some wells owned in partnership with other companies, and on April 1, 1953, Brown revived it as a management company to carry out all exploration and operations for both Home and Federated. The staffs of both companies were transferred to Oilwell Operators and it was agreed that Home would put up seventy-five per cent of its costs and Federated the remainder. (These percentages were reduced proportionately when other partners were involved, as they usually were.)

The merging of the two staffs, of course, led at first to some duplication of functions and overlapping jurisdictions, and a few staff members drifted away when they sensed that the wind was not blowing in their favour. Aubrey Kerr, for instance, who had been Home's chief geologist since his appointment by Jim Lowery in 1949, worked happily enough with John Carr, his self-effacing but brilliant counterpart at Federated since 1950. But he was less than comfortable with Alex Clark, who took over the initial direction of Oilwell Operators, commuting between Calgary and Williston's headquarters in Casper in a de Havilland Dove Brown had bought from Red Dutton—a modest precursor of the long, and increasingly luxurious, line of company aircraft with which he indulged his regal tastes. So Kerr resigned to become first a consultant to and later chief geologist of the National Energy Board.

There were a few other departures, but the combination of the two staffs was accomplished without any firings. Brown had the courage of a lion when it came to making business decisions, to the point that those who did not know him well sometimes considered him foolhardy. But he could never summon up the nerve to fire anyone—except perhaps during the exhilaration of a late-night party, when an employee blessed with less stamina than his boss and showing signs of wanting to go home to bed might find himself peremptorily and noisily discharged. Accustomed to this foible, the suddenly unemployed party-poopers would invariably show up at the office next morning secure in the knowledge that nothing more would be said about their dereliction of duty.

The most important effect of the pooling of resources—of both money and manpower—was that it made possible the creation of an integrated exploration group larger and more effective than either company could have afforded alone. Neither Home nor

Federated, for instance, had possessed a geophysical department. The seismograph is universally used in modern oil exploration to supplement the inspired guesswork of the geologist: skilfully interpreted, its recording of the time taken by the echoes of carefully placed dynamite charges to return to the surface helps to assemble the three-dimensional map of underground rock formations oil-finders are always seeking. The technique was pioneered in the United States before the Second World War but its use was still fairly new in Canada when Brown hired George J. Blundun to set up a geophysical department for Oilwell Operators.

Born in Grenfell, Saskatchewan, in 1907, George Blundun taught school on the Prairies throughout the Depression and played in small-town dance bands to finance the extracurricular studies which eventually won him his B SC. He joined the RCAF in 1940 and because of his academic qualifications was commissioned as a navigation instructor. Discharged with the rank of wing commander in 1945, he returned to Calgary, where he had spent a tour of duty at Command HQ, with the idea of selling life insurance, since he had "bloody near starved to death teaching school". Instead, at the age of thirty-eight, he was attracted to the new field of geophysics and managed to land a job with Gulf Oil. After three months' training at the Gulf laboratories in Pittsburgh he returned to Alberta to join a seismic crew and learn about geology and geophysics in the field, where, on one job or another through the years, he had met most of the men who now became his colleagues.

Much of the credit for welding Oilwell Operators into the most successful exploration and operating unit in the country over the next few years goes to the man Brown ultimately hired to run it, a man in whom he found all the organizational and inspirational qualities he had been seeking in Curran. When he arrived at the beginning of 1954, Bart W. Gillespie was nearing the end of a forty-year career in the oil industry that had taken him from the tip of South America to Alaska. He was tough, and he could be rough, but his combination of competence and fairness inspired an affection close to hero-worship among the younger men whose activities he now began to co-ordinate.

Bart Gillespie was born in Yuma, Arizona, in 1893, the son of a railroad conductor who later moved to California, where young Bart's studies in geology and petroleum engineering at Stanford University were interrupted by a hitch as first sergeant in a company of combat engineers during the First World War. He was awarded the Silver Star for gallantry in action in France toward the end of that war but was so anxious to return to his studies he never claimed it—and the army only got around to presenting it to him fifty-eight years later, in 1976.

In his graduating year at Stanford, Gillespie's coach urged him to try out for the U.S. team for the 1920 Antwerp Olympic Games —broad and stocky, he was a powerful thrower of the sixteen-pound hammer and the discus. But young Bart had been offered a job with an oil company in Tampico, Mexico, and as he recalled many years later, "I had to eat, and you can't make a sandwich with an Olympic medal." So he went to Tampico, and remained in the oil business until his retirement in 1961, apart from four years as a regimental commander with the "Seabees", the U.S. Navy's combat engineers, during the Second World War. When Bob Brown hired him for Oilwell, as vice-president, operations, he had just quit his job as manager of western operations in Canada for Gulf Oil.

Years later, Gillespie recalled to this author, "When I joined, I thought there were a hell of a lot of nice players in there—but they hadn't formed a team yet." With Bart Gillespie as captain—he was named president of Oilwell in March 1954—the team soon formed.

CHAPTER THIRTEEN

New Discoveries –
and a Consolidation

R. A. Brown, Jr., once told a journalist, "I have an effective arrangement with the senior employees who manage the operations of Home Oil. I find the money, and they find the oil."

The arrangement certainly was an effective one. During the next five years, Brown's genius for raising money, and his willingness—indeed eagerness—to gamble it once raised, enabled the Oilwell Operators team to achieve a spectacular expansion, in the course of which they discovered several new oil and gas fields and increased Home's reserves more than sixfold.

But when Oilwell first began operations money was still scarce—the track record had not yet been established—so in 1953 Brown reversed Jim Lowery's long-standing policy of paying out roughly $1 million a year in dividends to Home's shareholders and started to plough that money back into the business. To increase the size of the pie available for slicing, he also induced two sleeping partners to share the cost of the exploration program Oilwell was about to launch on behalf of Home and Federated.

In 1953, Alminex Ltd., an investment company funded by a diverse group of mining firms, agreed to put up 12.5 per cent of Oilwell's exploration budget. Alminex was the brainchild of Fred Burton, a Toronto-based consulting geologist and mining engineer who had enlisted the help of his close friend and fellow consultant Bill James to talk some of their clients into diversifying their interests by allotting part of their funds to investment in oil exploration. Burton became its president and in its early years the company's main returns came from its profitable association with first Oilwell Operators and later Home. Then, in 1954—when Williston Oil and Gas was foundering—Brown persuaded Thayer Lindsley that their joint company, Trans-Border, should take a twenty per cent interest in Oilwell's current program.

With this infusion of outside funds, Oilwell began to put into practice the policy laid down by Brown, which was described in the company's annual report some years later as "the development of exploratory plays based upon regional geological studies . . . followed by the acquisition of land, geophysical exploration and, if desirable, exploratory drilling".

The "regional geological studies" for Oilwell's first large successful play led John Carr and the promising young lieutenant he had hired while still at Federated, George Fong, to a virgin area around Cremona, about forty miles northwest of Calgary. Son of an immigrant from China who had opened a restaurant in Red Deer, Fong was president of his high school's student council and captain of its basketball team before graduating in geology from the University of Alberta in 1948. Like his boss, Carr, he had a nose for oil, and after poring over maps of the province and examining all the geological data they could lay their hands on they concluded that there was a good chance of finding oil deposits somewhere in the Cremona area, where the Mississippian rock beds to the south appeared to peter out among the other underground strata.

Carr and Fong took their supposition along to Oilwell's land man, R. E. Humphreys. The land man is an important member of an oil-exploration team, which can stand or fall on his ability to negotiate favourable deals, and it was the fencing and haggling inherent in negotiating oil leases that had attracted Humphreys into Federated. He had in a sense been born into the oil industry—his father was an engineer who built refineries all over Canada and the United States. After a peripatetic childhood and wartime service in the Royal Winnipeg Rifles, he graduated in law from the University of Manitoba in 1950 and took a job with Doug McDermid's firm in Calgary—McDermid had resigned from Federated in 1942 to go into private practice but he continued to act for Brown until his elevation to the bench in 1963. Humphreys found the work he was assigned to in the Federated office so congenial that he abandoned his law career and went to work as Brown's land man in 1952.

When Carr and Fong brought him their Cremona theory he got out his own maps, made some discreet inquiries, and discovered that a large part of the area they were interested in was still owned by the Calgary and Edmonton Corporation. The men who ran C. & E., they all knew, had collaborated with Home in the past;

perhaps the time had come to interest them in a new venture. So they took their idea to Brown.

His technical staff never hesitated to approach Brown with a proposal to drill a wildcat well, provided they had done their homework thoroughly. They knew he understood that successful oil exploration is based largely on individual hunches and the imaginative interpretation of facts turned up by much arduous research. He knew the risk of failure and accepted it with his eyes open, and without recrimination if the gamble did not pay off. George Fong's first assignment at Federated, for instance, had been to find the oil layer beneath the gas in the newly discovered Nevis field. Since there wasn't one, it was an inauspicious beginning to his new career. But time and again, when he telephoned head office in trepidation with the news that a well had struck water instead of oil, he was both relieved and pleased to find that instead of blowing up or bemoaning his fate Brown would merely say, "Fine. Where do we go for the next one?"

Typically, Brown reacted enthusiastically when Carr and Fong explained their theory about the Cremona area, and he readily authorized Humphreys to approach C. & E. and try to work out a deal. So Humphreys, with Carr along to explain the geology, flew to Winnipeg (where C. & E. was still managed from the offices of the brokerage house Osler, Hammond & Nanton), settled into the Fort Garry Hotel, and began a series of meetings with the C. & E. executives. Eventually, he managed to buy the rights to 72,000 acres of land in the Cremona area for the bargain price of $7 an acre—$3 down and the rest a year later. (In addition to the customary 12.5 per cent royalty, C. & E. retained the right to participate up to an interest of 25 per cent in any well drilled on the property. For some reason, it later decided to forgo this right, in return for an extra 5 per cent royalty.)

It was now the task of George Blundun and his seismic crew to find evidence to support the geologists' hunch. After a series of test shots, he and Carr decided the first wildcat well should be sited on a section of land near a little settlement with the romantic name of Westward Ho, immediately south of a section held by the Hudson's Bay Oil and Gas Company. Brown at this stage could not afford to put all his eggs in one basket—Oilwell was exploring in other areas besides Cremona and he was planning to bid on proven acreage in the vast new Pembina field, discovered in July 1953. So he proposed to Hudson's Bay that the cost of the new well should be shared. After weighing up the evidence presented by Carr and Blundun, Hudson's Bay agreed that the two sections should be pooled and the costs of the well split fifty-fifty.

George Blundun by now had embraced a new enthusiasm. No mean hockey player in his youth, he went out for the Gulf Oil team when he joined that company after the war but his first game, against a team of coal miners, persuaded him his aging legs might be better suited to figure skating.[1] And early in February 1955 he returned to Calgary after competing in an ice-dancing competition at Trail, B.C., to find a $2,000 bonus on his desk—the Westward Ho well had struck a prolific oil flow and opened a new field. By the end of the year, there were ten producing wells in the Westward Ho field, and Home had an interest in all but one of them.

Jim Lowery had felt himself very much left out of all the activity surrounding the setting up of Oilwell Operators and since he was not comfortable accepting a salary he knew he was not earning he suggested to Brown early in 1954 that they come to some agreement for his complete retirement from the company. Brown had helped Lowery financially with several private deals since his take-over of Home. He is known, for instance, to have paid him $125,000 for one of his houses at Qualicum—far more than its actual worth and many times what Lowery had paid for it. Now, in return for Lowery's surrender of the contract employing him as a consultant until 1961, Home paid him a lump-sum retirement allowance of $75,000 to supplement his normal pension. Later, in August 1956, in another deal that seems to have been inspired by the desire to help Lowery, Home bought a company called Calmar Petroleums from him for $150,000. Lowery's financial situation at the time can be judged from the fact that after he had repaid various notes outstanding (including a $10,000 loan from Brown himself) he came out of the deal with only $52,000. Soon after this transaction, while happily watching the East-West Shrine football game at Vancouver's Empire Stadium, "Hustling Jimmie Lowery" collapsed and died in his seat at the age of seventy-two.

In general, Brown seems to have completed his break with the old order with considerable generosity and without hard feelings. Upon Lowery's retirement, for instance, he asked George Hudson to move from Vancouver into head office in Calgary. A confirmed

Vancouverite, Hudson refused his request—as he had turned down Jim Lowery some years earlier—and his contract, which still had a few years to run, stipulated that he must be employed in Vancouver. Brown received legal advice that unless Hudson would settle for a negotiated severance payment he might as well keep him on for the full term of his contract as a sort of general factotum in Vancouver. Instead, Brown released him and paid up his contract in full, and Hudson went on to prosper in a partnership with the well-known Vancouver broker Sir Stephen Lennard.

The passing of the old management of Home was accomplished without any of the dislocations that might have been expected. It was one of Brown's strengths that early in his career he was able to attract to himself capable lieutenants secure enough in their own powers to bring with them, or hire, gifted understudies who eventually gave Home that valuable corporate asset, a strong middle-management team with continuity and the ability to step up the ladder as circumstances required. Alex Clark, for instance, brought with him Bob Campbell, who moved into Home after Williston Oil and Gas was finally wound up in 1955 and ultimately became executive vice-president and general manager. John Carr brought in George Fong, who would one day become exploration manager. George Blundun brought with him Gene Cook, another wartime RCAF navigator, who later became chief geophysicist.

The pattern was repeated on the financial side of Brown's organization. Bill Atkinson brought in Max C. Govier, who won a gold medal in accounting at the University of Manitoba at the age of twenty-two, went to work in the oil business in Tulsa, Oklahoma, and before he was twenty-five had opened his own management-consultant firm in Calgary. Govier, who went on to become vice-president and treasurer of Home, in his turn brought in two men who had been fellow students in the Winnipeg firm Govier had once worked for, who would eventually rise to the highest executive level. Ross F. Phillips, hired as chief accountant for Oilwell Operators in 1953, filled a variety of administrative and financial posts before succeeding Brown as president of Home. And Bart Rombough, who had joined Federated before Oilwell was activated, in due course became treasurer of Home and after Brown's death replaced Phillips as vice-president, finance.

With the aid of his strong financial staff, Brown early in 1954 devised an elegant feat of corporate juggling in which he switched his control of Federated and Home to the old established United Oils, took control of that company, and bolstered the holdings of his family company, Calta Assets, by a cool $2.25 million in cash. In the years since his father's death he had already established virtual direction of the all but moribund United, not by his share holding so much as by the sheer force of his personality and the confidence in his ability felt by his father's old associates such as Green and Compton. Under his influence, the company had once again become active in oil plays, if only on a modest scale.

His assumption of control was once again made possible by his banker friend Neil McKinnon, who lent United $3.25 million. That company, whose production and royalty income the year before had amounted to the puny total of $3,506, then bought 701,376 shares of Federated and 86,666 shares of Home from Calta Assets. Combined with the shares it already owned, these were enough to give United control of Federated, and through Federated, Home Oil. In return, Calta Assets—on top of the $2.25 million cash—received 2.2 million treasury shares of United. Added to those he held already, this gave Brown 2.8 million shares of United, 45 per cent of the 6.3 million outstanding, and quite enough to give him effective control of United, at the apex of the pyramid.

Profitable though it was, this transaction did not further Brown's objective of somehow putting Home and Federated together in one large organization. The creation of Oilwell Operators had protected him from any conflict-of-interest charges his control of the two separate companies might otherwise have exposed him to, and the pooling of the talents of both companies' staffs was already beginning to pay off. But only by some form of merger or amalgamation could he reap the full benefits of his control—in particular, the increased borrowing power he would have as undisputed possessor of Canada's largest independent oil company.

That it would be to his advantage to put the two companies together was no secret around Calgary, and that he intended to do so became fairly apparent in 1954 when Home and Federated agreed to share the cost of a new three-storey office building to be erected on a lot owned by Home at the corner of Sixth Avenue West and Second Street. But as always the problem was to arrange the marriage in a way that would preserve Brown's control of the much larger company that would emerge from it.

The search for a solution to this problem eventually engaged the attention of an eminent Wall Street banking house, Lehman Bros. Founded as a cotton-brokerage firm, Lehman Bros. grew rapidly under astute management until it was handling the financing for some of the largest businesses in the United States. It was, and still is, particularly noted for its expertise in the oil industry and when the Leduc discovery focused the eyes of the oil world on Alberta, Ross Faulkner, a Lehman oil specialist, was assigned to hold a watching brief on developments in Canada. After one of his periodic visits to Calgary, Faulkner told his boss, Ed Kennedy, about Brown and his interesting corporate problem. Lehman Bros. had close contacts with Wood Gundy in Toronto and Kennedy made inquiries there which eventually resulted in Jack McCausland taking Brown to New York to introduce him to Kennedy. And early in 1955 Lehman Bros. was retained by Federated "to study the corporate, physical and financial structure" of Home and Federated.

Ed Kennedy had become an oil specialist by one of those chance turns in the road that sometimes shape a man's career. He had graduated from the school of business at Ohio State in July 1929, hardly the most propitious time to enter the business world, and joined a financial publishing company that eventually became Standard & Poor's, the famous bond-rating agency. Then, in the depths of the Depression, he took on the job of liquidating eight failed state banks in Lackawanna County, Pennsylvania. One of the bankers had been so enamoured of the oil industry that he had put most of his own bank's funds into oil companies, persuaded the other banks to follow suit, and encouraged his customers to buy oil shares with loans he provided. To salvage something from the wreckage, Kennedy had been forced to become an expert on the oil industry and he joined Lehman Bros. as such a month before Pearl Harbor.

The formula he and the Lehman staff evolved for putting Home and Federated together was not particularly unusual in the United States but it was something of a novelty in Canada. It was decided to merge Federated into Home and for that purpose Home was given a new capitalization of eight million shares, divided into Class A, which carried the right to a twenty-five-cent annual dividend but no vote, and Class B, which carried a vote but no guarantee of a dividend. The market price of Home shares at the time was about double that of Federated—Home's high in September

1955, for instance, was $12, and Federated's $6. So Federated shareholders were offered one of the new Home shares for each two Federated shares they held, and Home shareholders were offered the new shares on a one-for-one basis.

To ensure that there would be enough funds to meet the dividend commitment, it was decided that the company could afford to issue only 1.5 million Class A shares. The prospectus for the merger, which described it as "the proposed corporate simplification", made it quite clear that it was hoped the ordinary shareholders of both companies would elect to receive the A shares, with their guaranteed dividend, but that United Oils, and Brown himself, would take only the B, or voting, shares, to maintain Brown's control of the new company. In fact, the prospectus warned that if this hope was not borne out United would vote its controlling shareholding against the merger, "which in all probability would result in the defeat of such proposals and the maintenance of the existing status".

Nowadays, such a division of a company's common stock would be frowned upon, at least, and perhaps not permitted at all; most financial jurisdictions would probably insist on one of the classes being a true preference share, with a prior right to the company's assets in the event of its bankruptcy. But the shareholders had apparently been chafing under Brown's policy of withholding dividends to increase Home's operating funds and after the merger proposal was approved by the shareholders of both companies on December 6, 1955, they were glad to take the opportunity to begin receiving dividends again: more Class A shares were applied for than were available, and the shareholders had to take some of their allotment in Class B shares.

When all the shares had been exchanged and the merger was complete, United Oils held almost thirty-six per cent of the Class B shares. Three subsidiaries of Federated which now came under the Home umbrella—Foothills Oil and Gas, Coastal Oils, and Southwest Petroleums—received a further thirteen per cent, giving Brown, at the top of the pyramid, secure control of Home, with almost fifty per cent of the voting power. And just three weeks after the shareholders had approved the arrangement there was a happy augury of good times ahead for the new company: Oilwell Operators discovered another important oil field on the Cremona acreage purchased from C. & E.

Top: Dingman No. 1 well in Turner Valley in May 1914 launched Alberta's first oil boom. The interested group examining the well's output includes R. A. Brown (second from right), whose infant son would one day take over Home Oil. *(Glenbow-Alberta Institute)* **Bottom:** Promoters promptly floated more than 500 short-lived companies, peddling shares from store-front offices and milking more than $1 million from a dazzled public. *(Glenbow-Alberta Institute)*

Above: Ontario farm boy Jim Lowery (left) moved to Alberta at the age of twenty-one in 1905 but found fame and fortune elusive until he launched Home Oil twenty years later, with the backing of Vancouver investors such as George S. Harrison (right) and W. C. Shelly (in cardigan), a millionaire baker who became Home's first president. Next to Lowery: drillers Chris Bennetsen and W. B. Nicholson. *(Courtesy of Mrs. Jean Frost)* **Right:** Major Lowery (centre) poses with the crew for a photo marking the completion of Home No. 1, the company's first well. Brought in originally in 1927, it was deepened and in 1929 became the most productive well in Turner Valley. *(Courtesy of George Hudson)*

Above: The big cars favoured by Jim Lowery were not mere ostentation: they often enabled him to negotiate treacherous roads in Turner Valley when others could not. Waiting here for Home No. 1 to come in, he spent three days and nights at the wellhead, then went home and slept on a couch for eighteen hours. *(Courtesy of Mrs. Jean Frost)* **Right:** Lowery in his later years. He lost a fortune in the Depression but stayed on to make Home the largest independent oil company in Canada by the end of the Second World War. *(Courtesy of Mrs. Jean Frost)*

Above and top of opposite page: By 1937, Turner Valley had made Alberta virtually self-sufficient in oil but conditions in the field were still primitive, as shown by these photos of a truck carrying an oil tank through Longview and derricks lining the main street of Little Chicago, one of the shanty towns that sprang up to house workers. *(Glenbow-Alberta Institute)* **Opposite page, left:** Dr. J. O. G. "Pete" Sanderson, rodeo-rider-turned-geologist, was hired by Home in the thirties to survey a wilderness area known as the Brazeau, where gas seeping from the ground raised hopes for a major oil discovery. *(Courtesy of Mrs. Jean Frost)* **Opposite page, right:** During the drilling of Home Brazeau No. 1, heavy gas flow blew a two-ton string of cable tools high into the air above the derrick, but the well had to be abandoned 8,728 feet down and the Brazeau did not live up to its promise until modern times. *(Home Oil)*

Opposite and above: R. A. Brown, Sr., gambled everything to bring in Turner Valley Royalties No. 1 well, which in 1936 established Turner Valley as an oil-producing area. He and his son Bob, Jr., went on to found dozens of oil companies before young Bob took over Home in the early fifties.

Top left: Soon after his takeover of Home, R. A. Brown, Jr., strolls through Calgary with his lifelong legal adviser, J. Ross Tolmie (left). They had become friends in Ottawa during the Second World War when Brown, nicknamed the "Oil Baby", was serving as a fuel-supply officer in the navy. *(Courtesy of Ross Tolmie)* **Right and bottom:** The first well at Virginia Hills presaged Home's opening of nearby Swan Hills field, one of the most important oil discoveries ever made in Canada. *(Mach 2 Film Productions Ltd.)* This base camp photo, taken in 1957, shows the primitive nature of wilderness terrain. *(Home Oil)*

The first field parties into Swan Hills had to contend with fearsome grizzly bears (some standing nine feet tall), believed to be remnants of the extinct Plains Grizzly. This specimen, captured as a cub in the Virginia Hills area in 1962, was four years old and weighed 800 lb. when he was photographed enjoying his "baby bottle" on naturalist Al Oeming's famous Alberta Game Farm. *(Home Oil)*

Winter temperatures in Swan Hills drop to fifty degrees below zero Fahrenheit and in the early days heavy rains turned forest trails into quagmires. Even tracked vehicles often bogged down and had to be winched through bad patches. *(Mach 2 Film Productions Ltd.)*

Above: The importance of pipelines was recognized by Bob Brown early in his career. Federated line, built by Home in 1958 to take Swan Hills production to Edmonton, had an initial capacity of 22,000 barrels a day and was eventually expanded to 450,000 barrels a day. Under Brown's direction, Home became the largest single shareholder in TransCanada natural gas line. *(Mach 2 Film Productions Ltd.)* **Below:** Carstairs gas field, discovered by Home in 1958, turned out to be one of the richest in Alberta. A plant built by Home and several other companies to process gas opened in 1960 and has been expanded several times. *(Home Oil)*

Top: In his heyday, Bob Brown enjoyed throwing lavish parties. A guest at this one, held during Calgary's famous Stampede week, was CNR President Donald Gordon, suitably garbed for the occasion. *(Home Oil)* **Bottom left and right:** As a company, Home was substantial enough to survive its multi-million-dollar loss on two dry wells drilled on the North Slope of Alaska. But his boundless faith in the area's potential proved disastrous for Bob Brown. *(Home Oil)*

Opposite page: After Brown's death in 1972, Oakah Jones ran Home Oil himself, displaying a bullish tendency that pleasantly surprised his associates. *(Home Oil)* **Above:** The management team that succeeded Jones was immediately faced with new industry ground-rules caused by OPEC's quadrupling of oil prices in 1973. Left to right: A. G. S. Griffin, chairman; M. P. Paulson, executive vice-president and general manager; R. B. Coleman, senior vice-president and general counsel; R. F. Phillips, president and chief executive officer. *(Home Oil)* **Below:** Bob Brown lost his last and biggest gamble, on the North Slope of Alaska. With his personal debt a staggering $26 million, he was forced to sell his control of Home Oil. The buyer: Oakah Jones (right), chairman of The Consumers' Gas Company, of Toronto. *(Toronto Star)*

Top: After gas discoveries in Yorkshire, England, for which high hopes were held, Home built a processing plant at Pickering. Unfortunately, the gas soon petered out and the plant was first closed, then dismantled. *(Home Oil)* **Bottom:** A self-propelled, semi-submersible drilling vessel, the *Odin Drill* cost $32 million and was built by Home in partnership with another Calgary company, Bow Valley Industries, and two Norwegian firms to explore North Sea concessions.

After the discovery of the Westward Ho field, Carr and Blundun had shifted their exploratory efforts some distance to the south and drilled a well in the Harmattan area. It proved to be dry, but it was not a complete loss: it found the Mississippian layer of rock from which the Westward Ho field was producing. So a second well was drilled a couple of miles to the east. That one found gas, and was capped awaiting a market—at the end of 1955, the planned pipeline to take Alberta gas to eastern Canada was still mired in the political complications that would in due course bring down C. D. Howe and the Liberal government of Louis St. Laurent.

Undeterred by these disappointments—oil men who found gas in those days reacted with roughly the same enthusiasm as the owner of a puppy who finds a stain on the new rug—Oilwell drilled a third well midway between the first two. And on December 27 it flowed oil, opening up what later became known as the Harmattan–Elkton field, one that proved much richer than its neighbour Westward Ho. This was Oilwell Operators' last discovery as such: as a result of the merger it ceased to function and its staff was transferred to Home Oil effective January 1, 1956, a formality that made no practical difference to either the composition of the team or its operations.

During 1955, Home had spent $2.2 million on exploration and $3.8 million on the acquisition of new land—most of it proven acreage in the Pembina field, where at one time it had seventeen rigs working, causing a good deal of overtime in the new office building, which was occupied that summer. Home had secured its first production from Pembina in 1954 and it went on increasing its holdings there. On November 1, 1955, for instance, Brown successfully bid a total of $5.8 million for ten parcels of land auctioned at a Crown sale, with Home putting up 50 per cent of the money, United Oils 33.75 per cent, Trans-Border 10 per cent, and Alminex 6.25 per cent. And on January 17, 1956, Home took a 60 per cent interest in the acquisition of a further 1,920 acres for a total price of $3.48 million. By the beginning of April 1956 the company had successfully completed forty-three wells in the Pembina field, which by the end of the year had taken over as the leading source of its production.

Since the combined gross revenue of Home and Federated in 1955 was only $6.2 million, much of this activity was financed by a $12-million loan Brown negotiated with the Bank of Commerce.

As soon as the merger had gone through he set his financial staff to planning the long-term security issues which would enable him to repay this loan and finance further expansion. Brown had no truck whatsoever with the sentiment expressed by Shakespeare, that "borrowing dulls the edge of husbandry"; if the creative use of credit is an art, he was its van Gogh. By the end of 1956 he had raised $22.5 million in three separate financings which, in their variety, set the pattern for the many more still to come.

The first of these, in July, was a $7.5 million issue of five per cent subordinated debentures due in 1971 and convertible into Class A shares of Home, half of which were sold to private investors in Canada and half in the United States. The second, in September, was the sale to financial institutions of $8.5 million worth of 5.5 per cent notes secured by a lien on some of Home's properties; most of this, $5.5 million, was sold in the U.S. and the rest in Canada. The third issue, $6.5 million in 5.75 per cent sinking-fund debentures in December, was probably unique.

Canadian investors by and large were still wary of the oil business and at first Brown's advisers told him that if the issue were to be successfully marketed in Canada it would have to be fully convertible into common shares. Since the first issue had been fully convertible and the 5.5 per cent notes also carried some warrants to buy Class A shares, Brown considered that another convertible issue following so soon would add up to too much dilution of Home's equity, and he resisted their advice. Eventually, as a compromise, he agreed to the highly unusual, if not totally unprecedented, course of making only half the issue convertible. It was sold, but it was not much of a bargain for the buyers: in due course, after the holder of a $1,000 bond had converted half of it into Class A shares, he was left with a stripped $500 bond which, since it bore only 5.75 per cent interest at a time when interest rates had already risen well above that level, was not readily marketable.

The essayist Charles Lamb once defined the human species as "composed of two distinct races, the men who borrow and the men who lend". Brown's success as an unrepentant member of the first category stemmed from the extraordinary rapport he was able to establish, often on first meeting, with members of the second. Like Neil McKinnon, his backer from the beginning, the men in charge of the lending departments of the insurance companies and other financial institutions that invested in Home Oil through the years, men not prey to undue sentimentality in their scrutiny of the bottom line, trusted in his judgment and integrity and admired his seemingly fearless assumption of risks that would have reduced lesser men to jelly. Perhaps just as important, they enjoyed his company—even though he could be a demanding host or, on occasion, an intimidating guest.

Brown always did a lot of his borrowing in the United States, and at various times such diverse entities as the Princeton Institute for Advanced Studies and the employees' pension fund of the giant U.S. Steel joined the major insurance companies in purchasing Home bond issues. But his main backer in the U.S., right from the days of Highland Leaseholds, was the Mutual Life Insurance Company of New York—which by coincidence Jim Lowery had worked for in Edmonton so many years before. Historically, Mutual was one of the first U.S. insurance companies to make production loans to the oil industry and by Brown's day its oil holdings amounted to its biggest portfolio.

Mutual's director of investments was Jack King, a brilliant lawyer with an unrivalled knowledge of the oil industry and a gift for personal relationships that matched Brown's own. The two became close friends and Brown took great pride in the fact that after the huge ATT—American Telephone and Telegraph—Home Oil was one of Mutual's biggest borrowers. Once, when he was seeking a loan for some United Oils project, King eyed him speculatively and said, "As far as I can see, the point of this deal is to make you a lot of money." Brown chuckled and replied, "Congratulations—you catch on quickly." And he got his loan.

When he was borrowing, Brown never quibbled about interest rates. He used to tell his staff, "We're in a high-risk business anyway. What difference does it make if we pay seven per cent or seven and a quarter? If it's *that* important, we probably shouldn't be borrowing at all. The main thing is to get the money." Jack King once agreed to take the lead in the purchase of an issue of Home bonds at 6.75 per cent. But the preparation of the bond documents was delayed by technicalities for a couple of months and when the time came to sign them—the formal "closing" of the transaction—the interest rates prevailing on the bond market had risen.

Just before the closing, King and Brown were dining out in New York with Ross Smith, of Home's financial staff, and Ronald B.

Coleman, a young lawyer who had recently joined its legal department. King mentioned the increased interest rates to Brown—without complaining, since to men like King a deal is a deal—and Brown said expansively, "Well, I don't want you to look bad with your board, Jack—we'll give you another eighth." King protested that was not necessary; he had agreed to the rate at the time the deal was made and that was that. Smith and Coleman, exchanging astonished glances, were not sure whether Brown was serious or merely mellowed by the wine and conviviality. But next morning he insisted they change the documents to make the interest rate 6⅞ per cent. "We have Jack's goodwill," he said, "and that's important. The eighth of a point doesn't matter, but the gesture will return itself one day."

Coleman, who went on to become Home's senior vice-president and general counsel, discovered years later how right he was. Home wanted to sell some properties that had been pledged to Mutual to secure a loan, so Brown picked up the phone and had a short conversation with King. And when Coleman arrived at the Mutual offices to discuss the release of the properties—which normally involves substituting other security or renegotiating the whole deal— he found the surprised Mutual staff prepared to hand over the properties on the spot. "We've been told to do this," said one of the Mutual men dubiously, "but that Brown must have some stroke around here to get away with it."

Behind Brown's borrowings, of course, there was always the security of the performance of Home Oil as a company, and the $22.5 million he raised in the first year after the merger was used to good effect. Home completed eighty-three producing oil wells during 1956, and its crude production increased by 43.9 per cent: by the end of the year it was running at the record rate of 10,000 barrels a day.

The new money also financed a successful new venture: Home's entry into the pipeline business. Early in his career, Brown had been fascinated by the fortunes made by pipeline builders in the United States, and as time went on he formed a theory that transportation was so important to Canada that whoever controlled it virtually controlled the country. Since his ambition knew no bounds, in 1951 he set aside $100,000 of Federated's then meagre funds to form a company he called the Independent Pipeline Company, and applied for a Federal charter to build an oil line from

Edmonton to Vancouver *via* the Yellowhead Pass through the Rockies.

The Pacific Northwest, the area including the major cities of Portland, Oregon, Seattle, Washington, and Vancouver, at that time received virtually all its petroleum products—a quarter of a million barrels a day—by tankers sailing up the coast from California. With the Second World War only six years in the past and a new war being fought across the Pacific in Korea, the security of the region's oil supply was a matter of concern—and Brown, like the rest of the Alberta producers, was always looking for new oil markets. So he commissioned an aerial survey of the proposed pipeline route, at a cost of $37,500, and engaged the well-known U.S. consulting firm of Purvin and Gertz to carry out a study which proved the feasibility of a line which could carry 50,000 barrels a day—enough to meet Vancouver's needs—and could be expanded to carry 110,000 barrels a day without using much more steel (a scarce commodity because of the Korean War) and at comparatively little extra expense.

Unfortunately for Brown, he had still to establish his track record and his credit was not yet good enough to enable him to finance such a major undertaking—it was estimated the line would cost at least $75 million. Moreover, there were several other applicants for the charter, and it was awarded at the end of 1951 to Trans-Mountain Oil Pipeline Company, of which the initial shareholders (later joined by several other major companies) were Imperial Oil and the huge U.S. engineering company Bechtel Corporation.

Brown was bitterly disappointed, and when his next opportunity to enter the pipeline business arose he resolved not to miss out again. In 1955 he incorporated Cremona Pipe Lines Ltd. as a wholly owned subsidiary of Home and applied for a provincial permit to gather all the oil from the Westward Ho and Harmattan fields, together with the Sundre field adjoining them to the north, and take it to the refineries in east Calgary through a sixty-five-mile pipeline. Bob Campbell, who had now finished winding up Williston's affairs in Casper, moved in to take charge of the application, with the help of Ian Drum, a school friend of Brown's who, as a chemical engineer, worked on special projects for Home.

The first hearings before the province's Petroleum and Natural Gas Conservation Board were held in the summer of 1955 and

Cremona's application was opposed by two competitors: Rangeland Pipe Line, owned by Hudson's Bay Oil and Gas (which had made the original discovery at Sundre, shared with Home in the Westward Ho discovery, and believed it had a prior right to build the line); and Pembina Pipe Line, owned by the Mannix construction firm and several other interests. Both Rangeland and Pembina wanted to build a line north from the Cremona area to take the oil to Edmonton, which since Leduc had begun to take over from Calgary as the refinery centre of the province. Brown held out for his plan to take it to Calgary—which at that time had three aging refineries served only by a pipeline from the declining Turner Valley and by railroad tank car from the minor field of West Drumheller—and the board adjourned without being able to reach a decision. The hearings were resumed early in 1956, and Brown's application was strongly supported by the city of Calgary, whose administration feared it would lose its refinery industry if new oil supplies were not forthcoming. In March, the board awarded the permit to build the line to Cremona Pipe Lines. Jack Balfour, Home's former public relations director, recalls that on the day the decision was announced Brown fairly skipped into his office and proclaimed, "This is the start of an empire."

In this, as it turned out, he was sadly over-optimistic: in the years ahead, his ambition to be a pipeline tycoon would cost him—and Home—dearly, and bring him little more than frustration and disappointment. But the Cremona line, built during the summer of 1956 at a cost of $2.6 million, proved a useful revenue-earner, and as a side-effect it increased the wellhead price received by Home and all the other producers for their Cremona crude. Hitherto this had been taken to Calgary by tank truck, at a cost of fifty-six cents a barrel; henceforth it was transported to market for thirty cents a barrel.

As usual in the oil business, not all of Brown's investments that year were as successful as the Cremona pipeline. At a Crown sale on May 24 he successfully bid the whimsical figure of $1,666,666.66 for a quarter-section of land at Bonnie Glen, south of Leduc. When George Blundun heard about this bid, after it had succeeded, he was astonished—and furious, because for some reason the geophysical department had not been consulted about the property and he was fairly sure it was off the field's oil-bearing reef. Neither, as it turned out, had the bid been recommended by John Carr, the company's chief geologist. It seems to have arisen from a private enthusiasm for the property shared by Brown and Alex Clark, who was then vice-president, exploration. It was one of the few occasions when communications within the exploration group had broken down—and Brown never let it happen again. For a well sunk on the property that summer was abandoned at 7,000 feet and the 160 acres never did produce a drop of oil.

Fortunately for Home, Brown had as usual enlisted other partners in the deal. United Oils, for instance, put up forty-six per cent of the money, and Home had to bear only thirty per cent of the loss. But as one of the company's production foremen, Jim Fraser, commented drily at the time, "He might just as well have bought beer for the boys."

CHAPTER FOURTEEN

Swan Hills:
A Triumph in the Wilderness

Early in his career, before joining Federated, George Fong had spent some time examining rock chips from a well being drilled south of Lesser Slave Lake, about 170 miles northwest of Edmonton. Some of them, from a layer of rock known as the Beaverhill Lake, contained fossils that aroused his scientific curiosity. The Beaverhill Lake formation had not previously yielded oil or gas but this evidence suggested that under certain circumstances it might contain oil-bearing reefs. Those chips stayed in his mind and after the discovery of the Westward Ho and Harmattan fields, when the time came to select another area for exploration, he mentioned them to John Carr and suggested it might be worth while looking for the Beaverhill Lake formation some distance south of where he had previously worked—in the Swan Hills, about 125 miles northwest of Edmonton.

While they were still vaguely speculating about the Swan Hills area and casting about for whatever geological information they could find relating to it, Bob Brown had a visitor whose call quickened their interest considerably. Dr. Hans Suter, a Swiss-born PH D in petroleum geology who had spent most of his life in the oil industry in Latin America and Trinidad, was exploration manager in Alberta for a company known as Regent Refining.[1] And he had a theory about the Swan Hills area which, while it differed from Fong's, made the proposition he brought to Home an intriguing one.

Suter had arrived in Alberta in 1952 and while familiarizing himself with its geology had noted with interest that there were Devonian reefs cropping out of mountains in the Rockies. The first oil-bearing reef found in Alberta had been Leduc and by now it was known that Leduc's Devonian reef extended across central Alberta in a straight east-west line. Suter reasoned that there could well be parallel reefs extending eastward from the outcrops in the

Rockies and picked on Swan Hills as a likely region in which to prove his theory. In 1954, Regent bid $287,252 at a Crown sale for the prospecting rights to a four-township block—92,160 acres— in the Swan Hills area, and Suter followed up his hunch with ground and aerial surveys and some seismic work. By 1956, when he came to Brown, he was sure there should be oil beneath Regent's four townships but he did not have enough money to drill a well and confirm his hopes. So he offered Brown a "farm-out" agreement under which Home could earn a forty per cent interest in the property in return for drilling an exploratory well.

The offer provided Carr and Fong with a useful opportunity to carry on their own investigations. They knew the middle Devonian thickened sharply eastward from somewhere in the Swan Hills area, and since the Beaverhill Lake formation in which they were interested lay below the level at which Suter expected to find his Devonian reef, if they came up dry on Suter's theory they could press on deeper in an attempt to prove their own. They recommended to Brown that he accept the deal.

Before the details could be worked out, however, Suter apologetically withdrew his offer, explaining with some embarrassment that his head office felt compelled to do so because Regent's parent company in London had begun the negotiations which eventually resulted in Texaco buying Trinidad Oil, and hence also Regent Refining.

Brown was now just as enthusiastic about the Swan Hills possibilities as the geologists, so he had Bob Humphreys look around for any other deals he might be able to make in the area. Humphreys found that another four-township block to the southwest of the Regent property, in an area known as Virginia Hills, was jointly owned by the Union Oil Company of California and Hudson's Bay Oil and Gas, who were apparently willing to consider an approach from Home. So the haggling began once again and by an agreement dated August 23 Home undertook to drill two exploratory wells at Virginia Hills, at a minimum expenditure of $400,000, in return for a one-third interest in any oil that might result.

Humphreys also reported that two reservations to the northwest of the Regent property, totalling more than 160,000 acres, were owned jointly by Canadian Fina and Imperial Oil, and by September 12 Home had negotiated another agreement giving it a one-third interest in this property—known as Grizzly Mountain—in return for the expenditure of a minimum of $350,000 on exploration work, including the drilling of a test well.

Meanwhile, Dr. Suter was still anxious to prove his own theory about Swan Hills. When his new bosses in Toronto had taken over direction of Regent's activities he had explained it to them and been disappointed by their reaction: they had shown no interest in drilling an exploratory well themselves and Suter even gathered that they thought he had paid too much money for what was still an unproved reservation. So he asked for, and was given, permission to renew his attempt to farm out the property. Since he had begun his negotiations with Home, he felt a moral obligation to return to Brown and this time, in view of Texaco's apparent lack of interest, he improved his terms and offered Brown a fifty-fifty deal. So, on November 6, Home agreed to pay Regent $50,000 in cash and spend a minimum of $900,000 on exploration of the four Swan Hills townships, once again including the drilling of a test well, in return for a fifty per cent interest in the property.

The $1.7 million Home undertook to spend on exploration under these agreements was to be split four ways, with Home putting up 62.5 per cent of the total and Alminex, United Oils, and Geoil Ltd. (the Frobisher subsidiary which had held half of the now defunct Trans-Border company with Federated) providing 12.5 per cent each. But as usual all the work was to be done by the Home team, and George Blundun immediately set about studying and re-interpreting the preliminary seismic work carried out by the other companies and comparing notes with John Carr and Fong on the best locations for the test wells.

This was no easy task, for the Swan Hills area was the wildest, most remote terrain in which anyone had yet looked for oil in Canada, a mountainous, thickly forested wilderness penetrated by only a few forestry trails and all but completely inaccessible except during the winter freeze-up, when the temperature drops to as low as fifty degrees below zero Fahrenheit. For the other nine months of the year, the heavy rainfall—on average, it rains on one day out of every three—turned the trails into impassable quagmires. Standing roughly 2,000 feet above the plains bordering it on the east, the area is dotted with lakes and muskeg, and its steep-sided peaks, rising to more than 4,000 feet, are divided by deep ravines and eroded gullies. It was inhabited in those days only by wildlife: fur-bearing animals of many species, moose, deer, wolves, lynx, and bears, among them the fearsome *Ursus arctos horribilis*, the huge Swan Hills grizzly, nine feet tall and thought by some naturalists to be a remnant of the long-lost grizzly of the western plains. There were many who thought Bob Brown was crazy to go looking for oil in such a benighted spot.

The Virginia Hills agreement called for the first well to be spudded in before December 31 that year, but no drilling rig could be taken into the area until a road had been built, and this could not be attempted until the ground froze. In September, Fred Willock, Home's construction foreman and an old Turner Valley hand, set off on horseback with an Indian guide to reconnoitre a route for the road. They faced a sixty-five-mile ride north from the isolated hamlet of Whitecourt, a mere handful of frame houses and a small hotel. For the first twenty miles, they wound along an abandoned logging road; then followed forty-five miles through virgin forest. They had a saddle horse each and a pack horse between them, and Willock, who later left Home to go into business for himself as a roads contractor in the area, recalls that no matter how carefully he tried to guide it, his mount kept sinking into the muskeg. Eventually, he dismounted and began to lead the horse— until it took over the lead itself and proved more adept than Willock at finding the dry ground.

Travelling light, the pair took no tent, but slept each night in the open. "We didn't see a soul," Willock recalls, "except for bears, moose, and birds." They were able to locate the site chosen for the first Virginia Hills well from the shot numbers posted on trees by the seismic crews who had been in before them during previous winters, and when they returned to Whitecourt three weeks later they had blazed what seemed to be a suitable route for the road.

As soon as the freeze-up arrived, Willock took a crew of ten men and four bulldozers, carved a forty-five-mile avenue through the trees—chiefly spruce, fir, lodgepole pine, and poplar—and packed down the snow so that the trucks could get in to the well site with the drilling rig and house-trailers for the crew. And on November 28, 1956, comfortably ahead of the contract deadline, the well was spudded in.

Then Willock and his road crew began to carve another trail through the wilderness to reach the site chosen for the first well on Regent's Swan Hills property, about twenty-five miles to the northeast as the crow flies. This time they started from Kinuso, on the south shore of Lesser Slave Lake, and headed south. And the first Swan Hills well was spudded in on January 21, 1957.

A few days later, 9,000 feet down, the Virginia Hills well struck oil in the Beaverhill Lake formation. With more land in the area due to be put up for auction at a government sale some months hence, Home had been trying to keep a "tight hole"—in other words, a clamp of secrecy had been put on the drilling results as the well progressed. But even in that isolated area the oil scouts were busy, and by next morning everyone in Calgary knew Bob Brown had hit oil again.

Without pausing to carry out production tests, the crew immediately began to dismantle the rig and move it six miles to the northeast so that a "step-out" well could be started before the spring thaw in an attempt to discover whether the oil-bearing structure extended in that direction. That well, spudded in on March 27, later proved to be dry.

But on that same day, a production test of the Swan Hills well, which had struck a gas flow earlier in the month, showed that it, too, had found oil in commercial quantities in the Beaverhill Lake formation.

The atmosphere on site and back at the office in Calgary was now electric. With two wells producing from the same formation and twenty-five miles apart, it looked as though Home might have made its biggest discovery yet—perhaps, though it was still too early to be sure, one of the most important discoveries ever made in Alberta.

And so it proved to be. Before the spring break-up, the Swan Hills rig was moved six miles to the southwest and a new hole, Edith Lake 11 of 19, was spudded in on April 8. Then the rains came, and the primitive winter roads turned into mud, thick and sticky and seemingly bottomless: even in four-wheel-drive trucks with winches to hitch on to trees and haul them through the worst spots, the men found journeys that in winter took a couple of hours might now take twenty-four or even forty-eight hours, and no one drove anywhere without a supply of food and sleeping bags. Under these conditions, it was impossible to keep the drillers supplied, so the rig was shut down and the crew lifted out by helicopter.

By midsummer of 1957 it had dried sufficiently for a start to be made on the upgrading of the road and the men went back in. And in August, the Edith Lake well "flowed oil at the surface"—in other words, as soon as the drill entered the Beaverhill Lake formation the oil rose more than 8,000 feet up the pipe under its own pressure in an hour and a half. It was one of the most exciting wells ever drilled by the Home team, and the "pay zone", the producing layer of rock, proved to be a satisfying 143 feet thick.

Bob Brown was now sure he had a new oil field, but neither he nor anyone else yet realized just how huge it would prove to be. One after another, new wells came in—Home drilled five successful "development" wells around Edith Lake during the winter of 1957–58—and still the boundaries of the field were not delineated. By now, other companies had joined the hunt. Mobil Oil Company discovered gas in the Beaverhill Lake formation a few miles south of the Home discovery. Then Phillips Petroleum found oil forty miles further west, in an area that was called the Kaybob field. And so it went on.

By the fall of 1957, Brown had already decided that even on the basis of the drilling done so far there would ultimately be enough oil in the area to justify the construction of a pipeline to take it to Edmonton. And with the profitable example of the Cremona line behind him, he determined he would be the one to build it. Before anyone could beat him to the punch, he commissioned an aerial survey to pick out a suitable route and applied to the provincial government for the necessary permit. This time, no hearings were required and on April 16, 1958, he was granted permission to build a comparatively modest ten-inch line with a capacity of 22,000 barrels a day.

The Swan Hills discovery, of course, had been made on what was now, since its purchase of Regent Refining, Texaco's land. Bob Campbell, assuming that Texaco was probably kicking itself for letting the land go instead of following up Dr. Suter's theory, suggested to Brown that since the two companies were henceforth to be fifty-fifty partners in the field, it might help to assure an amicable relationship if Home were to offer Texaco an interest in the pipeline. Brown, riding the crest of the wave, at first saw no particular need to concern himself with the susceptibilities of one of the world's seven major oil companies—a sentiment that was accentuated after he had permitted himself to be persuaded to offer Texaco fifty per cent of the company being formed to build the line, Federated Pipe Lines Ltd.

While Brown got along well with the Canadian management of

Texaco, he was an unknown quantity to the head-office executives in the United States. And his fighting spirit was roused when the Americans suggested that perhaps his proposal to build the line was a trifle premature. Brown viewed this as merely a stalling manoeuvre while Texaco's head office cast around for some way to take control of the project, and he stood firm. After all, Home had found the field, filed the application to build the line, and received the permission to go ahead. And he was going ahead, he let it be known, with or without Texaco.

Recognizing his determination, Texaco agreed to join him as a fifty per cent partner in Federated Pipe Lines, with Home as the operator of the project, and the line was built during the summer and fall of 1958 at a cost of $5.6 million, considerably below the original estimate. But even though the construction work was entrusted to the well-known pipeline-building company, Dutton–Williams Bros., which had built the Cremona line, the Americans evidently harboured lingering doubts about the ability of an upstart Canadian company to see the job through. Prominent among those who watched the initial stages of the construction was a colourful Texan pipeliner commissioned by Texaco, Jack "Ace" Diamond, a wartime p-38 fighter pilot and part-time Texas Ranger who apparently took his reputation as a trouble-shooter literally: he was reputed to wear six-guns back home, though discretion apparently restrained him from trying to bring them across the border with him.

Even after the line had opened for business, early in 1959, Texaco sent up a team of U.S. pipeline experts to conduct a surprise inspection of its operations. Only when its report turned out to be a glowing testimonial to Federated's efficiency did Texaco settle back to enjoy the fruits of Brown's enterprise: through the years, as the field grew, the original ten-inch line was "looped" twice with larger sixteen-inch pipe, so that there are now three parallel lines, expanding the system's capacity from the original 22,000 to 450,000 barrels a day.

Federated Pipe Lines now serves several oil fields in the general area—including Swan Hills itself, South Swan Hills, Judy Creek, Carson Creek, and Virginia Hills—and carries about a quarter of all the oil moved in Alberta. Swan Hills is the largest of the fields and it is considered to be one of the three most important finds ever made in Alberta. By 1963 it had taken over as Home's biggest source of oil, supplying thirty per cent of its total production. Ultimately, the field was found to extend over 115 square miles and to contain an estimated two billion barrels of oil in the ground. Ten years after its discovery it was supporting 450 producing wells. The neighbouring Virginia Hills field, though it turned out to be smaller, has reserves estimated at the useful total of 450 million barrels. But the Grizzly Mountain block, where Home drilled two dry wildcats, turned out to be off the structure.

To Brown's everlasting annoyance, Home narrowly missed picking up another four-township block in the area which in due course became the South Swan Hills field. It was at a Crown land auction in July 1957, after the discovery wells at Virginia Hills and Swan Hills had come in but before the Edith Lake well had fuelled the speculation that Home was on to something really big. Briefed by Carr and Blundun, Brown was rounding up partners to make a sealed bid on the 92,000 acres south of the Swan Hills block in the belief that the field extended in that direction.

His normal procedure before making a bid was to poll his own staff and the representatives of his potential partners to find out how much they thought the desired land parcel was worth. He would then review the previous prices paid for land in the area, take the highest figure suggested by anyone in the group—and usually raise it. If we really want this parcel, he would say, we'll have to go higher than that.

On this occasion, one of the potential partners was a Chicago-based company, Pure Oil (which has since merged with Union Oil). And each time Brown tried to talk up the bid at the meetings customarily held, amid great secrecy, during the days leading up to the sale, the Pure Oil representative would have to call Chicago for authority to commit the extra money. Eventually, on the day before the sale, Brown told the group he thought Home should bid something over $3.5 million to be sure of getting the land. This was higher than Chicago was prepared to go. It was now too late to recruit another partner into the group, so against his better judgment Brown scaled down his bid—and the parcel went to Pan-American (later Amoco) and British American (now Gulf Oil Canada Ltd.) for $3.35 million—$150,000 less than Brown had wanted to bid.

If Brown had followed his instinct, Home would have made the highest bid and its crude-oil production today would be somewhere between twenty-five and fifty per cent higher than it is. Understandably, no one was ever again able to persuade Bob Brown to lower a bid.

Even though this sale was held before the full magnitude of the Swan Hills discovery was realized, and with no guarantee that the field would extend to the south, the winning bid was almost twelve times what Dr. Suter had paid for his four-township block adjoining it to the north three years earlier. And as the field was developed the price of land in the area—all of it owned by the Crown—went on rising. But Brown continued to bid, both on new parcels and on land Home had to return to the Crown after its discovery. In 1958, for instance, he paid $6.8 million for 3,200 acres of leases adjoining the original Regent property to the north and east, on which six new wells were soon brought in. And in that same year he paid $6.5 million for a four-township block known as Morse River,[2] immediately east of the block he had missed. Home drilled several dry holes on this block in succeeding years, and while some production was obtained from it, Morse River never lived up to its promise.

As the years went by, a network of all-weather roads was constructed throughout the Swan Hills area and in 1961 a start was made on the permanent town of the same name, which now houses about 2,200 people—employees of Home and the other companies active in the various fields, their families, government employees, and the storekeepers and other small businessmen found in any town of similar size.

Inevitably, the arrival of modern man and his machines in the wilderness was not without its impact on the environment. It is estimated, for instance, that about nine per cent of the forest cover in the Swan Hills field was removed in its development, accentuating the erosion problem from which the area has always suffered naturally because of the sparse topsoil on its steep slopes and its heavy summer rainfall. At first, government regulations required that any wood cut when clearing a site or building a road had to be completely removed; marketable timber was therefore sold when possible and the rest, including the brush and undergrowth, was burned on the spot. This helped to keep the place tidy, but the wilderness is not naturally tidy and practical experience later demonstrated that distributing the smaller logs and slash over cleared surfaces helped to retain the topsoil in place until a new cover of vegetation could take hold, and the regulations were changed.

Great difficulty was encountered developing a mixture of grass seed that would grow in the poor soil, until co-operation between the provincial Department of Lands and Forests and Home's employees on the spot evolved a mixture popularly known as "tame hay", which contains creeping red fescue, crested wheat grass, timothy, white Dutch clover, a rambler variety of alfalfa, and Kentucky blue grass. This will grow if plentifully fed with a nitrogen-rich fertilizer for the first couple of years, and it is usually applied with a coating of a fine liquid plastic which holds the seeds in place until they germinate and then breaks up and disperses naturally.

Together with flood-control measures, such as the building of rock check dams in ditches to slow down the flow of water, the re-seeding of cut areas has reduced, if not entirely eliminated, the damage formerly done by erosion. Less is known about the impact of the new human inhabitants of the area on the wilderness wildlife. Fewer grizzlies are seen now—though some youngsters still occasionally turn up in town, to the general consternation of its residents—but grizzlies are cautious creatures who normally give mankind a wide berth and they may merely have retired into more remote regions: no one really knows if their numbers have declined because no count of them has ever been made.

The first crews into the area were advised by the Department of Lands and Forests to take high-powered rifles with them, and even though Home issued instructions that no one was to shoot a bear unless he was attacked, a few were shot in the early days. One old male was killed in the Virginia Hills area when he could not be induced to leave a site where a contractor had his wife and two young children living with him. More than nine feet tall, he was reputed to be the fourth-largest grizzly ever recorded in North America.

There are few more dangerous creatures on earth than a provoked grizzly, and construction crews were sometimes reluctant to work if a bear was known to be in the neighbourhood. On one visit to the field, two Home veterans, Jack Hamilton and Gordon Webster, were standing in a clearing listening to the complaints of a contractor. "You're going to have to let us do something about these bears," the contractor was saying. "Goddammit, they're all over the place." At that moment, Hamilton saw a large female grizzly walk around the corner of the contractor's hut and rear up on her hind legs, perhaps ten feet away from them. Behind her, over a dead tree lying on the ground, romped two cubs.

Hamilton gasped a warning, but the men were too far from their truck to make a run for it—particularly Webster, who had already sacrificed his legs to the pursuit of his chosen profession. Someone whispered, "Just keep talking and pretend we don't see her."

Understandably, the conversation flagged somewhat. But the female, after studying them briefly, barked a warning over her shoulder to the cubs, who promptly scrambled back the way they had come. Only then did the bear retreat, with a watchful eye still fixed on these unfamiliar intruders into her domain, who had probably startled her as much as she had terrified them.

The smaller and more numerous black bear is widely considered less deadly than the grizzly, but the horrifying experience of five-year-old Clint Emery at Swan Hills in the summer of 1971 demonstrated that it is not safe to make this assumption. The first crews into the area unwisely often made pets of the black bears. During the drilling of the Edith Lake well, for instance, three females and five cubs attached themselves to the camp and the cook regularly fed them pancakes. One of the cubs, to the great amusement of the men, became so tame he would wander into the mess hut and sit at the table. The danger of such fraternization becomes apparent when the rig moves on and the bears, deprived of both their regular diet and their instinctive distrust of people, roam elsewhere in their search for food. Sometimes they find what they want at a garbage dump safely removed from human habitation. But if not they can become dangerously unpredictable invaders within the town limits.

Clint's father, Cliff Emery, works for Federated Pipe Lines and one pleasant July evening in 1971 his wife walked over to the terminal where he was on duty to take him his supper. Little Clint stayed outside the building, playing with his elder brother Dwayne and their cousin, Murray Doherty. Suddenly a bear darted out of the bush, seized Clint's head in its jaws, and began to drag him away. Dwayne, with courage beyond his eleven years, dug his hands into its neck fur in a vain attempt to make it drop his brother while young Murray ran into the terminal screaming, "A bear's got Clint."

Fortuitously, someone had left a .303 rifle leaning in a corner of the operations room. By the time Cliff Emery had snatched it up and run outside, the bear had disappeared into the bush. But

Dwayne stayed right on its tail, and guided by his shouts Emery caught up with them after a chase of about a hundred yards, to find the bear climbing a tree, with Clint's head still clamped in its jaws. Emery yelled at Dwayne to get out of the way as he raised his rifle to take aim. His shout evidently startled the bear, who dropped Clint, giving his father a clear shot. It hit home—in Emery's words, "I got him right in the briskets." The bear, a male about two years old, at around which age the mothers usually abandon their cubs to fend for themselves, was dead when it toppled from the tree— which was fortunate for them all, since the rifle contained only that one bullet.

When Emery carried his torn and bleeding son back into the station, his wife ripped off her blouse to wipe the blood and pine needles from his face and head before bandaging him with gauze from the first-aid kit. Clint never lost consciousness as his father cradled him in his arms on the ambulance drive to the nearest hospital, at Barrhead, about sixty-five miles away. It took 150 stitches to close the wounds in his head and shoulder, and he was in the hospital for two weeks. But a month later, unperturbed by his shaven head, he rode his pony in a local horse show and took first prize in the parade class. For years afterwards, he suffered from occasional nightmares, but his only lasting physical injury was a slight deafness caused by scar tissue in one of his ears, which doctors hoped could be cured by surgery when he was older.

Young Dwayne—they had to clean hairs from the bear's neck from under his fingernails after it was all over—won four awards for his bravery, among them the Boy Scouts' Silver Cross and the Star of Courage, Canada's fourth-highest decoration for gallantry after the Victoria Cross.

CHAPTER FIFTEEN

Bob Brown Goes After the Montreal Market

The Swan Hills discovery was the most important ever made by the Home Oil team, but it would be a long time before either the company or Bob Brown would reap its rewards. Indeed—and this was only one of the many ironies of the Canadian oil industry in those days—while Brown was borrowing huge sums in his fever to expand and his staff was using the money to discover rich new fields, Home's oil production went down instead of up.

Home was not the only company to suffer this frustration: the decline in production was general, under the pro-rationing scheme which the provincial government imposed in its attempt to ensure that all companies received at least a share of a market that was severely limited by external forces.

Long before the Second World War the United States, then the world's dominant oil producer, had encouraged its oil companies to seek overseas reserves to meet the nation's rapidly growing demands. The phenomenal proliferation of these demands during and after the war spurred the major companies' overseas exploration efforts, which were remarkably successful—spectacularly so in the Middle East. By the early 1950s, the U.S. administration was beginning to feel that the country's strategic position was threatened by its mounting dependence on oil imports. Thanks to the low cost of finding oil in the Middle East, where almost any well anyone cared to sink turned out to be a gusher by North American standards, and the falling costs of sea transportation as tankers steadily grew in size, these imports could be landed at U.S. ports—in those palmy pre-OPEC days—at prices well below the cost of finding and producing domestic crude.

Late in 1955, fearing that its own producing industry would be driven out of business, the administration invoked the national security as the cornerstone of its oil policy and asked the companies to place voluntary ceilings on their imports, holding them to the same level, measured against domestic production, as had existed in 1954. In that year, Canada's exports to the U.S. had amounted to the paltry total of 6,000 barrels a day, though they had risen during 1955 to 46,000 barrels a day. Fortunately for the Alberta producers, this market was not at that time taken away from them: Canadian and Venezuelan oil was exempted from the quota system since the administration considered the discovery and development of more oil reserves within the western hemisphere important to U.S. national security.

Then, in 1956, Anthony Eden's attempt to safeguard Britain's oil supplies by seizing the Suez Canal backfired and the canal was blocked. Until a new line of supply could be organized by the much longer route around South Africa, Europe suffered a serious oil shortage and attempts to alleviate it by diverting supplies from other areas, such as Venezuela, spread its effects around the world. Deprived of their usual supplies of crude by the disruption, some U.S. refineries beyond the normal reach of Canadian exports—notably in California—turned to imports from Canada.

The Alberta government willingly raised well allowables to permit the producers to meet the increased demand, and exports to the U.S. rose steeply: to an average of 116,000 barrels a day in 1956 and 151,000 barrels a day in 1957. In January 1957, when Home made its first discovery at Virginia Hills, the province was producing oil at the record rate of almost half a million barrels a day.

The Suez crisis soon passed, however, and the U.S. refineries reverted to their customary sources of supply. And Canada's short-lived export boom was snuffed out in the summer of 1957 when Washington, thoroughly alarmed by the crisis, tightened up its import policy and this time decreed that henceforth Canadian and Venezuelan oil would be subject to the quota.

The result was an immediate decline in the production allowed in Alberta. Demand in those parts of Canada then served by Alberta oil was not enough to sustain the record rate of production and the province was forced to restrict wells to an average of about forty per cent of their potential production; some of the richer wells were even cut back to twenty-five per cent of their capacity.

Thanks to the record sales in the early part of the year, Home's drop in production during 1957 was not too marked: total output declined to 3.15 million barrels from the 1956 peak of 3.3 million barrels. But in 1958 the company's production fell by well over half a million barrels, all the way down to 2.5 million. And even after the Swan Hills wells began to come on stream, the recovery was slow: it was 1961 before it climbed back to the three-million-barrel mark.

This unsatisfactory performance, over which the company had no control, was reflected in the price of its shares. In 1956, Home's Class A shares sold at a high of $16.50 and a low of $10.25. In 1957, with the stimulus of the Swan Hills finds, they rose to a high of $23.75. But then—and the general market recession of the late 1950s did not help things—they began to slide downwards. By 1960, even though it was now clear that Swan Hills was a major discovery and Home's reserves were six times bigger than they had been five years earlier, the low was $7.10 and the high only $12.75. It was not until 1964 that the high again reached $23.

This paradoxical situation had several effects on Brown's career. For one thing, it helped to explain the variety and ingenuity of his many financings: with Home shares selling at far below what he considered their real worth he was always casting around for any means of financing the company's growth other than by equity issues of common shares, at prices which would have involved excessive dilution. Also, it directed his mind more and more to the possibilities for profit inherent in both oil and gas pipelines, and set his feet on two nearly parallel paths which, while they led only to failure and frustration, were as much a measure of his vision and his appetite for the attainment of the apparently impossible as his achievements in other fields.

The first path led to Home Oil's emergence by the fall of 1957 as the largest single shareholder in TransCanada PipeLines, the company formed to take Alberta gas to eastern Canada through the world's longest gas pipeline. The second launched him on a crusade whose objective—another pipeline, to deliver Alberta oil to the large Montreal market—would be resisted by successive governments until OPEC's holding of the western world to ransom vindicated his logic long after his death.

Bob Brown had neither the name nor the credit rating to become involved in the trans-Canada gas pipeline project when it was first proposed, by rival Canadian and American groups, at the end of the 1940s. But his associates from those days recall that he always viewed it as a modern version of the Canadian Pacific Railway, with the same potential for fostering Canada's prosperity and sense of national identity. He never doubted it would be built, even through the early years when political controversy and financing difficulties often threatened to strangle it before its birth. And while he always thought it should be an all-Canadian project, he accepted C. D. Howe's celebrated "shotgun marriage" of the rival groups in 1954 as inevitable, recognizing that American participation was essential to its financing—as he had found it essential to his own.

Howe believed as strongly as Brown himself in the national benefits to be obtained from the delivery of Alberta natural gas to eastern Canada, and he was determined to have the pipeline built, whatever government guarantees or assistance might prove necessary to its financing. His plan to subsidize that portion of the line which the country's developing nationalist sentiment demanded should pass through the inhospitable rock of northern Ontario—when a southern route through the United States would have been much cheaper, and hence more attractive to the private investors who were being asked to finance the line—provoked the clamorous House of Commons pipeline debate of May 1956, which paved the way for John Diefenbaker's defeat of the Liberals in 1957.

That debate was still a month away when Brown recommended to the Home Oil board "that the company take a position in Trans-Canada PipeLines". His recommendation was accepted readily enough, since his directors knew as well as he did that with its oil production held down by lack of markets Home's best chance of expansion lay in selling the natural gas it had found through the years but had so far been unable to exploit, and that TransCanada, as the only vehicle in sight for the achievement of that objective, deserved all the support the company could give it.

Whether he could have carried his directors with him had they realized his ultimate objective is a moot point: for Bob Brown, at least, could see that a period of phenomenal growth lay just ahead for the natural-gas industry as a whole and—as audacious as ever—he had already resolved to profit from it by one day getting control of TransCanada, no matter how much it cost him.

The Liberals' forcing through of Howe's plan to have the government finance the uneconomic northern Ontario portion of the line and then recoup its investment by selling it back to the company when its profits enabled it to buy it, though widely interpreted as a frontal assault on the rights of Parliament, removed the last obstacle to TransCanada's financing, and the company was able to make its first offering of shares to the public early in 1957. Before the issue, Brown let it be known that he was willing to buy $15 million worth of its common shares, the price of which had been set at $10. He was turned down, because that amounted to no less than half of the common stock the company proposed to issue as such: the "mix" of the $234 million financing had been set at $144 million in first mortgage bonds, $60 million in subordinated debentures (with each $150 unit consisting of a $100 debenture and five common shares), and only $30 million in common shares.

Notwithstanding all the controversy the plan to build the line had caused, the public enthusiasm for its shares was such that the underwriters had to ration them among the eager buyers. So Brown supplemented his initial allotment of debentures and common shares by buying on the open market which developed immediately after the issue and soon pushed the price of the stock up to $20. By October that year he had accumulated more than 700,000 common shares and Home Oil was the largest single shareholder in TransCanada, with twelve per cent of its issued shares. Early in November, Brown was elected to TransCanada's board, and he went on buying its shares on the open market. By the end of 1958, Home owned 1,044,073 shares—almost eighteen per cent of the company—acquired at a cost of $30.4 million, most of it advanced by Brown's invaluable ally Neil McKinnon in the form of demand loans from the Bank of Commerce.

In the course of his buying, Brown spearheaded the "Canadianization" of TransCanada—the repatriation of its control from the American companies which had helped to launch it. One of these, though a latecomer to the group, was the huge Tennessee Gas Transmission Co. (later Tenneco), probably the most powerful pipeline company in the United States. Before TransCanada was successfully financed, its directors decided they needed Tennessee's support—among other things, to guarantee U.S. supplies of the large-diameter steel pipe needed for construction of the line, which at that time could not be manufactured in Canada. Gardiner Symonds, president of Tennessee and a no-nonsense executive of the old school, did not believe in getting mixed up in any venture whose success could be affected by anyone other than Gardiner Symonds: he insisted that as long as he had any liability for Trans-

Canada's undertakings he must have control of the company, and the board, though reluctantly and only temporarily, yielded it. After the company was successfully financed and construction had begun, Symonds agreed to sell his shares—a large block of them to Bob Brown.

Hindsight is, of course, the clearest vision with which one can be blessed, but in retrospect Brown's long campaign to win control of TransCanada was a mistake: it saddled Home with huge debts and for years tied up money that would probably have been better spent enlarging the company by acquiring more producing properties. And on this occasion, certainly, it induced him to break what some oilmen consider a cardinal rule of the business: that is, a company should never sell production, because oil in the ground almost invariably appreciates in value with the passing years.

In October 1957 Brown negotiated a deal with Symonds under which Home acquired 189,227 TransCanada shares from Tennessee in return for forty per cent of Home's gas reserves in the Nevis field, which Federated had discovered back in 1952, together with Home's interest in nine Harmattan and eight Pembina wells representing a total daily production of 675 barrels of oil. The properties he sacrificed, valued at $5.79 million, had produced gross income of $635,000 during 1956, even though the Nevis gas wells were not yet producing, pending construction of the Trans-Canada line. The TransCanada shares he bought—including the Tennessee block and another block purchased subsequently from Hudson's Bay Oil and Gas (a subsidiary of the U.S. company Continental Oil)—paid no dividend for five years.

As it happened, however, the luck of the Irish held, and the loss of the Nevis gas properties was more than made up soon afterwards, when in mid-1958 Home discovered the Carstairs gas field, a short distance south of its Westward Ho and Harmattan oil discoveries. Carstairs turned out to be one of the richest gas fields in Alberta and by 1970 it was producing almost half of the revenue Home was obtaining from the sale of natural gas and its products. The find came at a particularly fortunate time for the company: to make the line economic, TransCanada had negotiated its first gas contracts with Alberta producers at the low price of ten cents per thousand cubic feet, but by the time the Carstairs wells began to produce, its need for supplies to meet the demand in eastern

Canada—which rapidly exceeded the most optimistic forecasts— had increased the contract price to 13.25 cents, a bonus gratefully accepted by Brown and Home.

It was at Carstairs, also, that Home (as a 50.4 per cent partner with Canadian Superior and several other companies) built the biggest of several gas-processing plants in which it now has an interest. The plant opened in 1960 and its original purpose was to "condition" the gas for sale by removing such "impurities" as hydrogen sulphide. This was then considered a waste product but nowadays the sulphur is extracted from it and sold. The Carstairs plant, expanded several times as new companies found gas in the area and joined the original partners, now also extracts such marketable liquid components from the gas as propane, butane, and natural gasoline. It proved successful from the start—so much so that its original cost, $3.7 million, was repaid within eighteen months, even though the gas only fetched what today seems the ridiculously low price of thirteen cents per thousand cubic feet.

By 1961, only sixty per cent of Home's revenue was being provided by its crude oil production, which had accounted for virtually all its income five years earlier. Twenty per cent now came from natural gas and its products and twenty per cent from other sources, including the Cremona and Federated pipelines.

Since Brown had played no part in the setting up of Trans-Canada, he was not involved in the national uproar that accompanied the pipeline debate. But one of its sequels provided him with a public forum in which to lobby for his other pet pipeline project, the opening of the Montreal refinery market to Alberta oil. One of John Diefenbaker's first acts as prime minister was to establish a royal commission—inspired largely by the TransCanada controversy—to take what amounted to an inventory of Canada's resources of all forms of energy, under the chairmanship of a prominent Toronto businessman, Henry Borden. And when Brown appeared as a witness before the commission at its hearings in Calgary in April 1958, pleading the case for a Montreal pipeline, he represented not just Home Oil but a dozen independent oil-producing companies.

The initiative for the formation of this loose coalition of otherwise competing companies had come from Charles Lee, president of Western Decalta Petroleum Ltd. The independent companies shared a common concern over the twin effects of the government-imposed restrictions on their production: their revenues had sunk to the point at which the rate of return on their capital investment was dangerously low for corporate health, and too little money was available for finding or acquiring the new reserves without which any oil company must wither away as its existing reserves are used up. Independently of Brown, Lee had also come to the conclusion that the solution to the problem was access to the Montreal market. In 1956, Canada consumed a little over 700,000 barrels of oil a day. Alberta, which was capable of producing far more than that—900,000 barrels a day—actually supplied less than half of the country's total requirements, about 350,000 barrels a day. The gap was made up by imports, mostly in the form of Venezuelan and Middle Eastern crude shipped into Montreal, where the refineries were using about 250,000 barrels of crude a day.

The delivery of Alberta oil to Montreal (either by an entirely new pipeline, as Brown wanted, or an eastward extension of the Interprovincial line already in place as far as Toronto) could thus serve a dual purpose: it would vastly expand Alberta's production and save the country millions of dollars in foreign exchange into the bargain. But could Alberta oil be laid down in Montreal at a price which would compete with the overseas supplies? Lee realized he needed some facts before he could make a public pitch for this solution to the Alberta producers' problem, and so he commissioned the engineering firm of Pryde Flavin to study the economics of a Montreal pipeline.

At the same time another, more ambitious, study was taking shape in his mind. Through his brother-in-law, he had met and become friendly with a remarkable refugee from Nazi Germany, Walter J. Levy, who had become one of the world's leading oil consultants. Levy had fled Hamburg for London in 1936 and found a job with Shell Oil which entailed the apparently humdrum task of studying the rail transportation of oil within Europe, particularly in Germany. He performed his duties with such thoroughness that after the outbreak of the Second World War, when he crossed the Atlantic and joined the U.S. intelligence organization, the Office of Strategic Services, he was able to follow and interpret the significance of oil shipments within Germany by piecing together snippets of information gleaned from a careful reading of German trade journals available to the State Department. Armed with his reports, the Allies were often able to pinpoint those refineries on which bombing raids would wreak most havoc. After the war, Levy set up a consulting firm in New York and his analytical mind and encyclopedic knowledge of the industry established him as a petroleum adviser to world governments and major oil companies alike.

Lee knew that any project aimed at supplying Montreal with Alberta oil would involve more than simply the engineering of a pipeline. It would need government approval, for one thing, and since it would presumably run counter to the interests of the major companies which were shipping their overseas crude into Montreal the government would have to take into account in its deliberations such factors as the balance of international supply and demand, world pricing policies—in fact, all the controversial complexities of international oil politics. No one could speak with more independent authority on this subject than Walter Levy, and Lee formed the idea of commissioning a study by Levy's organization that would define the issues at stake. But a study on that scale, he realized, would cost more than Western Decalta could afford. So he took his plan to Bob Brown. As he wrote in a memoir years later: "I was fully aware that if Bobby came to the conclusion, for whatever reason, that he should put his organization and dynamic personality behind the Montreal pipeline, it would be pursued with relentless energy and a disregard for expense which I, myself, was unable to do."

Brown welcomed this unexpected ally warmly. He had, of course, already decided not only that a Montreal pipeline was a national necessity but that he would further his own fortunes by building it and owning it, using as his vehicle the Independent Pipe Line Company he had set up years before in his frustrated attempt to take Alberta oil to the west coast. Confident that any independent, objective inquiry would support the case for the line, he readily agreed to share its cost.

On his part, Lee was aware of Brown's purchases of Trans-Canada shares and recognized his "clearly demonstrated personal drive towards dominating oil and gas transportation systems across Canada". While he himself would have preferred to see the line built under wider ownership, with every taxpayer in the country given an opportunity to share in its equity—the phrase "a citizens' pipeline" was later applied to this concept—he saw no reason to let Brown's personal ambitions prevent their co-operation to achieve a mutual objective. The main thing, in Lee's view, was to get a pipeline built, regardless of who owned it.

Mapping out the details of their campaign, he worked closely with James H. Gray, a newspaperman better known later for his popular histories of life on the Prairies, who had been hired by Brown as Home's public relations manager after espousing the cause of the Montreal pipeline in the now-defunct *Western Oil Examiner*. As their discussions progressed, Lee and Brown agreed that any representations ultimately made to the government should come from as broad a segment of the industry as possible, so together they sought the support of other independent companies, ten of which eventually agreed to join Home and Western Decalta in financing the study.

The Levy Report, as it became known, was ready in December 1957. It nowhere actually recommended a Montreal pipeline, but its exhaustive analysis of the oil industry—its "summary and conclusions" section filled eight and a half single-spaced typewritten pages—gave Bob Brown and Charles Lee plenty of ammunition for their campaign.

"Since 1951," the report said, "Canadian crude has extended its market frontier in several directions." In the east, it was now moving to refineries in Toronto; in the U.S. Midwest it had established itself in the Minnesota–Wisconsin area, which was a long way from most U.S. sources of supply; and in the west it was supplying British Columbia and the Puget Sound area of the state of Washington. Failing a major expansion of refining capacity in those areas, the only way the Canadian producers could expand their market would be to reach out to the next large refining complexes: San Francisco in the west; Chicago or Detroit to the south; or Montreal in the east.

Access to the first two of those three potential new markets would depend on U.S. import policy, and might require the U.S. to give Canadian oil preferential treatment—though the report gave no indication there was any likelihood of this happening. As to the third market, Canadian oil would cost about twenty-five cents a barrel more than Venezuelan oil by the time it reached Montreal, but this price disadvantage could be overcome by a combination of three possible actions. For one thing, given the increased production that access to the Montreal market would bring, Alberta producers could afford to cut their wellhead prices by ten cents a barrel without sacrificing revenue. Second, the Canadian government could follow the U.S. lead and impose a tariff of ten cents a barrel on imported oil. And last, the price of transporting the oil could be reduced a further ten cents a barrel by a more modern pipeline: the report pointed out that when the Interprovincial line to Ontario was built, the Canadian oil industry was still at an early stage of its development; its builders did not then realize the full extent of Alberta's reserves or how they might supply Canada's expanding requirements; and large-diameter pipe—which could carry more oil at less cost—was not then available.

A combination of all these measures, the report said, could give Canadian oil a price advantage over imports at Montreal. But there—as in any other potential new market—the Canadian product would have to overcome a stumbling block for which the report coined the term "commercial preference": the natural inclination of refineries owned by the major companies to use their own crude from low-cost areas such as the Middle East and Venezuela. Milton Lipton, the Levy partner who did much of the research for the report and most of its writing, told this author, "We didn't use the term 'commercial preference' in any pejorative sense . . . but any company which has as an alternative either buying a barrel of crude oil from itself, on which it makes its own producing profit, or buying a barrel of crude from a competitor, on which its competitor makes the producing profit, is damn well going to have a natural commercial preference for its own source of supply. It's as simple as that."

To establish Canadian crude at Montreal, the report concluded, would therefore require more than just the efforts of the Canadian industry to meet the price competition of imports: "It would probably further require an explicit formulation of public policy in support of Canadian markets for Canadian crude oil."

Without expressly recommending this course of action by the government, the report clearly hinted that there was a precedent for it in the United States' imposition of quotas to protect its domestic producing industry, "whose development is deemed essential to its national security". And it added, "The cost of oil imports could be an additional consideration in the determination of Canadian policy. In 1956, crude oil imports were valued at $271 million and were an imposing item in Canada's $734 million deficit in the balance of merchandise trade. An expanded export market for

Canadian crude or the replacement of foreign crudes in eastern Canada would contribute significantly to the nation's foreign trade balance."

Summing up, the report said that the Montreal market "was not an obvious direction of expansion from a logistic point of view," and if the possibilities of exports to the U.S. appeared adequate to its future development, the Canadian industry could reasonably await the growth of an export market without seeking an outlet in eastern Canada. "On the other hand," it continued, "if the uncertainties of the U.S. export market appear to inhibit the balanced development of Canadian resources, or the cost of waiting for expanded market opportunities in the United States is too high, then the Canadian producing industry might have to seek relief where its own national policies could prove effective. This would, in fact, mean a penetration of the Montreal market."

Even before the Levy report was completed, Brown had begun his personal campaign to mobilize support for a new line to Montreal. He managed to arrange a private meeting with Prime Minister Diefenbaker for a delegation representing the independent companies, and came away with the impression—a mistaken one, as it turned out—that they had won his support. And he embarked on a series of speeches to financial groups and service clubs across the country which would eventually extend over more than a decade. The texts of those speeches show how his ideas developed as he gave more thought to the problem, and commissioned more studies of it, during succeeding years.

In September 1957, before the Levy report was ready, he spoke in fairly general terms to a delegation of Toronto Stock Exchange members visiting Calgary. Energy, he pointed out, was essential to our civilization, and Canada should establish a national energy policy aimed at achieving the maximum possible development of its energy resources and their best use for the national benefit. No energy should be exported at the expense of preventing industry from being located in Canada, but he was confident an inventory of the country's resources would show that some surpluses were available for export. That being so, then mutually advantageous arrangements must be worked out between Canada and the United States. For instance, while the U.S. wanted electrical energy and natural gas from Canada, it seemed unwilling to buy Canadian oil. But the search for oil and gas went hand in hand and without the incentive to drill for oil the Alberta producers would not find enough gas to supply the demand. So if the U.S. continued to exclude Canadian oil, the only way Canada could have a healthy producing industry would be to fill all its needs from its own fields— which would mean "servicing the Montreal market to the exclusion of United States-owned oil coming from South America and the Middle East".

By January the following year, when he addressed the Toronto Society of Financial Analysts, Brown had begun to incorporate in his speeches some of the points made in the Levy report. He explained how the interests of the Canadian independents and the major world companies conflicted because of "commercial preference", and permitted himself to be somewhat more pejorative than the Levy report had been, describing crude from the Middle East and Latin America as "dictatorship oil". When oil was found in those areas, he said, great pressures were created: "The dictatorships become eager to have the maximum of oil produced so as to obtain the largest possible income. The oil companies, simultaneously, are extremely eager to produce as much oil as possible before their reserves are confiscated or their royalty payments heavily increased." In contrast, the reserves built up in Canada were the safest in the world, so it was naturally in the major companies' interest to hold them in the ground for future use and supply Montreal with "dictatorship oil".

The U.S. had recognized this and acted to protect its domestic industry at a time when American companies were being allowed to produce their wells at seventy per cent of capacity. With Alberta wells producing at less than fifty per cent of their capacity, the Canadian government should follow suit: "It is my suggestion . . . that the economics of moving Alberta crude to Montreal can be simply resolved and that this is a matter of serious national interest and becomes a question of government policy. All that is required in order to put Alberta crude in Montreal refineries is the decision on the part of the government that Canadian oil will be given a preference in that market. This can be accomplished on a voluntary basis as a result of government pressure, or by a quota system. . . . In this world in which we are now living the national security of Canada clearly dictates that Montreal cannot be dependent upon the hazardous oceans for its supply of crude. The decision with regard to the Montreal market would be made very quickly if a few Russian Nautilus were found cruising the Atlantic."

Brown returned to this theme, though in more restrained terms, when he appeared before the Borden Commission in April of that year. "Our economy would be seriously impaired," he said, "if, for any cause, our ability to import were taken from us. We would pay a heavy price for not recognizing that nations must set high the principle of being able to accomplish their own aims without external aid. . . ." During 1956, he pointed out, the United States had imported only 15 per cent of its oil requirements; Canada, in the same year, imported 54.4 per cent of its total consumption, and "a comparison between the two nations in terms of the ability of each to maintain the function of its economy must inevitably lead one to conclude that Canada has far greater concern in time of crisis. . . ."

Spoken two years before OPEC was even founded, and fifteen years before the exporting countries fully realized their power to bring the industrialized world to its knees, those words have a prophetic ring today. But they failed to win over either the Borden Commission or the government to the cause of a Montreal pipeline. Nor did the other exhibits Brown filed with the commission: the Levy report, a report on the feasibility of the proposed line he had commissioned from the pipeline construction company Dutton–Williams Bros., and a report on the suitability of Alberta oil for use in Montreal refineries commissioned from the U.S. consulting firm of Purvin & Gertz.

The public case against a Montreal line seemed to be based on the assumption that it would mean higher prices for Quebec consumers. While the representatives of the major companies who appeared before the commission did not actually say so, the impression seemed to gain currency that Quebec motorists might be asked to pay as much as five cents more for a gallon of gasoline. With pumps in those halcyon days still registering less than forty cents a gallon, even that sacrifice might seem, in retrospect, to have been worth while. But Brown countered that the consumer would not have to pay even one cent extra. Toronto refineries were already using Alberta oil, he said, and the price of gasoline in Toronto and Montreal was approximately the same; so if any saving was being made on so-called "cheap" overseas oil, it was not being passed on to the Montreal consumer.

Furthermore, he contended that the Dutton–Williams report,

commissioned after the Levy report had been prepared, demonstrated that Albertan oil could be entirely competitive with Venezuelan oil in Montreal. It showed, Brown said, that a thirty-inch pipeline could be built from Edmonton to Montreal for $353 million. (In passing, he mentioned that the line would provide 6,000 jobs directly and 25,000 indirectly during the two-year construction period, and would lead to the manufacture within Canada of 700,000 tons of steel.) And provided the refinery market were assured, the oil could be transported for 51.8 cents per barrel—considerably less than the 82-cent figure the Levy report had used in its calculations. This meant that even without lowering the wellhead price of Albertan oil or imposing an import tariff, domestic oil could be delivered to Montreal for $3.16 per barrel, compared with Venezuelan prices that ranged from $3.07 to $3.28 per barrel according to grade. (A later study by Dutton–Williams estimated that if 36-inch pipe were used from Edmonton to Superior, Wisconsin, and 34-inch pipe from there to Montreal, a transportation price of 48.1 cents per barrel could be achieved—less than it cost at that time to take Alberta oil to Toronto.)

When it handed down its two reports, the Borden Commission accepted some of Brown's premises, but not the conclusions he drew from them. "It is undoubtedly in the national interest," it said, "that Canada should at least be in a position readily to make itself as independent as possible of imports, which may be subject to interruption. . . . The present level of production in Canada is low relative to capacity and it is highly desirable that it should be substantially increased. . . ."

As to how this "highly desirable" objective was to be achieved, the commission rejected the idea of a Montreal pipeline, apparently agreeing with the major companies' proposition that it would be healthier for the industry to expand by increasing its exports rather than clamouring for "protectionist" policies which would allegedly shield inefficient companies from competition. While the United States was the only outlet in sight for Canadian exports, the commission could offer no specific formula for making Canadian oil more acceptable to U.S. refineries. It contented itself with saying the Canadian industry "should pursue a vigorous policy and have the initiative to take full advantage of exemption from quotas in the U.S.A. to find markets. . . . Refiners should strive assiduously to work out private exchange agreements. . . ."

Instead of fostering the construction of a Montreal pipeline, the commission said, the government should limit the area supplied by imported oil to that portion of the country lying east of the Ottawa river. And in what was probably its most important recommendation, it suggested the government should set up a national energy board, among whose responsibilities would be the policing of the voluntary use of Canadian oil by refineries elsewhere in the country. In this way, it should be possible to achieve "a target level of production by the end of 1960 approximating 700,000 barrels per day". In any case, the commission agreed, "the time has come to restate Canada's national policy on oil."

Pending the government's promulgation of that policy, Brown redoubled his proselytizing for the Montreal pipeline, in speeches, letters to Home's shareholders, and statements to the press. In 1960, Canada's U.S. exchange deficit was more than $1 billion, and he hammered home in his speeches that year the point that the admission of Alberta oil to the Montreal market would eliminate more than $300 million of that deficit. By now he had found another ally to reinforce his economic case: Don Armstrong, director of the school of commerce at McGill University in Montreal. Armstrong, who was born in Alberta—"within the sight and smell of Turner Valley"—had been following the Montreal pipeline controversy from the sidelines and he mentioned in a speech one day that the economic arguments being advanced against it were "just incorrect".

When Brown heard this, he descended on Armstrong at McGill and immediately recruited him into his growing circle of advisers. Among Armstrong's contributions to the cause was his contention that the classical economic argument in favour of free trade did not apply to oil, because such a large proportion of its selling price consisted of revenue to governments—in the form of prior payments for leases, royalties, and other taxes. In other words, if Canada paid Kuwait three dollars for a barrel of oil, that was a real cost of three dollars going out of the country, and it had to be paid for by three dollars' worth of wheat or steel or some other export. But of the three dollars paid for a barrel of domestic oil, slightly more than one dollar consisted of revenue to Canadian governments. The government "take" on a barrel of oil is far more than that now, of course, but even in those days, had the Montreal market been supplied with domestic oil, not only would the country have saved $300 million a year in foreign exchange but the extra domestic production would have put $100 million or so into Canadian government treasuries.

The end of 1960 came without either the promised new oil policy or the fulfilment of the Borden Commission's production target. In a letter to Home shareholders published as a pamphlet in January 1961, Brown complained that while the commission had proposed a minimum production of 700,000 barrels of oil a day by the end of 1960, actual production during the year had reached only 525,000 barrels a day. Even though Canada had been exempted from the U.S. oil-quota system in the summer of 1959, the hoped-for boom in exports had not come about: the daily average during 1960 was 113,000 barrels, considerably less than the rate achieved during the post-Suez boom.

In Home's case, this meant that while the company's reserves had increased threefold during the previous four years—from 53 million to 158 million barrels—its production had decreased from 8,900 barrels to 7,100 barrels a day.

And so the argument raged on, to no better effect than before. When the Diefenbaker government at last introduced the new national oil policy in February 1961, it clung fairly closely to the Borden Commission's recommendations without attempting to break new ground. It set a target production rate of 800,000 barrels a day by 1963—which, since it included natural-gas liquids, the market for which was expanding rapidly, was not much of an improvement on the target set by the commission for 1960. George Hees, the minister who announced the policy, said this target was "approximately as high as the figure which would be achieved if the Montreal pipeline were to be constructed". It would be reached, he added, "by increased use of Canadian oil in domestic markets west of the Ottawa Valley, and by some expansion of export sales, largely in existing markets which can be reached through established pipelines." The policy would involve the displacement of a small quantity of imported crude from Ontario and a progressive reduction in imports to the province of refined petroleum products from foreign sources and the Montreal refineries, and while the program would be voluntary it would be policed by the National Energy Board established in response to the Borden Commission's recommendations.

Most of the independents, more interested in producing and selling their oil than in how it was transported to wherever it was going, regarded the new policy as at least a step in the right direction. Brown considered it a pitifully small and weak-kneed step and would have preferred to see the government take a self-confident stride toward national self-assertion. How much he was influenced by concern for the national interest and how much by his personal ambition no one ever really knew. But he continued to campaign for the Montreal pipeline. In Home's annual report for 1960, a few weeks after Hees's announcement, he said, "Your Company supports the adoption of a National Oil Policy and is hopeful that [its] minimum objectives may be achieved. At the same time, it does not believe that such minimum goals are a substitute for the dedication of the Montreal refining market to Canadian crude. The Canadian economy needs a rapidly expanding natural resources industry. Oil and gas development must proceed at a much faster pace than will be possible under the modest incentives provided by the above objectives. These targets plus the construction of a pipeline to Montreal, on the other hand, will stimulate our industry to rapidly expand its reserves, which are so vital to the defence of this continent."

While the production figure set by Hees for 1963 was not quite achieved—the country's total output fell short of the target by 25,000 barrels per day—the new policy did have a beneficial effect. Exports to the United States began a steady rise, accelerated after representations were made to Washington by Ottawa, and the increase was reflected in Alberta's production figures. In Home's case, the effect was immediate: the company's production of oil and natural-gas liquids rose by more than a thousand barrels a day in 1961, the year the policy was introduced; by 1963 it had surpassed the 10,000-barrel-a-day mark; and it went on rising year by year.

But by the mid-1960s there was new evidence to support the contention that Canada's oil industry could not be viewed in isolation from the world picture. One after the other, large new discoveries were made in places like Libya, Algeria, Nigeria, and the Middle East, to the point where there was a glut of oil on world markets, and overseas oil once again began to seep into Ontario. Between 1965 and 1968 almost all the increase in Alberta's production was accounted for by exports: the use of Canadian crude in Toronto refineries increased hardly at all.

The independent companies now became concerned that the

national oil policy, if it had not already been abandoned, certainly needed revision to adapt it to the changing international circumstances. This concern was finally expressed to the federal government in 1969 by an industry-wide organization, the Independent Petroleum Association of Canada, which had grown out of the original group of companies put together by Lee and Brown to make their case to the Borden Commission.

The evidence given before the commission a decade earlier had convinced a growing number of independent companies that their true interests were not being adequately articulated by the Canadian Petroleum Association, which was naturally dominated by the big foreign companies that controlled more than eighty per cent of the oil and gas reserves and production in Canada. So in 1960, before the Diefenbaker government had yet acted on the commission's recommendations, thirty-one companies combined to form an association with the provisional title of the Independent Canadian Petroleum Producers, whose first action was to send telegrams to Prime Minister Diefenbaker, the members of his cabinet, and the chairman of the newly formed National Energy Board pleading for the immediate introduction of the promised national oil policy. The association was incorporated under its present title a year later and by 1978 its membership had increased to 304 companies (of which 175 were exploration and production companies, 124 companies indirectly involved in the industry, such as banks and service companies, and 5 companies operating pipelines).

While he helped to form IPAC, and Home Oil belonged to it from the beginning, Bob Brown never played as large a role in its activities as might have been expected, largely because after the introduction of the national oil policy most of its members proved lukewarm at best to his continued campaign for the Montreal pipeline. Brown was, however, a member of the four-man IPAC delegation when Prime Minister Trudeau and his cabinet received representatives of the oil industry, including a similar delegation from the Canadian Petroleum Association, in June 1969. IPAC's delegation was headed by its chairman at the time, Carl O. Nickle, a Calgarian who had published an influential oil journal and been a federal Member of Parliament before forming his own oil company.

The brief presented by IPAC made many of the same points that had been laid before the Borden Commission and reiterated in several studies carried out for Home and various other independent companies during the subsequent decade. But it also covered some new developments that were worrying the domestic producers, notably the wave of new refinery construction being subsidized by both Ottawa and the provincial governments in Quebec and the Atlantic provinces. While the brief did not challenge the principle of government action to create jobs in depressed areas, it pointed out that the new refineries would all be using imported oil and if they were all completed they would increase refining capacity east of the Ottawa Valley by about half a million barrels a day. Since this would far exceed the forecast growth in demand in that area over the coming decade, it would put irresistible pressure on refiners and marketers west of the Ottawa to avoid further refinery construction there and buy their requirements of gasoline and other refined products from Quebec—thus diminishing even further the use of Canadian oil in the area supposedly reserved to it by the national oil policy. Canada, the brief said, "with subsidies borne by all Canadians, could be permitting a massive loss of revenues within Canada, and a massive burden of expenditure for overseas petroleum."

The brief contrasted the treatment accorded "three products which have, over the past twenty years, become important to Canada and Canadians"—television sets, natural gas, and oil. The government had decreed that in the national interest Canadians should use television sets built within Canada, and had forbidden the import of sets from the United States. Canadians thus paid from fifty to one hundred per cent more for their TV sets than Americans, but since their manufacture had contributed to the economy of Quebec and Ontario the higher costs of "buying Canadian" could be justified.

Similarly, the national interest had been invoked when, before the TransCanada pipeline was built, western producers had asked for the freedom to market the natural gas they had found but been unable to sell to the only buyers then in sight, those in the United States. The government had ruled that natural gas was "an asset to which all Canadians within economic reach must have priority", so that western gas was now serving the whole country from the Pacific to Quebec, with only surplus supplies available for export at higher prices.

What eastern Canadians did not realize, the brief went on, was that without a constant search for oil, not enough gas would be found to meet their growing needs. And while a large part of the independent companies' productive capacity was "shut in" for lack of markets, they would have neither the funds nor the incentive to go looking for new oil reserves.

The national oil policy had gone some way to increase Canadian production—but mainly because of the increase in exports. Canadian exports of crude to the United States had grown from 92,000 barrels a day in 1959 to 457,000 barrels a day in 1968—a tremendous expansion of four hundred per cent. In contrast, the use of Canadian oil within Canada had risen by only fifty per cent during the same period: from 415,000 to 615,000 barrels a day. Imports had risen by more than that—from 422,000 to 686,000 barrels a day, an increase of sixty-six per cent. In the meantime, Alberta had an estimated 660,000 barrels a day of "surplus productive capacity"—almost enough to eliminate imports entirely—shut in because there was no way to move it to markets.

Perhaps because the rest of the independents were still leery of Brown's desire to run his own oil pipeline across Canada, or perhaps because his long advocacy of it had swayed so few eastern minds, the brief did not press for a new line. In fact, its plea was a modest one: it suggested extension of the existing Interprovincial system from Toronto to Montreal so that western Canada might, by the fall of 1970, supply between 150,000 and 200,000 barrels of crude a day to the Montreal refineries—between a quarter and a third of the market then held by overseas crude and refined products.

In support of this plea, the brief said, "Canada is the only nation capable of oil self-sufficiency which gives only limited priority to domestic oil; permits a drain of hundreds of millions of dollars for overseas oil; leaves half the nation totally dependent on overseas supply, thus ignoring the problem of security in emergencies; and leaves it to another nation—the United States—to provide the lion's share of market growth for a Canadian resource."

The format for the meeting with the cabinet provided for a fifteen-minute opening speech by each delegation's leader, followed by an informal discussion lasting an hour and a half. In conversation with the politicians, the IPAC delegates went further than they had in their brief, warning them that by the mid-1970s the world would depend on OPEC for ninety per cent of all the oil moved in trans-oceanic trade among nations, and that this was placing tremendous power in the hands of that organization's member states. "We correctly forecast," Carl Nickle recalled in an interview with this author, "that within a year the squeeze would begin. . . . We correctly forecast, though we couldn't, naturally, pinpoint the exact year in which it would happen . . . that prices would be raised as the OPEC nations saw fit and that cheap oil would be a myth before the mid-1970s. And it had now, as we saw it, become vitally important that Canada extend the oil pipeline on to Montreal—not to help western Canada but to ensure security of supply in the crisis that lay ahead in the 1970s."

The minutes of the meeting at which the delegation reported back to the IPAC board of directors on its session with the cabinet record that: "The responses by Cabinet to this potential issue indicated that government simply would not be persuaded by the security argument to a point where they would force eastern Canada to accept western Canadian oil." Well over half the meeting, the delegates reported, had been devoted to the question of giving western oil access to the Montreal market, and in the words of the minutes:

"The principal points raised by Cabinet with respect to Montreal were:

"That Canada, along with the U.S., must protect Venezuela's interest and ensure that this country remained within the western hemisphere community of democratic nations;

"That Canada's best oil market was represented not by Montreal but the U.S. Midwest, and the prospect for expansion in these U.S. markets was highly favorable in the 1970s;

"That Canada's oil price structure was simply too high to meet the competition of off-shore oil moving into eastern Canadian markets. . . .

"It was fairly obvious from discussions at that particular meeting, and more obvious from meetings held both before and after this meeting, with individual Cabinet Ministers, that the Federal Government were unwilling to impose their jurisdiction or press for a pipeline to Montreal in the face of opposition from Quebec. . . ."

The industry representatives spent three days in Ottawa, discussing their problems with government officials as well as ministers. At the end of their meetings, Jean-Luc Pépin, then Minister of Industry, Trade and Commerce, summed up the impressions of the cabinet. "I think he had a better understanding than some of the other cabinet ministers," Nickle recalls, "but he was speaking for the cabinet as a whole. And he told us our proposals would have the effect of raising the price of petroleum products in the Province of Quebec by one cent a gallon, and that was a price tag the Government of Canada was not prepared to pay. Bobby [Brown] of course, as well as the rest of the independent sector of the industry—we all could see the shape of things to come. So could the major oil companies. But governments were very slow to realize it, not only here but in other countries. The answer Ottawa gave—in mid-1969!—boiled down into simple English, though it was said more diplomatically, was: 'Go peddle your surplus oil where you can south of the border; we don't want it.'"

Bob Brown did not live to see the about-face forced on the government when, with successive increases in the four months between October 1973 and January 1974, OPEC quadrupled the international price of oil and plunged the whole western world into economic chaos. Fifteen years after Brown first proposed his own line, the government agreed to provide a deficiency guarantee to make possible the extension of the Interprovincial oil line from Sarnia to Montreal. Brown's initial plan for a line all the way from Edmonton to Montreal envisaged a construction cost of $350 million. Because of the inflation of the intervening years, the much shorter Interprovincial extension, completed in May 1976, cost $250 million.

Bob Brown, as he demonstrated time and again throughout his remarkable career, was blessed with a resilience given to few men. But perhaps he was fortunate to be spared contemplation of this dénouement to a chapter of his life that cost him a million dollars. Such was the estimated expense of feasibility studies and presentations to various groups, plus the time devoted to the project by his staff through the years.

Looking back on the long controversy, Charles Lee, of Western Decalta, said in the memoir quoted above, "No more remarkable indication of the lack of attention being paid to those who really know what they are talking about can be cited than this particular instance of the eleven-year fight to try and introduce some sense of responsibility and security into the minds of our administration."

It seems safe to assume that Brown would not have quarrelled with that verdict.

CHAPTER SIXTEEN

The Wildcatter
Weathers a Crisis

The 1950s were Bob Brown's most active and productive years, but his hectic pursuit of ambitions that sometimes proved to be beyond even his considerable reach imposed a crushing financial burden on Home Oil and as the decade neared its end the company faced a grave crisis.

His $30 million investment in TransCanada PipeLines stock coincided with heavy outlays to develop the discoveries at Swan Hills, Virginia Hills, and Carstairs. There was money to find to build the Federated pipeline from Swan Hills to Edmonton and the Carstairs gas-processing plant, and bills to be paid for the studies he commissioned to further his case for the Montreal pipeline. And while its exploration program suffered to some extent during those years, the company went on taking up leases and permits, some of which, inevitably, came to nothing. In 1957, for instance, after an oil discovery on the Kenai Peninsula in Alaska, Home took a one-eighth interest in 1.6 million acres in the Bristol Bay and Bethel Basin areas of Alaska. And a couple of years later it negotiated the largest "farmout" deal ever made in Canada up to that time, committing itself to spend $1.6 million to earn a one-eighth interest in 1.25 million acres in the Celibeta Lake area of the Northwest Territories, about thirty miles north of the substantial Petitot River gas discovery in northern British Columbia. Neither venture worked out.

Home entered 1959 owing the Bank of Commerce almost $20 million on a demand loan (secured by properties) and with an overdraft of more than $1 million. None of this deterred the unsinkable Robert A. Brown. That summer his associates discovered he was shopping for a new executive aircraft. He had soon found the de Havilland Dove he bought from Red Dutton back in the Williston days inadequate, and in 1953 had sold it in favour of a Lockheed Lodestar, a much bigger plane capable of flying him and eight passengers non-stop from Calgary to New York. But the Lodestar was powered by two piston engines, and by 1959 the jet age had arrived.

His choice now fell on the Grumman Gulfstream Mk. I, the first big turbo-prop executive aircraft built anywhere in the world. With twin Rolls-Royce Dart engines—the same as those in the Viscount passenger planes then being used by Trans-Canada Air Lines—the Gulfstream could fly Brown and whichever eight passengers he chose to accompany him both faster and further than the Lodestar. He resolved to own the first one imported to Canada—and its $1.3 million price tag only increased its appeal.

When he heard this, Brown's friend and legal adviser in Ottawa, Ross Tolmie, was aghast. Still devoting his best efforts to the campaign to convince the country and the government that the Montreal market was vital to the health of the Alberta oil industry, Tolmie wrote immediately to Jim Gray in Calgary, warning him about the possible public-relations repercussions of the proposed purchase. "Public opinion in the east," he said, "is already prejudiced against the western Canadian oil industry, with its expensive cars, airplanes, gin rummy, etc. The popular idea of the booming conditions and display of wealth in Alberta does not fit in with the present facts or the probable future of the oil industry if the Montreal market is not made available to it. However, it is going to be an uphill battle at best to educate public opinion, including eastern Cabinet Ministers, on the need for government action to save the western oil industry. The danger of a feature article in *Time* as soon as this latest, fastest, most expensive executive plane appears on the airports of Calgary, Toronto, Ottawa, and Montreal, should not be under-estimated."

Tolmie did not question the need for a private aircraft: as a director of TransCanada PipeLines, Brown now had monthly board meetings to attend in Toronto and he was travelling more than ever, chasing hither and yon across the continent in the furtherance of his multitudinous activities. But if a new plane was required at this juncture, Tolmie suggested to Gray, the most advisable course would be to lease it, rather than buy it for the potentially headline-grabbing price of more than a million dollars.

Brown, always consciously trying to build up his image as the consummate promoter, was not swayed. He had a full measure of the gambler's philosophy that it is always easier to borrow money if you look as though you don't need it, and the plane was duly purchased. If there were those who thought its acquisition reflected an unwarranted prosperity they were mistaken, at least in Home Oil's case: by the end of 1959, the company's bank debt had escalated to the daunting total of $31.4 million, and with its total assets standing at only $82 million, even the obliging Neil McKinnon had begun to insist that Brown should do something to reduce it.

In 1959, Home was still adding to its reserves by finding ever more oil at Swan Hills and Virginia Hills—that year it brought in the best well found in Virginia Hills up to that time and a successful wildcat a full four miles away from the Swan Hills discovery well. But its production rose only disappointingly: from 6,770 to 7,227 barrels a day. Brown told the shareholders in his annual report that if markets had been available, wells in the Swan Hills field would have been permitted to produce a daily average of 230 barrels; instead, they were restricted to 88 barrels a day.

So, with the company's gross income from all of its operations only $7.7 million for the year, there was no hope of repaying the bank loan out of production. And, with Home's shares selling for their lowest price since the merger with Federated, it was clearly no time to raise money from the public with an equity issue. Brown's choice was thus to go out and seek new long-term financing, in the form of one or more bond issues—none too easy a task given the depressed state of the market generally, and the state of Home's affairs in particular—or to realize some of his corporate assets. This came down to selling either some of the company's producing properties—or its hoard of TransCanada shares.

Most of Brown's friends and associates had already concluded that his attempt to get control of TransCanada was doomed to failure; they felt, correctly as it turned out, that the company was just too big for his resources. But Brown did not give up easily and he refused to countenance the sale of any of the TransCanada stock, even though it had not yet begun to pay a dividend. Practically, also, since there was as yet no large purchaser in the wings cherishing the ambition to take over the still unprofitable Trans-Canada, he could not have dumped $30 million worth of its stock on the open market without disastrously depressing its price and taking a heavy loss.

Neither did he wish to commit the cardinal sin of selling production. Instead, he decided to use the TransCanada shares indirectly in the financing blitz he now launched, which, at a time of tight money and with the U.S. oil industry in the doldrums, demanded all his impressive self-assurance and powers of persuasion.

In the summer of 1959, with the help of Lehman Bros. in New York, he managed to ease the pressure temporarily by charming a short-term loan of $15 million in U.S. funds out of the Chase Manhattan Bank, putting up some of the TransCanada shares as collateral. With the favourable exchange rate then prevailing, this amounted to $15.8 million in Canadian funds, and Neil McKinnon was greatly impressed that Brown had been able to persuade such an eminent U.S. financial institution as Chase Manhattan to play Peter to his Paul.

With this welcome respite, Brown next turned his energies to planning what was probably the most unusual of all his many financings. It is normal practice for a company to sell bonds that the purchaser can at some future date convert into—in other words, exchange for—that company's common shares. But this issue was a novelty: $20 million worth of six per cent Home Oil debentures convertible into the shares of another company altogether, namely TransCanada shares at $27.

In effect, Brown was borrowing $20 million on the understanding that if and when the market price of TransCanada shares rose to a reasonable margin above $27, the people who had lent it to him would be given the opportunity to make an instant profit by surrendering their Home debentures to the company in exchange for TransCanada shares at below the going price. When the time came for the conversion, Home would be relieved of its $20 million debt, but would have to give up—if all the debentures were converted—740,741 of its TransCanada shares.

The issue was successfully sold in January 1960, half of it in Canada and half in the United States, and Brown's willingness to part with such a large number of his TransCanada shares, even at some unspecified future date, was seen by his associates as an admission that he would never control the world's longest gas pipeline. In fact, though, he later bought more shares and probably never entirely abandoned his ambition until Canadian Pacific acquired control of TransCanada in the mid-1960s.

Any financing involves an immense amount of detailed work

for a company's financial and legal staff, who must prepare the prospectus for it, the legal document disclosing the company's precise financial position, setting out its balance sheets, outstanding debts, its ownership and control, future plans and prospects—all the information, in fact, that a potential investor needs to judge the soundness of his investment. In this case, the task of Brown's team—Max Govier, Ross Phillips, Bart Rombough, Ron Coleman, and their staffs—was doubly complicated: in effect, they had to prepare two prospectuses, one on Home Oil and the other on TransCanada PipeLines. And the resulting document was said at the time to be the most voluminous prospectus ever filed with the U.S. Securities and Exchange Commission.

As if this were not enough to keep the midnight oil burning in Home's offices, the staff was simultaneously engaged in the preparations for another important financing: with the help of his friend Jack King at Mutual of New York, Brown had managed to sell $10 million worth of 6.5 per cent secured bonds to a group of U.S. insurance companies headed by Mutual and New York Life, which took $3 million worth each. That issue was successfully closed on January 31, and having borrowed $30 million in a month Brown would have to wait a while before going to the market again.

But Home was not yet out of the red, and some of his directors now told him that to clear off its bank debt entirely he would have to part with some of his producing properties. Reluctantly, he was persuaded to put out feelers for potential buyers. The situation, in fact, was considered so desperate that for a time he even contemplated selling the jewel in Home's crown, Swan Hills.

On November 10, he reported to the Home board on some of the options open to him. Mobil, he said, had offered to buy all the interests of both Home and its parent, United Oils, in Swan Hills, Virginia Hills, Morse River, and Pembina, for a price somewhere between $31 million and $39 million. Shell had offered $17 to $20 million for the Swan Hills and Morse River interests— which was considerably less than British American's offer of $23 to $25 million for Swan Hills alone.

For Brown to have accepted any of these offers would have been, in effect, a confession of failure in his life's work: he would have been wiping out most of the expansion Home had achieved since he took over from Jim Lowery. It seems incredible that he would even have considered selling Swan Hills while he still held so many unproductive TransCanada shares, and perhaps he was merely playing for time.

At any rate—fortunately for Home's subsequent progress—while he was still mulling over his decision he had a visit from his friend Ed Kennedy of Lehman Bros. They had a long talk over dinner and Kennedy said that while the oil industry generally had been going through a tough period, he thought the tide was on the turn. "I told him," Kennedy recalled to this author, "that I thought we were about to see the start of a recovery. I can still remember his great interest in my views. Then it came out that he was under heavy pressure from some of his directors to reduce Home's debt by selling some properties."

Predictably, Kennedy was horrified. "That's just what you shouldn't be doing," he told him. "You should be buying—if you had any money."

This optimism, from someone whose opinion he always respected, was all Brown needed. He had not wanted to sell any production anyway, and henceforth there was no more talk of selling Swan Hills. Home's plight, though, did force him to accept a compromise at the end of 1960: he sold all its interests in the rich Redwater field—including the wells it had inherited from his old creations, Highland and Riverside Leaseholds—to Triad Oil (which later became part of BP). The purchase price: $7 million.

And a few months later, when the industry recovery predicted by Ed Kennedy was under way, he managed to pay off the last of Home's bank debt by negotiating the sale of $14 million worth of 6⅛ per cent secured bonds to two U.S. insurance companies: his old ally Mutual of New York and the Prudential Insurance Company of America.

In planning the measures that enabled Home to weather this storm and embark on a new decade of continued growth, Brown no longer enjoyed the services of the two men who had been his closest associates from the beginning: John Scrymgeour and Bill Atkinson. Back in the mid-fifties, Scrymgeour had introduced him to an American screen-writer and advertising man named Charles F. Spalding. "Chuck" Spalding had impeccable Ivy League credentials —he was a close friend of John F. Kennedy's—and he wanted to get into the oil business. So with his boss at the J. Walter Thompson agency, Jim Meek, he formed the Meek-Spalding syndicate and among its first investments was a 7.6 per cent interest in Brown's ill-fated venture at Bonnie Glen. Brown accepted responsibility for the failure to consult George Blundun before the purchase of that $1.66 million lease and when the hole turned out to be dry insisted on refunding the syndicate's contribution to it.

Understandably, this led to a warm friendship between Spalding and Brown, and when Meek and Spalding decided they would like to buy an oil company of their own Brown, as a favour, sold them Southwest Petroleums, the small but sound company he had inherited in the Foothills deal with Imperial, for half a million dollars. Soon afterwards, however, Spalding became more interested in a new venture in the United States, and in 1958 he sold Southwest—not back to Home, as might have been expected, but to Scrymgeour and Atkinson.

The merits of disputes between close friends—like those between man and wife—are often impossible for others to adjudicate. But this purchase infuriated Brown. John Scrymgeour told this author years later that when Spalding announced his intention of selling Southwest, he and Atkinson asked Brown whether he would mind if they bought it. Southwest was only one of Brown's minor interests and it was characteristic of him that he never became enthusiastic about anything other than a big deal. Also, he often encouraged other members of his staff to make investments he thought would pay off for them. At any rate, Scrymgeour recalls, he offered no objection to their purchase and they went ahead and bought Spalding's shares.

Perhaps Brown later forgot that conversation; maybe he did not take it seriously. But when Max Govier saw the names Scrymgeour and Atkinson on some shares being transferred and mentioned the fact to Brown, he exploded. And ever afterward, he considered himself to have been betrayed. He had often told friends he felt closer to Scrymgeour than to his own brother Ronnie (who, though still a director of Home, was beginning to take less interest in the oil business as the years went by), but from then on he treated both Scrymgeour and Atkinson with icy remoteness and began to rely on Bob Campbell as his right-hand man. After weeks of virtual ostracism, Scrymgeour and Atkinson went to see Doug McDermid, who was still Brown's lawyer, and it was agreed that whatever the misunderstanding had been it could only be resolved by their resignations.

The episode was a considerable blow to Brown's self-esteem. He prided himself on his own loyalty to his friends and employees and he expected it to be fully returned—so much so that he could become quite upset if even a comparatively junior employee left Home. It was almost as if the act of resigning to take another job implied some form of personal rejection of Brown himself. "More and more," Scrymgeour recalls, "he was tending to become patriarchal."

The departure of his two chief lieutenants precipitated an executive reshuffle at Home Oil which Brown somewhat mystifyingly announced to the press in September 1958—it made headlines in Calgary—as "a change from administration through executive vice-president [Scrymgeour's title] to administration by a management committee". The composition of this body made it clear, at least to those on the inside, that Home was no more likely to be run by a committee than it had ever been. It consisted of Brown himself and his father's old friend John Moyer, who was still chairman of Home's board but no longer in the prime of life; Bart Gillespie, who was about to retire to California but had consented to return to Calgary for a few days each month in the capacity of consultant; Alex Clark, who was still vice-president, exploration, but would soon resign to become president of the C. & E. Corporation; Max Govier, who now became secretary-treasurer (combining the posts of secretary, formerly held by Atkinson, and treasurer, formerly held by Jim Hamilton, the last survivor of Lowery's company officers, who retired soon after the reshuffle); and Bob Campbell, who, while he would within a few years be given the title of executive vice-president supposedly eliminated by the reorganization, had not yet clearly emerged as Scrymgeour's successor and was designated general manager, production and pipelines.

There were a few other promotions or changed titles lower down the line which did little more than confirm the continuity that had been built into the Home organization. The unassuming John Carr reluctantly accepted the title of chief geologist and, no more anxious than ever to be boss of anything, continued his geological cogitations as before; George Blundun remained chief geophysicist until, after Clark's departure, he replaced him as first manager and then vice-president, exploration; Maurice Paulson, who had first caught Jim Lowery's eye at Leduc, became operations manager but retained his old responsibilities as chief engineer; and Ross Phillips replaced Govier as comptroller and chief accountant.

Essentially, the Oilwell Operators team was still in business at the old stand. And once the financial crisis of 1959–60 had been surmounted and the national oil policy of 1961 took effect, Home began to reap the fruits of its early work. Thanks to the development of the discoveries of the 1950s, and the growing use of secondary recovery techniques—increasing the flow of oil from a field by pumping water or gas down some of its wells to increase the pressure in the reservoir—Home's production of crude oil and natural gas liquids more than doubled during the 1960s: from 7,849 to 16,666 barrels a day. Its natural-gas sales rose even more: from 30.6 million cubic feet per day in 1960 to 69,945 m.c.f. per day in 1969; and the sale of sulphur recovered during the processing of natural gas, which had not yet begun in 1960, reached a total of 31,947 tons during 1969. The increase in the company's gross revenue was even more satisfying: from $9.2 million in 1960 it more than tripled, to $27.7 million, in 1969.

In contrast, Brown himself entered the 1960s heavily in debt. He had taken out a large personal loan from the Bank of Commerce to acquire control of United Oils back in 1954, and had had to increase it substantially when a United share issue he sponsored early in 1958 backfired on him. United's position at that time, despite its holding of the control block of Home stock, was at least outwardly a shaky one. Simultaneously active on a dozen fronts, as always, Brown had put the company that was at the apex of his pyramid into a number of Home's ventures and it had invested large sums in leases which had greatly expanded its reserves: it had, for instance, a 6.25 per cent working interest in the Swan Hills discovery. But while he had increased the annual income from its operations from a paltry $5,549 to over $1 million in five years, the full returns that could ultimately be expected from these investments had not yet begun to flow in. Meanwhile, United owed the bank $11.3 million, and more than half of the total assets on its books consisted of its holding of Home's Class B shares—valued at $6.5 million—which had not yet begun to pay any dividends.

Plainly, an infusion of funds was needed, and Brown decided to offer United shareholders the right to buy one common share for two dollars for each three shares they already held. Such an issue would normally be "underwritten" by one or more brokerage houses—meaning that they would guarantee to "place" all the shares, themselves buying any that were not taken up by the public. But Wood Gundy, while it consistently supported Home Oil's financings, considered United something of a private preserve of Brown's and declined to underwrite the issue.

Brown went ahead anyway and issued a prospectus in which he stated his intention of taking up all the shares to which he was entitled by his two-million-plus holding. In addition, he privately guaranteed to take up any shares not claimed by the rest of the shareholders. Perhaps because United had not paid a dividend for five years, the issue was not a popular one. Many of the shareholders did not claim their allotments of shares and Brown himself had to put up a large part of the $3.9 million by which the issue bolstered the company's treasury (only $2 million of which was used to reduce its bank debt, the rest going to finance its continuing operations). Fortunately, McKinnon continued to support him, but his bank loan was now so large that he could not pay it back without selling a substantial portion of his assets—and possibly losing his control of Home. He lived at the time like a millionaire, and along with everyone else the reporters who wrote about him from time to time assumed that he was one. But whatever millions there were in his personal bank balance were on the wrong side of the ledger. If this description of his precarious financial situation and his many borrowings suggests that his "empire" was as flimsy as a house built with playing cards, it must be remembered that the men who advanced him all this money were shrewd, seasoned professionals; their security was not simply their faith in Brown's genius as a builder, which they undeniably had, but their knowledge that oil in the ground was at least as good as money in the bank.

Now that the "energy crisis" is an accepted part of all our lives, it seems strange that ordinary investors seldom realized this. One reason is that Home and United, like most other oil companies in those days, carried their reserves on their balance sheets at "book value"—in other words, at how much it had cost to discover them, rather than how much the oil when brought to the surface would fetch at the refinery. Given this conservative method of accounting, Home's shares sold during those years at far less than their actual "break-up" value—that is, how much the company's assets would really be worth in the event of its sale or bankruptcy. The control block of Home shares was thus worth far more than the $6.5 million at which it was carried on United's books. But Brown, nevertheless, was trapped: he could not repay his personal loan without selling so many United shares that he would lose control of that company, and hence also of Home.

Perhaps because of his anxiety over this seemingly insoluble problem—or, more probably, given Brown's nature, out of sheer frustration that his upward climb was at least temporarily stalled—he stepped up his already heavy drinking. He was now in his late forties and the recuperative powers which had always been the envy of his friends were beginning to wane: more and more he would show up at the office late and sometimes he would be unable to attend even important business meetings if they were held early in the day.

He had now become as fond of the house at Qualicum as Jim Lowery had been and in the summer he would wind up his work on Friday morning, have lunch in his opulently furnished executive dining room,[1] then fly to Vancouver Island in the Gulfstream. After a relaxing weekend with Genny and his three daughters, he would usually decide to stay on another day and not get back to the office until Tuesday. His frequent business trips to the east—he was now a director of Canadian National Railways and Trans-Canada Air Lines as well as TransCanada PipeLines—also reduced the amount of time he spent on Home's business and provided further excuses for drinking far into the night.

One evening in November 1963, when he and Bob Campbell had just flown in to Toronto for a week of business meetings, they went together to a cocktail party at the York Club. Campbell, who restricted himself to a glass of sherry on such occasions, was surprised to feel a tug at his sleeve before the party had really begun and hear Brown saying, "I don't feel too well—do you mind if we leave early?"

They took a taxi back to the Royal York Hotel, had a light dinner in Brown's suite, watched television for a while, and then went to bed. Next morning, Brown, looking pale and shaky, told Campbell he did not feel well enough to attend a meeting scheduled in the Wood Gundy offices. Campbell was feeling queasy himself—he thought he was developing flu—but he went to the meeting and afterward returned to the hotel with Jack McCausland.

McCausland had suffered a heart attack some time before, and he was alarmed by Brown's appearance. "He never had too much colour to his face ever," McCausland recalled to this author, "but now he looked like putty and I told him he should get back to Calgary and see his doctor. But he was too busy for that, of course."

After McCausland had left, Brown complained of cold shivers and Campbell, who could see he was sweating heavily, managed to persuade him to get into bed. The house doctor, summoned by Campbell, made a quick examination and recommended that they call in a heart specialist, who arrived at about 4 p.m. and concluded Brown had had a heart attack. It did not seem too serious, he said, and he could remain at the hotel for the night, under the care of a nurse, but he must be admitted to hospital next day, a Thursday.

One of the reasons for Brown's visit to Toronto was to make the final arrangements for the redemption of the 1960 Home debenture issue that was convertible into TransCanada shares at $27. With the market price of TransCanada now above $30, it was expected that most of the bond-holders would exercise their conversion privilege and exchange their debentures for TransCanada shares, thus relieving Home of the burden of paying the interest charges on them.

After Brown had been spirited out of the hotel in a freight elevator and taken to hospital, Campbell spent the rest of Thursday arranging the last-minute details of the redemption with Wood Gundy and the various trust companies involved. The plates for the financial-page advertisements announcing the "call" were handed over to the trust companies and everything was in readiness for the announcement to be made as soon as the stock market closed next day, Friday, November 22.

After their trip to Toronto, Brown and Campbell had planned to fly on to Dallas to discuss another deal there. When he was taken ill Brown told Campbell to go on without him, but Campbell, still feeling wretched himself, decided to postpone the Dallas trip and go home to Calgary for the weekend. On his way out to the airport on the Friday morning he stopped in at the hospital to say goodbye to Brown and assure him all the arrangements for the call had been completed. Then he took off in the Gulfstream with Don Douglas, a wartime RCAF ferry pilot with international airline experience who had been hired by Brown to head Home's aviation department when he bought the Lodestar.

Hardly were they airborne when the shocking news was flashed around the world from their former destination: President John F. Kennedy had been assassinated in a motorcade through the streets of Dallas. Immediately, stock markets in both the United States and Canada were beset by a wave of panic selling.

Agonizingly immobilized in his hospital bed, Bob Brown watched the news on television and realized its implications for him: if Home went ahead with its call a couple of hours hence and the stock market slide carried TransCanada shares down below the $27 mark the bond-holders would not claim them and he would have to come up with $20 million he didn't have to redeem their debentures.

In vain, he telephoned the control tower at Winnipeg airport, trying to pass a message to Bob Campbell. But Campbell, nursing his flu, cruised on toward Calgary blissfully unaware of the panic on the ground below. And so it fell to Ross Phillips and Ron Coleman to make the crucial decision: should they go ahead with the call? They spoke to Wood Gundy on the telephone and were told that if the market plunge continued it was highly unlikely any bond-holders would convert their debentures into TransCanada shares. But they also knew that to cancel the call at the last minute might shake investors' confidence in Home's stability, particularly with Brown out of action, at least temporarily.

There was no way Phillips and Coleman could consult Campbell, but they did manage to reach Brown in his hospital bed. Exhausted, he could only tell them, "You'll have to do whatever you think best."

Then came the news that the stock exchanges had closed early to try to halt the rout. Phillips and Coleman waited about twenty minutes to see if Brown would call them back with new instructions. He didn't, so they took the bold course and told the trust companies to go ahead with the call as planned.

The markets remained closed on the following Monday, the national day of mourning for Kennedy, and when they reopened on Tuesday, November 26, the panic had subsided and share prices, including TransCanada's, recovered. When the dust cleared, almost all the $20 million worth of debentures were exchanged for 662,521 of Home's TransCanada shares (the rest were redeemed for cash), and the company's net income benefited to the tune of $1.03 million—the difference between the average price it had paid for the TransCanada shares and the $27 conversion price.

By the end of 1963, the amount of money Home had tied up in TransCanada shares had been reduced to $31.5 million, and while the interest on those shares and its other long-term debt during the year was $3.3 million (more than its net income of $3.09 million) the company finished the year in reasonably good shape. It owed the bank $5.25 million but this was a normal loan for operating purposes and it was paid back with part of the proceeds of a $15 million issue of 6.25 per cent collateral trust bonds sold to financial institutions in the United States and Canada in October 1963.

Brown himself, however, while he seemed to be making a satisfactory recovery from his heart attack, was still in deep financial trouble. Only he and his bankers knew the full extent of his personal debt but it was thought to be around $2 million and his senior executives at Home, who were close enough to him to recognize the gravity of the situation, spent months trying to evolve some formula that would enable him to realize some of his tied-up assets without sacrificing his control of Home.

The solution, which emerged early in 1964, was attributed to the combined brainstorming of Bart Rombough, Ross Smith, Ron Coleman, and Earl Lomas, who had replaced Doug McDermid as Brown's personal lawyer on McDermid's elevation to the bench. Quite simple in outline but by no means so in detail, it was to split United Oils into two, separating its control block of Home shares into a new subsidiary and leaving the oil and gas properties in the original company, which Home, as part of the transaction, offered to buy.

United's position by now was better than it had been a few years earlier. Its bank debt, for instance, had been reduced to $3.65 million, thanks partly to a $6 million bond issue Brown had managed to sell to Mutual of New York and the Prudential in 1961. And an independent appraisal carried out by the firm of McDaniel Consultants Ltd. early in 1964 as the first stage of the company's reorganization found that its oil and gas properties were actually worth $14.06 million, rather than the $6.5 million at which they were being carried on the books.

The next step was the creation of the new subsidiary, which was called Cygnus Corporation Ltd., partly because of the comforting echo of E. P. Taylor's successful Argus Corporation, and partly because "cygnus" is the Greek word for swan, and all concerned realized the importance of Swan Hills to Brown's empire. Cygnus adopted the Class-A-and-B-share formula which had served Brown so well in the Home-Federated merger (with its four million Class A shares carrying a ten-cent dividend but no vote, and its four million Class B shares carrying the vote but not necessarily a dividend) and in return for the control block of Home shares it issued 868,789 Class A and 2.6 million Class B Cygnus shares to its parent company, United. United then distributed these shares to its shareholders in the proportion of one Class A and three Class B Cygnus shares for each ten United shares they held—a legal process known as a reduction of capital.

A United shareholder—who might have been forgiven for being somewhat bemused by this whole proceeding—now held two parcels of shares: one in a holding company which controlled Home Oil and had announced that it intended "to pursue an aggressive policy of investment and participation in other business ventures" and the other in a producing oil company whose gas and oil properties were worth $14 million, and which Home had promised to buy at seventy-five cents a share (a price established as fair by independent appraisals of both companies involved).

United was still not paying a dividend, and its share prices had not risen for years, so its shareholders were glad to ratify the reorganization at a meeting in May 1964. Most of them also promptly accepted Home's offer for their "reduced" United shares.

Brown, who had owned 2.6 million United shares, emerged with 780,000 Class B shares of Cygnus, almost a third of the total issued, which—until he received an unpleasant shock a few years later—was considered enough to ensure his continued control of Home, but henceforth through Cygnus. In addition, he received 260,000 Class A shares of Cygnus, worth a little over $4 each, which, since they did not affect control of the company, he was free to sell if he wished. And then the sale of his reduced shares of United to Home brought him $1.95 million in cash.

At last, and probably for the first time since he had wound up his appliance business, R. A. Brown, Jr., was free of debt. It was a happy state he would not, alas, enjoy for very long.

CHAPTER SEVENTEEN

A Raid
Is Beaten Off

Ever since Swan Hills, back in 1957, there had been no major oil discovery in Alberta. But in February 1964 the California Standard Company drilled a wildcat well about 150 miles north of Edmonton that opened up the big new Mitsue field, southeast of Lesser Slave Lake. To Brown's delight, Home's 1.8-million-acre land inventory in Alberta included 21,000 acres near by (held 87.5 per cent by Home and 12.5 per cent by Alminex) and he immediately ordered the drilling of two exploratory wells. Both found oil—ten miles apart—and by the end of the year Home had eight producing wells in the new field.

The Mitsue discovery substantially increased both the company's reserves and its production, as did the acquisition of United Oils. Home had purchased ninety-two per cent of the issued shares of United by the end of the year, and the inherited production increased its gross income by $1.3 million. (The purchase of United Oils, financed by bank loans, cost almost $10 million, which was repaid out of the proceeds of an issue of 5.5 per cent convertible debentures sold on a rights-to-shareholders basis which raised $20 million in December 1964.) During 1964, also, TransCanada Pipe-Lines at long last paid its first dividend—one dollar per share—and with Home still holding 1.28 million shares this made another welcome contribution to its revenue. Net income for the year was up sixty-four per cent, at $5.08 million, and the annual dividend was raised from twenty-five cents a share to thirty-five cents.

That better times were on the way had been signalled the year before, when the company paid a dividend on its Class B voting stock for the first time and distributed a stock dividend of one Class A share for each ten A or B shares held. And the improvement in his corporate fortunes had encouraged Brown to launch his first venture overseas, which was widely heralded as a major departure for a Canadian company. On a visit to England, his brother Ronnie had been intrigued by the interest being shown in the North Sea, where the first large-scale exploration for oil and gas was about to begin. With its fierce and unpredictable storms, such a contrast to the sun-baked deserts of the Middle East, the chilly North Sea seemed an improbable place to drill for oil. But some of the world's largest companies had been drawn to the area by the discovery in 1959 of the second-largest gas field in the world, at Groningen, on the coast of Holland. There were indications that the gas-bearing structure extended beneath the North Sea toward the English coast, and perhaps beyond into Yorkshire.

When he returned to Calgary, Ronnie Brown—who would soon give up his active participation in the company's business and move to Vancouver—convinced his brother that Home should become involved in the North Sea play, and Ron Coleman and Bob Humphreys were promptly despatched to England to work out a deal with the major British company, British Petroleum. After weeks of almost daily negotiating sessions, Home undertook to drill seven wells on BP land in Yorkshire in return for a half-interest in 993,600 acres in the northeast part of the county.

George Fong was astonished one day when John Carr walked into his office, plunked down a pile of books and charts, and told him, "Okay, your responsibility now is England." But after a preliminary visit to find a house, Fong moved his wife and two young sons across the Atlantic and settled down to investigate the geology of Yorkshire.

Soon after the company had spudded in its first well—Crayke No. 1, twelve miles north of the historic city of York—Britain was awarded thirty-five per cent of the North Sea by an international agreement drawn up in Geneva. It then began to issue two types of licence to the oil companies: one for exploration, covering searches and experimental drilling only, and the other a full production licence, permitting the holder to take and sell whatever oil or gas he might find. Perhaps because its on-shore drilling in Yorkshire provided a satisfactory earnest of its intentions, Home (in partnership with Canadian Pacific Oil and Gas and Alminex) was awarded two production licences covering 750,000 acres: 400,000 acres just off the coast of Yorkshire opposite its land holdings and the rest fifty miles further out to sea. A marine seismic program begun immediately had to be suspended because of rough weather in October 1964, and it could not be resumed until the following spring, by which time Home had been awarded another production licence covering a further 19,000 acres.

By now, the on-shore drilling program had run into frustrating delays. Crayke No. 1 was drilled with a British rig, and true to the relaxed English fashion the crew worked only the day shift, instead of round the clock like their Canadian counterparts. Ed Ratke, an Albertan born on a farm within sight of the old Atlantic No. 3 well—scene of the most spectacular oil-well fire in Canadian history, back in the days of Leduc—was in charge of the drilling, and when Crayke No. 1 turned out to be dry, late in 1964, he made arrangements to hire two German rigs and crews to sink the four wells planned for 1965.

Then a new complication arose. The sites chosen for the four new wells were on the Yorkshire Moors, beloved of all readers of the Brontës and many others whose hearts thrill at their windswept bareness, and Home's applications for drilling locations began to encounter passionate opposition from environmental groups and hiking clubs. Much time was expended at hearings trying to persuade the authorities that the wells could be drilled without damage to the local scenery, and whether they proved to be producing wells or dry the surrounding area would be restored to its pristine grandeur at Home's expense. At one site, Home's subsequent landscaping was judged to be altogether too efficient: the local hikers complained that it looked too much like a golf course and clumps of heather had to be planted to roughen up the vista.

Britain's need for fuel ultimately outweighed the desire to preserve the moors undisturbed and permission was duly obtained for all four wells. And all four turned out to be dry. But in 1966, the next well drilled—Lockton 2A—came in with a roar: it was the largest gas strike ever made in England and a giant even by Alberta standards, with a calculated open flow potential of 510 million cubic feet a day.

Bob Brown was elated at this success. He went around chuckling to his friends, "Imagine, a little Canadian company like us—we send a Chinese geologist over there and find gas where BP couldn't." He had formed a new subsidiary to handle his U.K. operations, Home Oil of Canada Ltd., and as its chairman had secured the services of a man with a name redolent of Britain's maritime glory: Earl Beatty, son of the famous admiral who commanded a squad-ron at the Battle of Jutland in the First World War and a much-decorated naval veteran in his own right.

Brown revelled in the *entrée* to British society provided by his new associate, though he later confessed to having some qualms when, at a reception he gave at the Mansion House in London, it fell to his lot to introduce the Earl—who had been a Conservative Member of Parliament before his elevation to the House of Lords—to the Labour government's Chancellor of the Exchequer, and later Prime Minister, James Callaghan. He need not have worried. Callaghan shook Beatty's hand warmly and said, "I'm a Beatty man and always have been—and my father was a Beatty man before me." He then explained to the gratified but somewhat puzzled Earl Beatty that his father had served on Admiral Beatty's flagship during the First World War, and he himself had been a stoker on a ship commanded by Home of Canada's chairman during the Second World War.

For the final production test of Lockton 2A, Brown ordered a marquee set up at the wellhead and entertained the local gentry at a moorland version of a garden party, to which Earl Beatty and a group of distinguished guests from London were delivered by chartered helicopter. Soon afterward, Home's seventh well, drilled beside an ancient stone monument known as Ralph's Cross, also struck gas, though in lesser quantities than Lockton 2A. This completed Home's obligations and earned it a half-interest in what was universally considered to be the most important gas field in Britain, since it was close to the large potential markets of the industrial Midlands. Both wells were then capped pending negotiations for the sale of the gas to the Gas Council, the government-owned agency with a monopoly on the manufacture and distribution of gas within the United Kingdom.

This discovery, and Home's licences in the North Sea, where seismic work continued during 1966, were considered especially important because oil discoveries were becoming fewer and farther between in Alberta. Home continued to branch out, however, and with propane and butane sales still rising in 1966 it entered the field of liquid petroleum gas marketing, forming Hardisty Storage Ltd. in partnership with Canadian Superior and a U.S. wholesale marketing firm named Union Petroleum Corporation, based in Tulsa, Oklahoma. Hardisty, by pumping water into a large salt bed 4,000 feet underground, leached out four caverns capable of storing a million barrels of propane and butane, which are, of course, produced all year round, until the winter months, when demand for them is heaviest. In association with this project, Home and Union Petroleum, as equal partners, formed Can-Am Liquids Ltd., to buy propane, butane, and condensates from producers and resell them on a wholesale basis, and Can-Am Transportation Inc., to move the products to market in a fleet of railroad tank cars.

These ventures were considered a normal and profitable diversification for an oil company.[1] But during the 1960s Brown began to be criticized for applying too much effort—and money—to outside investments which sometimes lacked even a tenuous connection with the business he knew best, the finding and development of oil and gas. In 1965, for instance, he heard that a group of Winnipeg investors was seeking a buyer for a block of 500,000 shares of Calgary Power Ltd., the company that supplied two-thirds of Alberta's electric-power requirements. This holding amounted to about ten per cent of Calgary Power's outstanding shares and Brown bought it—without even consulting his board in advance—for $13 million. While Alberta's growth was increasing its demand for electricity by leaps and bounds, his associates could find no better rationale for the purchase than that he believed a local company of such importance should be at least partly owned by a home-town boy. Uncharacteristically, at around this same time he made several other investments which for Bob Brown could be considered minor: for instance, in partnership with Crown Trust Company, Home built a ten-storey office building and adjacent parking structure in downtown Calgary.

His next major purchase—which raised the amount of money Home had tied up in outside investments to $64 million—was within his own field, but once again his associates were never entirely sure of the reason for it. In 1967, he had Home buy the largest single block of shares in Union Gas Company of Canada Ltd., a utility supplying natural gas to customers in southwestern Ontario. The 650,000 shares cost Home $9.65 million, and they amounted to slightly less than five per cent of the total outstanding. In addition to buying gas from TransCanada for resale, Union owns pipelines and more than a thousand producing gas wells in Ontario. It also has about fifty billion cubic feet of storage capacity in old depleted wells in the counties of Lambton and Essex, and when Canada sent extra gas to the beleaguered northeastern United States during the vicious winter of 1976–77, eastern-Canadian consumers were supplied from Union's stored reserve, permitting TransCanada to divert part of its flow directly into the United States.

In retrospect, some of his associates thought Brown saw the potential value of this storage capacity long before most other people and was attracted by the prospect—since he was already involved in the production and transportation of gas—of diversifying into its distribution as well. He certainly put his staff to work on a variety of "scenarios": how Home might get control of Union, for instance; how Union might then be able to take over the considerably larger Ontario distribution company, Consumers' Gas Company, of Toronto; how this larger entity might even take over TransCanada PipeLines; or what would happen if Union were taken over by some other company, possibly Consumers' itself.

Others in Brown's circle thought it was this last possibility—a takeover of Union by Consumers'—that accounted for his purchase of the Union shares in the first place. Brown took his responsibility as a director of TransCanada seriously, and he was always concerned that if Union and Consumers' merged it would not augur well for TransCanada, which would then be faced across the bargaining table by one dominant buyer.

If indeed this was a threat, it was not perceived as such by the rest of TransCanada's directors, and Brown was unable to interest them in forestalling the possibility by purchasing either an interest in or control of Union. So when Home needed funds a year or so later he sold his Union shares to Consumers' come what may (at $2.28 million more than he had paid for them).[2]

If Brown was unable to sway the TransCanada board on this occasion, he was certainly given full credit for helping to resolve a problem the company encountered in the mid-sixties which once again brought it into unwelcome conflict with the federal government. Faced with an ever-increasing demand for its natural gas on both sides of the border—the government was still encouraging exports of oil and gas at the time—the company needed to expand the capacity of its line and it applied for permission to build a new thousand-mile stretch of thirty-six-inch pipe from Manitoba south through the states of Minnesota, Wisconsin, and Michigan to Sarnia.

The route through the United States had several advantages: it was shorter than the original route through Northern Ontario which had caused such a fuss in the company's formative years; it was cheaper, because it avoided the need to blast another trench through the rock of the Laurentian Shield; and it would permit sales to U.S. customers along the way, which would benefit the company and keep down the price of gas to consumers in Ontario and Quebec. But the proposal aroused opposition on both sides of the border.

In Canada, it was approved by the National Energy Board but then disallowed by the cabinet, which feared it would reduce the quantity of gas carried on the all-Canadian Northern Ontario route and revive the controversy that had brought down a Liberal government once before. And in the United States, when TransCanada formed a wholly owned subsidiary, Great Lakes Gas Transmission, and applied to the Federal Power Commission for permission to build the line, its application was opposed by rival U.S. gas companies, one of them American Natural Gas of Detroit.

When Brown applied himself to this problem he soon decided that if its application was to be successful TransCanada would need an ally in the United States. He went to see Ralph McIlvenny, president of American Natural, and quickly won his confidence. The result, after a long series of negotiations in which Brown played the role of honest broker, was a fifty-fifty partnership in Great Lakes between TransCanada and American Natural, and an episode during the courtship leading to their marriage showed that Brown had not lost his wildcatter's spirit. McIlvenny and James Kerr, president of TransCanada, were having difficulty agreeing on the price at which American Natural would be able to buy gas. Eventually they narrowed the gap between them to half a cent per thousand cubic feet and Brown—making light of this difference, even though it would amount to many thousands of dollars a year—suggested they toss a coin for it. Kerr won, and McIlvenny accepted his defeat in a good-humoured way that augured well for the future relations between the two partners—though in later years he would sometimes enliven social gatherings by twitting Kerr about his two-headed coin.

With the support of American Natural, Great Lakes' application for the line won the unanimous approval of the FPC, and after receiving a high-level delegation of TransCanada directors the cabinet reversed its rejection of the National Energy Board's recommendation and approved the line, provided—on pain of a $1 million "fine"—that TransCanada did not permit the quantity of gas flowing through Northern Ontario to fall below guaranteed levels: fifty per cent of its total deliveries to eastern Canada when the new line opened, rising to sixty-five per cent by 1976. Far from having to pay any fine, TransCanada easily met these requirements and in subsequent years, as the demand for gas continued to rise, it "looped" the line through Northern Ontario to more than double its previous capacity.

Not all of Brown's exertions in the cause of TransCanada were as fruitful as this one. Some of his fellow directors found him far too much the activist for their more conservative tastes, and on his part he was often frustrated by their refusal to be galloped in the direction he was convinced they should take. Occasionally, especially if he had given one of his legendary parties the night before, he would tacitly signify his lofty detachment from the minutiae of whatever business was at hand by dozing off at directors' meetings. But on the whole he was acknowledged to be a valuable and important member of the board.

The grasp of business he brought to their boards was welcomed also by Donald Gordon and Gordon McGregor, the presidents respectively of Canadian National Railways and Trans-Canada Air Lines. Brown and Donald Gordon, in particular, became good friends, though they seemed an unlikely combination: Gordon bluff and hearty, a rumpled giant of a man with an intellect to match his physical size; Brown neat and by comparison formal, reserved, and—in the view of some of his friends—excessively sensitive about his short stature.

Once, when Gordon was visiting Calgary, Brown gave a cocktail party for him on the lawn of the Italianate mansion he now occupied in the exclusive Mount Royal district. At the front of the house is a massive flight of steps leading up to a balustraded balcony, the sort of vantage point from which a South American dictator might be imagined reviewing his troops. As the conviviality induced by his native spirit took hold of Gordon, he planted his huge feet squarely on the balcony and began to regale the guests with Scottish songs—until the proceedings were interrupted by a wail of sirens denoting the arrival of a squad of motorcycle police.

It was Stampede Week in Calgary, and among the attractions that year was a troupe of Mexican dancers, musicians, and equestrians. Accompanying them was the wife of President Lopez

Mateos, with her children and a considerable retinue, all of whom, at the request of the Stampede committee, were guests in Brown's home. The sirens had announced the arrival of a police honour guard to escort the presidential party to the evening performance of the Stampede—and no sooner had the commotion caused by their departure subsided than the other guests, outside on the lawn, were drenched by a cloudburst. Gordon, who appeared to enjoy the confusion, was interviewed by a reporter next day and he congratulated Brown for "being able to cope with the First Lady of Mexico, me, and a flood, all at the same time and without batting an eye".

Invitations to Brown's lavish parties were eagerly sought and freely given. But the guest list was more restricted at another series of parties which he made into a tradition, his annual fall weekends at Qualicum Beach, apparently modelled on Cyrus Eaton's Pugwash thinkers' conferences. These spirited get-togethers had their genesis in an annual management meeting initiated by Bob Campbell in the late 1950s. Then Brown began to invite his directors, to give them a chance to mingle informally with his executives, and friends such as Ed Kennedy, of Lehman Bros., and Milton Lipton, of the Walter Levy firm, together with other eminent oil men, who were invited to give short talks on current developments in the industry on the Saturday morning. The rest of the weekend was spent, according to the guests' predilections, on salmon-fishing, golf on a nine-hole course between Brown's house and the sea—which he had bought in case someone put a housing development on it and spoiled his view—and just general high-level horseplay, such as the occasion when a couple of his junior executives who had caught a small shark instead of a salmon spirited it back from their boat and into Brown's swimming pool.

While not notably witty himself, Brown enjoyed hearing jokes (and retelling them, when he managed to remember them) and he took such pranks in good part. He laughed as hard as anyone when Ed Kennedy easily won a contest to find the most fitting words to be inserted in a cartoon-type balloon emanating from the mouth of a life-size cut-out photograph of Brown in a typically animated pose, obviously issuing instructions he knew would be obeyed. Wall-Streeter Kennedy's winning entry: "I don't want to hear a word from any of you about the bloody Americans—until after we get the money."

Brown was not much of a fisherman, but he did sometimes accompany his guests on to the golf course, where he displayed a conspicuous lack of mastery of the game. His friend David Williams, of the U.S. pipeline company Williams Bros., had presented him with an antique Oldsmobile, and he had had it fitted out as a mobile bar, which accompanied the golfers on their rounds. And when playing with Brown, his guests soon learned not to count the shots too carefully. "I own the course," he would grin, "so I make the rules."

He had a similar attitude to the shots that were consumed around the barbecue pit and the poker table after the day's sporting events were over, and one night Milton Lipton sought refuge from the revelry in the library, where he found Harry Thompson, a Home director who was also chairman of Calgary Power and an old friend of the Brown family. The talk turned, with sadness on both sides, to Brown's apparent inability to control his drinking, and Thompson said he had warned him about it often in the past—but not since the occasion, about a year earlier, when Brown had put his arm around the older man's shoulder and said, with a mixture of penitence and fatalistic acceptance, "Harry, it's just my life, and I'm going to have to live it the only way I know how."

Home continued to make steady progress during these years, but as with the rest of the industry it was by the development of its existing reserves rather than the discovery of new ones. Perhaps this lack of excitement led to a lessening of Brown's interest in the day-to-day running of the company. At any rate, he spent more and more time away from Calgary, travelling the continent in pursuit of his various ventures—until he was galvanized back into action by a telephone call from Toronto at the beginning of February 1967.

Brown listened to the call with dismay—and mounting fury. It informed him that if he had not already lost control of his whole empire, he was in grave danger of doing so, in circumstances that were spelled out in a registered special-delivery letter he received a couple of days later.

The letter came from Westburne Industries Ltd., and it informed him in starkly formal terms that one of that company's subsidiaries, Petrobec Ltd., had accumulated 676,258 Class B voting shares of Cygnus Corporation, which amounted to 25.9 per cent of the total outstanding; and that it had an option to purchase a further 145,356 shares, which would give it 31.5 per cent of the total outstanding. This, while the letter did not say so, would give West-burne more shares of Cygnus voting stock than Brown himself held. In view of the size of Petrobec's holding, the letter suggested, "We feel that discussions should be held at an early date with a view towards the seating of mutually acceptable nominees to represent our interest on the Board of Directors of Cygnus Corporation Limited. . . ."

At this suggestion, Brown exploded. For Westburne Industries, as he well knew, was owned by another company, Commonwealth Petroleum Services Ltd. And Commonwealth Petroleum was owned by none other than his old friends and lieutenants, the men he had broken with almost ten years earlier—John Scrymgeour and Bill Atkinson.

After Scrymgeour and Atkinson had bought Southwest Petro-leums from Chuck Spalding and gone into business as proprietors themselves, they had used their financial acumen to good effect and built up a network of oil and drilling companies. Then they had branched out into the construction field by establishing Westburne, a highly successful nation-wide plumbing and electrical supply company. As their own empire prospered, they had watched from afar the formation of Cygnus Corporation, and had wryly admired its astute preservation of Brown's leverage over Home Oil.

In the first few years after its formation, Cygnus had not fulfilled the ambitious hopes entertained for it. It had raised $2.5 million capital with an issue of preferred shares and Brown's aides had investigated dozens of potential investments suggested for it by him and others. For various reasons, most were found wanting, but its first venture was the construction of the Thio-Pet chemical plant, opened in Edmonton in 1965. This was designed to produce carbon disulphide, used as a solvent in natural-gas wells and in the manu-facture of a wide variety of industrial products, and hydrogen sul-phide, used in metallurgical processes and the production of heavy water for nuclear-power generators. The plant ultimately cost $2 million—far more than the original estimates—and since the de-mand for its products did not develop as envisaged it never became profitable. As its next investment, Cygnus bought Empire Manage-ment Ltd., an Alberta company administering a small mutual fund, and this, too, proved disappointing. (Both the Thio-Pet plant and Empire Management were eventually sold.)

At the beginning of 1967, Cygnus Corporation was certainly no Argus Corporation. But it remained solidly based on its main asset —its control of Home Oil. And Petrobec had begun to buy its shares on the open market two or three years previously, through nominee brokers, in an operation reminiscent of Brown's own take-over of Home—and financed, ironically enough, by loans from Brown's old ally, now the Canadian Imperial Bank of Commerce. Even more ironically, the shares as they were bought were lodged in a branch of the bank housed in the west corner of the Ritz-Carlton Hotel, where Brown always stayed on his visits to Montreal.

Brown was blissfully unaware of the threat to his well-being until Scrymgeour and Atkinson, faced with the need to raise more funds with a public financing, had to disclose Petrobec's holding in their prospectus, in accordance with Ontario Securities Commission regulations. The bombshell burst on Home's startled employees, and the whole city of Calgary, in a news item in the *Herald* on Saturday, February 4, 1967, under the headline "HOME OIL CONTROL MAY BE CHANGED". The story quoted Lucien Cornez, president of Westburne, as saying he did not know whether Petrobec's holding represented control of Home. Brown was hardly mollified by this statement—and he was provoked to near-apoplexy by another attributed to Bill Atkinson: that no changes were planned in Home's management.

The announcement prompted a series of meetings on Home's executive floor that went on all that weekend and into the wee hours of many subsequent mornings, as Brown planted his back against the wall and prepared to do battle. The question of whether he held firm control of Cygnus was complicated by the fact that a block of B voting shares representing about twelve per cent of those outstanding was held by Coastal Oils Ltd., one of the early Brown companies that had lived on as a subsidiary of Home, and there was some doubt whether those shares could legally be voted by Brown. Assured of them, he was safe: added to his personal holding they would give him close to fifty per cent of the voting stock, more than Westburne could hope to have.

Ron Coleman, his "in-house" lawyer, considered that the Coastal shares *could* legally be voted in his favour but Neil McKinnon, when Brown consulted him, suggested that he should take no chances and see Alex MacIntosh, one of the country's leading corporate lawyers, who was McKinnon's own counsel and confidant and a director of the Bank of Commerce. MacIntosh, who thereafter became an invaluable adviser to Brown, mapped out a defensive strategy for him. And so that his whole future would not depend on a legal opinion, Brown set out to increase his holding of Cygnus voting shares by buying them on the open market. Some of his friends also rallied round and picked up shares wherever they could, and in the process the price of the stock was driven up from about $8 to more than $14.

But Brown won his fight. By the end of February he had increased his personal holding of Cygnus Class B by more than 146,000 shares, to 962,383 shares—enough to give him clear control even without the Coastal shares. Home's annual meeting in April passed off without any of the expected fireworks; Westburne, in effect, had no choice but to vote its entire holding in support of the existing management.

The subsequent year, nevertheless, was an uncomfortable one for the president and managing director of Cygnus Corporation. He had refused Westburne's request for representation on the board and he was still in control of its operations. But he could not make a move without trying to anticipate the possible reaction of Scrymgeour and Atkinson, with whom he was still not on speaking terms. As holders of 31.5 per cent of the voting shares they were entitled to consideration: would they approve of any course of action he might propose, or could they reasonably object? Cygnus was a swan with pinioned wings.

Then, tragically, in January 1968, Bill Atkinson was found to have cancer of the lymph glands. By April he was dead, at the age of forty-six.

Brown had always blamed Atkinson more than Scrymgeour for the assault on his position, but with so many B shares remaining in Westburne's hands he still felt uneasy. So he consulted MacIntosh, and with McKinnon's promise that the required funds would once again be available to him he telephoned Scrymgeour, suggested that the Cygnus situation was an impossible one for them both, and to resolve it offered to buy all Westburne's Cygnus shares for what they had cost, plus interest. Scrymgeour accepted his offer, and after the accountants had gone over the books 825,247 shares changed hands for $5.75 million.

With 69.3 per cent of the Cygnus voting shares now in his own portfolio, R. A. Brown, Jr., was restored to impregnable command of Cygnus, and his control of Home Oil was preserved. But he had borrowed heavily, first to raise his own holdings and again to buy out Westburne's. And so his personal bank account was again millions of dollars in the red.

CHAPTER EIGHTEEN

The North Slope:
A Slide to Disaster

The discovery of the biggest oil field ever found on the North American continent went quite unnoticed by the public, perhaps because it was made in a place so impossibly remote and climatically forbidding, but more probably because oil was still taken for granted—there were plenty of "cheap" foreign supplies around and no one yet realized how badly new reserves would soon be needed.

Atlantic Richfield, one of the top ten American oil companies, started drilling a wildcat well in April 1967, more than three hundred miles north of the Arctic Circle on the shores of the icy Beaufort Sea. Arco Prudhoe Bay No. 1, as the well was called, struck oil in December, but the company's reporting of that fact seems to have attracted scant attention, even within the industry.

It was not until six months later, when a second Arco well drilled seven miles to the southeast also struck oil, that anything more than casual interest began to be focused on the now-famous North Slope of Alaska, whose recoverable reserves are today estimated at ten billion barrels of oil and twenty-five trillion cubic feet of natural gas. Even then the full significance of the find was not recognized: reporting it, the *Calgary Herald* said, "The gas phase of the discovery is believed large enough to support several northern communities in terms of space heating, cooking fuel and other domestic and community uses of natural gas."

It was a situation tailor-made to set Bob Brown's entrepreneurial blood racing. In phone calls and personal visits, he began to pump his friends for any scrap of information they might have about the North Slope. He even flew to Dallas, where he knew some of the people in the oil world's pre-eminent consulting firm, DeGolyer and MacNaughton. Since that company had been retained to make an independent assessment of just what Brown wanted to know— the likely extent of the North Slope reserves—his friends in Dallas could only tell him their lips were sealed. But everywhere he went

Brown detected the scent of "big oil" in the air. Eventually, he concluded that Alaska was another Middle East.

Bob Brown was now fifty-four. As the owner of Canada's biggest independent oil company, he had a large circle of friends among the rich and influential on both sides of the Atlantic. He flew everywhere in his private jet, which was now a $3 million Gulfstream II, widely considered the most luxurious executive aircraft in the world—its washroom taps took the form of gold-plated dolphins. He had three imposing homes, having added a ranch-style bungalow in the wealthy retreat of Palm Desert, California, to his mansion in Calgary and the Qualicum Beach house he had bought from Jim Lowery. Even though he had borrowed heavily to fend off the loss of his empire, his debt was a manageable one, far outweighed by his assets. Had he wanted to sell out, he could have lived in idle luxury for the rest of his life.

But none of this was enough. The inner demons still possessed him. Herein lies the enigma of the wildcatter: success, riches, the awe of friends, public esteem, power even—all pale before the compulsion to look for oil. And with Bob Brown there was something else. Of course he wanted money; he could not achieve his ambition without it. But more than anything he craved recognition as a *builder*. He wanted—indeed whatever secret fires and torments drove him *demanded*—the respect accorded to the true artist, the creator of a masterpiece no one else could have accomplished.

It was inevitable, then, that he would sink every cent he could raise into the play for which he had prepared himself all his life. Here at last was the opportunity he had always known would one day come along, his chance to prove himself beyond all others.

Even so, the heroic size of the stakes he tossed on the table astonished all his friends, and worried many of them. The long-retired Bart Gillespie, for instance, watched from afar in California. He knew there was oil in Alaska—he had been in charge of the operation that discovered U.S. Naval Petroleum Reserve No. 4 during the Second World War, one hundred million barrels of oil to the west of Prudhoe Bay and eight hundred miles inland. But he was frightened for his old boss. "I knew the problems of drilling up there," Gillespie told this author, "the *enormous* costs."

But Bob Brown had played for high stakes all his life. He had taken apparently impossible gambles before and won. Who was to say he could not do it again? To have done so would have been to challenge his judgment, and even had there been anyone possessed of such temerity, Brown would certainly not have listened: he never had much time for those circumspect souls whose touchstone is caution.

The word went out: Bob Brown is buying, and buying big. He sent off his land men with instructions to pick up all the leases they could lay their hands on, however high the bidding. And within months of the Arco discovery Home[1] had bought up 287,225 acres on the North Slope—not quite in the prime area but all around it.

He also approached Robert O. Anderson, head of Atlantic Richfield, and late in 1968 put his signature to a "farmout" agreement under which, by spending $23 million in a two-stage exploration program, Home would earn a fifty per cent interest in 313,000 acres and a twenty-five per cent interest in a further 137,000 acres of Arco lands extending to within thirty miles of the Prudhoe Bay discoveries. As part of the first stage of the agreement, Home paid Arco $3 million in cash and committed itself to spend a further $8 million by November 30, 1970—most of it to drill a well which became known as Nora Federal No. 1. After that, it was agreed, Home could either pull out of the deal or proceed to its second stage, which entailed the drilling of another well as part of the expenditure of a further $12 million.

Home was indeed "plunging into Alaska with the will of a salmon heading upstream", as a reporter for the *Anchorage Daily News* put it when Brown and a group of his executives paid a flying visit to the North Slope in November 1968.

Driven by an instinct no less compelling than that of a spawning salmon, Brown had only just begun. He was so determined to take advantage of the greatest oil play in North American history that he also embarked on a costly shopping expedition for Atlantic Richfield shares. These had sold for $74 early in the year. As news of the discovery spread they rocketed upward and the 400,000 shares Home had acquired on the open market by the end of the year cost an average of $108 each—a total expenditure of more than $43 million. Brown had Cygnus Corporation buy 50,000 shares, too, for $5.6 million—and then he started buying on his own account, increasing his already large debt to do so.

As Christmas neared, his closest lieutenant, Bob Campbell, decided it was time to call a halt. Brown had started buying Arco shares when they were between $80 and $90. In November they reached $130, and Campbell began urging him to take his profit—to sell his own shares, which would enable him to pay off his Bank of Commerce loan and still have a comfortable sum left over; and to sell Home's shares as well, since the company's purchases had increased its bank debt to $44 million—the highest in its history—and it was now faced with spending many millions more to explore its own lands on the North Slope and the Arco farmout.

Brown had other plans for the company, however. Home shares, which had started the year at $18, were now selling at $40 and more, and his advisers had suggested to him that the developing North Slope fever on the U.S. stock markets provided a golden opportunity to market an issue of Home Class A shares. While Brown had always resisted making equity issues in the past—when Home shares were selling for much below their real value—he realized that if his advisers were right he could probably raise enough money from the U.S. public to pay for the Arco shares Home had bought. So he decided to hang on to them.

But on Christmas Eve, over a drink with Campbell, he permitted himself to be persuaded to part with his personal holding. He picked up the phone, called his friend Ed Kennedy in New York, wished him a Merry Christmas, and told him to sell. And his friends gathered later that he had made a profit of about $3 million on the transaction.

The equity issue was sold without difficulty in the United States in February 1969—900,000 Class A shares at $43 each in U.S. funds, which buttressed Home's treasury by almost $40 million Canadian and enabled most of its bank loan to be paid off.

Brown also improved his personal financial situation considerably two months later. The rise in Home shares had carried the value of his Cygnus stock up, too, and with virtually seventy per cent of the voting shares in his own hands since his acquisition of the Westburne block he was able to sell some of them without imperilling his control. He made a public issue of 500,000 Class B Cygnus shares which, after commissions, netted him $5.4 million—almost as much as he had paid for Westburne's 825,427 shares. That left him a profit of almost 300,000 shares (after the various costs involved), or more than $3 million at the existing market price—though it was at the moment a paper profit, since he had determined that henceforth he would never permit his holding of

Class B shares to fall below 50.1 per cent of the total outstanding, thus preserving his absolute control of his empire and warding off such ugly shocks as he had lately received.

Brown should now have been sitting pretty, his personal debts paid off and Home poised for potentially lucrative discoveries in the two most exciting oil areas in the world—the North Slope and the North Sea. But the lure of what he saw as the biggest opportunity of his career had been too powerful for him to resist: he had not paid off his loan; instead, he had left the money he received for his Arco shares sitting in the bank in New York while he turned over in his mind a plan that was breathtaking in its audacity.

Early in 1969, there had been yet another rich discovery on the North Slope, this time by BP, the major British company which, with admirable foresight, had acquired the largest acreage held by any company in the area. Once again, the stock markets were gripped by oil fever, and Brown became convinced Arco shares would ultimately soar to $200. They were selling at that time for $120, and he decided to begin buying again on his own account. He realized, though, that with his personal loan now standing at almost $10 million even his usually obliging friend Neil McKinnon would probably refuse to advance him any more money, particularly for what still seemed to all but Brown to be merely a gamble on the stock market.

So, without McKinnon's knowledge, he called on the Bank of Nova Scotia. The Nova Scotia's chairman in those days, F. William Nicks, is no longer alive, so it is not known whether Brown explained to him the full extent of his grand design. In fact, he mentioned it to only a handful of his closest associates. And when he did, it seemed such an impossibly grandiose dream that most of those he confided in did not take him seriously. For Brown was now seized by the conviction that he could get control of Atlantic Richfield which, with more than $4 billion in assets, was one of the twenty largest industrial corporations in the United States.

He still spent many hours every week on the telephone, exchanging information with his continent-wide network of influential friends. And with his highly tuned antennae he had located a single block of 900,000 Arco shares that was thought to be for sale in the United States. At the going market price, that block would cost more than $100 million—but Brown had long since proved himself a master of the art of leverage, and long rows of noughts on balance sheets had never intimidated him.

Home already held 400,000 Arco shares, and Cygnus 50,000 more. If he could build up a substantial personal holding—and if Home's wells on the North Slope and in the North Sea found oil, which with the typical wildcatter's sanguinity he assumed they would—he would be big enough to assemble the financing to go after that U.S. share block. That would make him the largest single shareholder in Atlantic Richfield. Then, surely, he could make Robert Anderson see the wisdom of a merger between Home and Arco—controlled, of course, by Cygnus. And he, Bob Brown, would have pulled off the spectacular feat for a Canadian of taking control of a giant U.S. corporation.

Whether or not he set out this inviting vision of the future for Bill Nicks, Brown had lost none of his old charm and persuasiveness. The Bank of Nova Scotia lent him $12 million. With this, and every other cent he could lay his hands on, including the proceeds of his sale of Cygnus Class B, he plunged into the market for Arco shares.

There were signs in 1969 that foreshadowed the end of "the Go-Go years", that frenetic Wall Street decade of proliferating conglomerates and apparently magical mutual growth funds specializing in their "wonder stocks"; signs indicating to the wary that up through the roof was perhaps not the only direction share prices could go. But all that spring and summer, while other stocks faltered, the North Slope fever raged unabated and some of the more adventurous mutual-fund managers picked out this little Canadian company, Home Oil, as something of a "sleeper". Bob Brown sat happily by as their operations pushed Home's Class A shares up to the unheard-of price of $81. Arco shares continued their upward movement, too, though not so spectacularly. And upwards, too, went the estimates of how many billions of barrels of oil were locked away under the snows of Alaska.

Exhilarated by all this activity, and with his old affinity for pipelining, Brown managed to talk his way into the charmed circle of big operators planning to build the Alyeska pipeline south across Alaska to the port of Valdez, whence the North Slope's fabulous riches could be conveyed by super-tankers to the waiting world outside. At that time, it was estimated that the line would cost $900 million and would be operating by 1972. Brown managed to deal Home in for a two per cent interest, which committed the company to a further expenditure of $18 million.

But still he was not satisfied. He had heard on his grape-vine that a U.S. firm, Hamilton Brothers Oil Company, had headed a drilling group which had sunk a well on the shores of the Arctic Ocean not far from the Arco discovery wells. It had turned out to be dry but Fred Hamilton, head of the firm, had been encouraged by what its cores disclosed and was putting together a group of U.S. companies to bid at a huge lease auction scheduled by the state of Alaska for September. Included in the group were such well-established independents as Sun Oil, Continental Oil, Cities Service, and the rapidly expanding Ashland Oil of Kentucky—fitting company, in Brown's eyes, for Home Oil.

He had lately become friendly with the head of Ashland, a tall, live-wire lawyer named Orin E. Atkins. They had been introduced by Ed Kennedy a couple of years earlier, when Neil McKinnon had warned Brown his financial position was such that he would have to find a partner to buy into Cygnus if he was to have any hope of paying off his personal loan. Brown had managed then to work his way out of his difficulties without the need of a partner, but during their discussions he and Atkins had recognized each other as kindred spirits and he now asked Atkins to introduce him to Fred Hamilton.

The meeting, in Denver, was not an auspicious one, since Brown had flown down in the Gulfstream and it was quite apparent when he walked into Hamilton's office that he had whiled away the journey with more than his usual quota of drinks. His customary graciousness, as it sometimes did on these occasions, had given way to a manner that could most charitably be described as high-handed, and Hamilton, understandably, showed no great inclination to welcome him into his group. Atkins, however, like those who had known Brown much longer, had come to accept his occasional departures from decorum as lapses which, while regrettable and embarrassing, were far outweighed by his normal warmth and generosity. He knew, too, that they did not fairly reflect his brilliant business sense. After Brown had left the unproductive meeting, Atkins interceded on his behalf. Mollified, Hamilton agreed to admit Home Oil to his bidding group. But, he insisted, he did not want that man on "the train".

The slogan "Careless Talk Costs Lives" was a familiar one designed to foster security-consciousness during the Second World War. And careless talk before a lease sale has sometimes cost oil companies millions of dollars. So to preserve secrecy before the Alaska land auction Hamilton Brothers chartered a twenty-car train from Canadian National, aboard which it was proposed to sequester the representatives of all the companies in the group during the week leading up to the sale, while they worked out details of the bids they proposed to make. Other companies took over whole floors of hotels in Alaska and mounted guards in the corridors, in the best Howard Hughes tradition.

Bob Brown was no more anxious to subject himself to a week's incarceration on a train that was going nowhere than Fred Hamilton was to have him aboard—to the private relief of Home's executives, who feared that in his fervor for the North Slope he would incur heavier commitments than the company could bear. In fact, his own exploration men tried to dissuade him from bidding at all, on the grounds that they did not have enough information to evaluate the leases that were for sale. Also, everyone was now worried over the way he had put all his eggs in one basket. Even those few who were aware of his grand design—the takeover of Arco—felt he had plunged too heavily; that he *must* win or lose everything. And neither his geophysicists nor his geologists were particularly encouraged by their preliminary investigation of the land parcels Home had already bought in Alaska.

A few of Brown's close friends even urged him to lay off some of his risk. Home's land position was such that he was several times approached by other companies willing to take "farmouts" and shoulder the costs of exploration and drilling in return for a part-interest in any wells that resulted. It was the Williston Basin all over again, on a larger scale; a promoter's dream. Back then, he had *sought out* Thayer Lindsley and persuaded him to share his risk. Now, in defiance of all the rules of the game, he turned down all suitors.

As far as Home was concerned, he considered he had already taken in a partner—the U.S. investors who in effect put up a large part of the money the company invested in the North Slope play by subscribing for the equity issue in February. And as far as his personal investment was concerned, he was certain he was going to win, and he had no intention of sharing his winnings with anyone. In the words of one of his former associates, "He started to *wish* oil into the ground." He also stopped listening to his technical advisers. So Bob Campbell, George Blundun, and Maurice Paulson climbed aboard the CN Special, authorized to spend yet another $50 million worth of Home funds.

For the next week, the train wandered aimlessly up and down the line to Edmonton, the men inside clustered around maps pinned up in an empty baggage car or immersed in their calculations in smoke-filled compartments, unable to escape their imprisonment even long enough to call home. Predictably enough, this attracted the attention of the press, which began to speculate excitedly about the dark goings-on aboard what was variously dubbed the "Blue Sky Special" and the "Mystery Train". The speculation might even have been fanned by Bob Campbell, who scrawled a large "HELP!" on a laundry bag and held it up to a window as the train rolled through a station.

When all the bids were agreed upon, they were drawn up in duplicate and handed over in sealed envelopes to be flown to Anchorage in two jets Hamilton Brothers had standing by at Calgary airport—the duplication being in case one of the planes did not get through because of bad weather or accident. And only after the last lease was knocked down were the tired and dishevelled oil men permitted to leave the train.

In the event, the Home representatives spent only $11 million of the $50 million Brown had been prepared to commit, taking a twenty-five per cent interest in the $44 million bid made by the Hamilton group on Tract 73, an area extending to within two miles of the nearest production established on the North Slope at that time. The bid was successful—but there was some dismay that no one bid on the adjoining tract. Arco, the company that had found the field, did not bid on any land at all. And the state coffers were augmented not by the $2 billion everyone had expected but by less than half that sum: $900 million.

It was the turn of the tide, the first break in the Prudhoe Bay euphoria, and the ebb that now began to gather momentum swept Bob Brown to disaster in its undertow. For him there lay ahead a fall as stark as any in Greek tragedy, eighteen months of slow torture during which his hopes of rescue faded one after the other in a collapse so complete it exceeded the worst forebodings of his friends.

The warning note sounded by the land sale was detected far to the south, and North Slope stocks on the U.S. market immediately began to slide downward. By the end of 1969, Home had accumulated 476,380 shares of Atlantic Richfield. They cost $52.8 million. But their market value at the year-end was only $42.5 million —a loss of more than $10 million. The extent of Brown's personal loss at this stage is not known, but it was probably more than $2 million. And worse was to come, as the Klondike aura that had enveloped the North Slope quickly faded.

Everything seemed to fall out of the sky at once. The dread term "dry and abandoned" began to figure more often in reports from the field. The problem of building a pipeline to transport the oil to the south acquired a new and disturbing dimension: from being largely technological it became quasi-political. There were native land claims to be settled and well-organized objections by environmental groups to be overcome. Delay was piled on delay. New construction standards were constantly demanded or imposed. And costs that were already rising almost daily because of inflation spiralled right out of court.

Then, to complete the disaster, came the general stock market crash of early 1970. Arco shares that sold for $133 in the fall of 1969 were worth only $55 by the end of February 1970, and the bottom had not yet been reached. Home shares fared even worse. Much of the buying that had pushed them up to $81 had come from "hedge accounts", private investment groups which, owing to a quirk of the regulations, were exempt from some of the restrictions imposed on publicly held mutual funds. They could, for instance, "sell short" and thus profit from a falling market. When they decided to unload a stock, they got out quickly, with no attempt to preserve an orderly market. And when they pulled the plug on Home, its shares plunged all the way down to below ten dollars.

This price was just as unrepresentative of Home's true value as the eighty-one-dollar figure to which its shares had been pushed before the land sale, and shrewd Canadian buyers took advantage of it, reaping handsome profits later—Home's 1971 low was above twenty dollars—and in the process repatriating almost all the stock that had been sold in the United States in February 1969.

Some time early in 1970—so well did he conceal his plight that no one among his former associates knows exactly when—Bob

Brown must have recognized that he faced not a temporary setback, of the kind he had faced and surmounted many times before, but total and irrevocable bankruptcy. With his investments shorn of well over half their value, his loss was at least $10 million and mounting daily, his personal debt more than twice that sum. Forgotten now was the all but impossible dream of taking over Arco; instead his aim became the hardly less impossible one of salvaging enough from the wreckage to preserve his control of his beloved Home Oil.

There was only one development that might save him: a big new oil find, on the North Slope, in the North Sea—anywhere on the 4.5 million acres of land Home held in its inventory at the end of 1969.

In April 1970—when his closest associates knew he must be in trouble but did not yet know how desperately—Brown addressed the annual general meeting of Home's shareholders. The company's gross revenue during 1969 had reached $27.7 million, the highest figure in its history. But because of Brown's headlong plunge into Alaska it had spent more than that—the grotesquely top-heavy sum of $31.5 million—on exploration. Then there was the greatly increased cost, caused by generally rising interest rates, of carrying its investment portfolio, which was now, with the Arco shares superimposed on the TransCanada PipeLines and Calgary Power shares, tying up more than $100 million in company funds. The result: net earnings for 1969 had fallen to $4.5 million, less than half the previous year's $10.7 million, and the value of the company's securities barely equalled the outstanding bank loans they were pledged to cover.

Trying to put a brave face on the situation, Brown told the shareholders in his speech that Home's production of crude oil and natural-gas liquids had reached an all-time high during the first quarter of 1970: 21,300 barrels a day, compared with 17,100 barrels a day for the corresponding quarter of 1969. Natural-gas sales were up considerably, too: from 69 million cubic feet per day to 97 million cubic feet.

Unfortunately, this trend was not being carried through to the second quarter of the year, because of an "unexpectedly sharp cutback" imposed by President Nixon on Canadian imports to the U.S. Midwest. This prompted Brown to return to his old complaint about "the reluctance of the Canadian government to move resolutely to protect the interests of the Canadian oil producers in the way the U.S. government protects American interests." Wearily, no doubt, he reiterated the theme he had expounded so fruitlessly for so long: if only the Canadian government would "enforce the National Oil Policy and expand the eastern Canadian markets for our oil", Home could look forward to a steady growth in its production. In the meantime, "the market value of our investments has decreased substantially due to a severe decline in security markets."

For Brown, it was a subdued speech, but he tried to end on a confident note he can hardly have felt: "We learn from experience that things in the oil business are seldom as good, or as bad, as either the extreme optimists or extreme pessimists believe. There is no doubt that the Alaska oil discoveries were the most important made anywhere in the world since the discovery of the huge Middle East reserves after the Second World War. In the tidal wave of optimism that covered the industry last year, there was a tendency to overlook some of the harsh realities of moving the Alaska oil to market. Now the pendulum seems to have swung the other way and there is a tendency to magnify the difficulties out of all proportion. However, despite the delays and the unexpected opposition to the Trans-Alaska Pipeline System from the organized naturalists, Alaska oil undoubtedly will move to market in the United States in the not too distant future."

This "not too distant" future would turn out to be more than seven years away—much too far in the future to save Bob Brown. And by the time he made that speech, the prospects for a last-minute rescue were becoming dimmer by the day. One after the other, the two wells sunk in the North Sea had been found to be dry. Then came the bitter news that Nora Federal No. 1, also, had been abandoned, at a depth of more than 17,000 feet. Only one shred of hope remained—Bush Federal No. 1, the second North Slope well, which had been spudded in at the beginning of 1970.

Soon after the annual meeting, Brown flew off to Louisville to attend the Kentucky Derby as a guest of Orin Atkins, of Ashland Oil. Given the desperate straits in which he found himself, this might have been taken as a case of Nero fiddling while Rome burned. But Brown, though he had still not admitted it to his staff, now realized that unless Bush Federal No. 1 turned out to be a new "wonder well" his only hope of salvation would be to find a partner with sufficient resources to purchase a substantial interest in Home Oil. And he had already begun to test the air with Atkins, taking up their talks again where they had left off a couple of years earlier.

Ashland Oil began life half a century ago as a small family-owned company engaged in the transportation of oil by barge on the Ohio River. Gradually it expanded into the refining and marketing of oil products, among them the well-known Valvolene lubricating oil, and some years after Leduc it established a small exploration and production division in Calgary under Earl Joudrie, an Albertan who had taken a degree in history and political science before gravitating into the oil business. Through the years, it had also inherited a number of other Canadian branch-plant operations, including the nation-wide Warren Brothers asphalt paving and construction firm, mostly through its acquisition of their U.S. parent companies. When Brown revived the idea of a partnership between Ashland and Home, Atkins and Joudrie were considering the formation of a new subsidiary, Ashland Oil of Canada, to bring all the company's Canadian operations together under one umbrella. Brown suggested, in a general way, that perhaps somehow Ashland Canada could fit into Home Oil.

Even before Brown's predicament became public knowledge, the spectacular plunge in the price of Home shares and the company's heavy load of debt prompted occasional references in the business press to "the financially troubled Home Oil". In fact, though, the company's difficulties were only temporary; there was no serious basic weakness that could not be corrected. Home was still setting new oil and gas production records, its pipelining and liquid natural gas marketing activities were gratifyingly profitable, and despite the North Sea disappointments Brown could take some comfort from its operations in England. There, after four follow-up wells to Lockton 2A had proved dry, the company had made another promising gas strike and had now negotiated an agreement with the Gas Council for construction of a processing plant whose sales were expected to be forty-five million cubic feet per day when it went on stream early in 1971, rising to eighty million cubic feet per day after four years.

And by the time Brown reopened his talks with Atkins the retrenchment necessary to restore Home's position—it could perhaps be described as a shifting down of the gears—was already under way. Late in 1969, Ross Phillips, as Home's vice-president, administration, had begun to write worried confidential memoranda to Brown warning him, in effect, that the company was over-extended, that its future commitments were far too heavy for safety. In response to these and other warnings from his top executives, Brown agreed to sell the Calgary Power shares and 500,000 of the company's 1.3 million TransCanada shares. This brought in $25.5 million, enough to take off the worst of the immediate pressure.

Phillips also warned Brown that the company's commitment to the Alyeska pipeline was escalating dangerously as the months passed without any date being set for the start of its construction. Because of the continuing inflation and rising interest rates on the U.S. bond market, each delay led to an upward revision of the line's estimated cost. Brown had originally committed Home to contribute $18 million to the project. Phillips warned him in a memo dated December 23, 1969, that since the estimated cost of the line had already more than doubled, Home's share would now be a minimum of $35 million, with every likelihood that that figure, too, would continue to rise. Bob Campbell also urged Brown to try to negotiate out of the pipeline commitment, and he man-aged to do so—mercifully for Home: the line, which did not open until the summer of 1977, eventually cost more than $8 billion; Home's share of that figure would have amounted to the staggering sum of $360 million.

To further restore the company's liquidity, Phillips also man-aged to renegotiate the long-term debt issues held by Prudential and Mutual of New York, reducing the principal amounts it had to pay out every year by stretching out the repayments over a longer period. So when, in response to Brown's approach, Atkins and Joudrie examined Home's position, they felt no concern for its stability and realized both companies would gain from a merger of Ashland's various Canadian ventures into Home. The result, they could see, would be a large, fully integrated company with all the advantages that size and diversification bring in their train.

Brown liked and admired Atkins—a sentiment that was fully reciprocated—and he was confident they could work harmoniously together. But naturally, having decided he had to sell, he did not want to restrict himself to one potential buyer. In June, he sounded out a fellow-Calgarian, Fred Mannix, the hard-driving and im-mensely successful son of the CPR contractor Jim Lowery had courted so assiduously when he was putting Home Oil together almost half a century before. Fred Mannix had built the business founded by his father into the world-wide Loram International group of companies which, while it was still held privately by the family, was well able to contemplate the purchase of Home, and representatives of both companies began to "go over the figures".

Well aware now that he was fighting for his life, for all that he had built and still hoped to achieve, Brown cut down on his drinking and his old habit of work returned. After a day on the telephone he would labour long into the night, bent over his desk pad covering sheet after sheet with concise but thorough notes, keeping track of stock prices and the progress of the various wells Home was drilling, analysing prospects and proposals in his old incisive way. But he also found time that June to appear before the House of Commons standing committee on finance in Ottawa and present a brief on the government's White Paper on Tax Reform, which had shocked the Canadian business world when it was published the previous November.

One of this strange document's stated aims was to encourage the development of Canada's natural resources and their ownership by Canadians. Brown told the committee many of its provisions would have the opposite effect, and illustrated his contention by pointing out the ludicrous situation Cygnus would have found itself in if one of them, the proposed tax on unrealized capital gains, had been in effect during 1969. The dramatic rise in the price of Home shares before the Alaska land sale had increased the market value of Cygnus's holding of Class B shares by more than $51 million. Even though this was purely a paper profit—the corporation had not sold any of its shares—under the "unrealized gain" provision it would have subjected Cygnus to more than $17 million in tax, payable on March 31, 1970. By that time, Home shares—along with most others—had reverted to their more normal 1968 levels, and the only way Cygnus could have raised the money to pay the tax would have been by selling its entire controlling holding of one million Home shares to the highest bidder.

Brown warned the committee that the only buyers with deep enough pockets to have contemplated such a purchase would almost inevitably have been American. And to further demonstrate the futility of the proposal he pointed out that the forced sale of its Home holding in 1970 would have subjected Cygnus to a loss approximately as large as the unrealized gain that was taxed in 1969, a loss which could then have been carried back to the previous year, entitling Cygnus to recover the $17 million it had paid in tax. As a result of this naively unrealistic provision—perhaps surrealistic might be a more appropriate term—Cygnus would have lost control of Home Oil, a wholly Canadian enterprise since its inception; the already heavy foreign ownership of the Canadian oil industry would have been increased; and the country, in the shape of the income tax department, would have gained nothing at all.

"On a more personal note," Brown told the committee, "I might add that I, as a taxpayer, would have a similar fate at the hands of these proposals. I have had many opportunities to sell my holdings to large integrated companies during the past twenty years. However, I have never yielded to this temptation. The reason is quite simple. I have wanted to be a part of the ever-challenging business scene in Canada by building a truly Canadian resource company. The White Paper proposals would make it more difficult, if not impossible, for me to continue as a long-term investor in resource companies. Like other investors, it would be financially more attractive for me to own securities of well-established industrial companies rather than high-risk resource companies such as Home and Cygnus. . . ."

The members of the standing committee, of course, had no way of knowing how "difficult, if not impossible" Brown's personal situation was at that time; how unlikely it seemed that he would be able to continue as an investor in anything. But some of them may have wondered about his physical appearance. He had become so ashen-looking, so frail and short of breath, that some of his associates had doubted that he would be able to go through with his scheduled appearance before the committee.

A month later, the battering Bob Brown was receiving at the hands of not the government or the framers of income-tax regulations but fate, took its toll: on July 6 he was admitted to Holy Cross Hospital in Calgary with another heart attack.

CHAPTER NINETEEN

Ottawa Lowers
the Boom

When Neil McKinnon, chairman of the Canadian Imperial Bank of Commerce, discovered some time after the fact that Bob Brown had gone across the street to borrow from the Bank of Nova Scotia he was, to put it mildly, displeased. As Brown must have known it would, his action opened a distinct rift between the two former comrades-in-arms. But McKinnon, presumably for old times' sake, continued to carry Brown's personal loan. By the summer of 1970, however, the stock-market slump and the North Slope setbacks had so eroded the value of the shares Brown had pledged with the bank as his collateral that McKinnon knew something must be done about it. And so, early in July—before the news of Brown's heart attack had reached Toronto—a letter went out to Calgary from the bank's head office.

For three days after his admission to Holy Cross, Brown lay all but insensible in the intensive-care ward. Then, still hooked to an electro-cardiograph machine, he was moved to a private room for the rest and quiet he would need if he was to make a satisfactory recovery. But trying to persuade Bob Brown to rest was a thankless task at the best of times; given the strain he was under now it was, of course, impossible. He constantly importuned the few visitors he was permitted to make telephone calls for him, and questioned them anxiously about stock prices and the progress of the wells Home was drilling.

He also insisted on his mail being delivered to the hospital, and when this was done, among the first envelopes he opened was the one from the Bank of Commerce. The letter inside, while it did not actually foreclose on him by "calling" his loan, requested quite firmly that by August 20 he should present the bank with some mutually acceptable arrangement for the repayment of the $9.4 million outstanding on his account. It struck him, one of his closest friends told the author later, "like a dagger in his heart".

Here, surely, was the end of the road. Brown at this time held 145,900 shares of Atlantic Richfield, with a market value of around $8 million, much less than half what he had paid for them. Even if he sold them all—and assuming that the unloading of such a large block on the market did not depress their price any further—he would still not raise enough money to pay off the Bank of Commerce. In the meantime, taking into account his unpaid interest charges, he owed the Bank of Nova Scotia more than $14 million. The question now was whether all the rest of his assets combined— chiefly his 1.3 million shares of Cygnus and the 173,540 Home shares he owned personally—would be enough to cover that huge sum.

What he needed most desperately was time—time to work something out, time during which the market might turn around and rescue him or Home might make a dramatic new oil discovery. From his hospital bed, he called Neil McKinnon in Toronto, but was told he was away on vacation, no one seemed to know where. So he left a message for McKinnon to call him as soon as he returned. Then he called the Bank of Nova Scotia and explained his position to Arthur Crockett, an old navy man like himself, a Nova Scotian who had joined the bank at the age of seventeen and recently been appointed its president. Crockett expressed his sympathy and promised to talk to the bank's chairman, Bill Nicks, to see what they might be able to do to help.

But fate had not yet finished with Bob Brown. As his strength gradually returned and he began to fret for the day when he could return home and begin to grapple seriously with his problems, his family broke the sad news they had been shielding him from almost since the day he had entered the hospital: his mother, Christina, whose indomitable character had been an important influence in his life ever since his boyhood, had collapsed with a stroke, her second in three years. And at the age of eighty-three, she was not expected to recover.

The grief-stricken Brown now demanded to be released from hospital, and he was permitted to return home provided he remained in bed under the round-the-clock care of private nurses—a condition he accepted grudgingly so that he could at least see his mother before she died.

The last week of July and the first two of August were busy ones for the Brown household. The invalid chafing upstairs was not an easy patient, and Genny found herself escorting a steady stream of invited visitors up to his room, despite the protests of his nurses, one of whom startled and mightily offended the indignant Brown by telling him, "You don't need a nurse, Mr. Brown, you need a custodial officer." And when he was not pumping his visitors for news, Brown would be on the telephone, covering his desk pad with page after page of shakily scrawled notes.

On July 29, the wellhead team on the North Slope carried out the first series of tests on Bush Federal No. 1, which was now down 17,000 feet. Brown was so eager to hear the results that reports from the well site were telephoned to Ed Ratke in the drilling department every half-hour. Ratke would then telephone Brown at home—and if he was five minutes late with his call Brown would be on the telephone to him. "Have you heard anything more, Ed?" he would ask, in a voice so polite and controlled that Ratke never suspected how much hung on the result of the tests. The calls from the well continued far into the night, but the tests proved inconclusive and it was decided to resume them a few days later.

On August 4, Brown was well enough to attend his mother's funeral, but his friends were shocked by his haggard appearance and immediately afterward he returned to bed. He was still there on August 7, the day chosen for the final drill-stem test of Bush Federal No. 1. This time, he had arranged to have the half-hourly reports from Alaska phoned directly to his room, so that afternoon a group including Bob Campbell, Ratke, Bill Lundberg from the production department, Ray Smith, the area geologist for Alaska, and Jack Balfour, Home's public relations man, gathered around his bedside. As the calls came in, Brown gave them what amounted to a running commentary on the progress of the test.

First came the expected rush of gas. As usual, it was ignited, and the men around Brown's bed settled back to wait while the flare burnt itself off. As the afternoon wore on into the evening and the calls kept coming, the suspense mounted. What would rise up the drill hole next? Would it be more gas? Or oil? Or—well, no one wanted to think about that.

Around 10 p.m., the phone rang again. Brown's face was impassive as he listened to the report from Florian Desrosiers at the wellhead. The others could not hear what their colleague was saying, but Brown's heart sank. "I've tasted it," Desrosiers said disgustedly, "and it's pure drinking water."

The state of California was at that time enduring one of its periodic droughts. The men around the bedside knew the North Slope adventure was all over when they heard Brown chuckle and say to Desrosiers, "Well, Rosie, it's a pity we didn't have it in California—we could sure sell it there."

It was the end of all the hopes that everyone at Home had pinned on Bush Federal No. 1, and the North Slope of Alaska. Among the visitors, only Bob Campbell knew how much more it meant to their boss. No one felt much like talking. What was there to say? One by one, they rose to leave.

Typically, Bob Brown uttered no word of disappointment, much less of complaint. As courageous as ever, he climbed out of bed and in his dressing gown escorted his guests to the front door. "Thanks for coming, fellows," he told them. And only then did he let slip a hint that this latest dry hole might be far different from all those that had gone before. "This little problem," he said, "could change a hell of a lot of things."

After the visitors had left, each pondering that ominous remark, Brown returned wearily to bed—but not to rest. For the thousandth time, he went over his situation in his mind. Clearly he must sell out, but to whom, and on what terms? The negotiations with Loram were not going well. Fred Mannix had made him an offer a few days before, but among its provisions was one, in particular, that Brown shied away from accepting. Mannix wanted fifty-one per cent control of Home right away. Where would that leave Bob Brown? Mannix seemed willing to let him stay on as president and managing director, but Brown sensed that would be merely an empty title. What he really wanted was a partner, not a boss. He was sure he could make a better deal with Ashland, and Orin Atkins had let him know he was still interested.

But since he had entered the hospital rumours that he was in trouble had begun to circulate and he had received several other approaches, one of them from an unexpected quarter: Jacob Austin, the recently appointed deputy minister of the federal government's Department of Energy, Mines and Resources. A Calgarian by birth, Jack Austin had been a corporate lawyer and businessman in Vancouver before his appointment, and when he heard from his business contacts that Brown might be about to sell his control of Home he raised the matter with his minister, J. J. Greene.

Walter Gordon, the Liberals' controversial Minister of Finance, had retired from politics a couple of years earlier, but Austin knew his brand of economic nationalism was still a growing force not only in Ottawa but elsewhere in the country. And at that time, Herb Gray, the Minister of National Revenue, was preparing the report on foreign ownership of Canadian business that paved the way for the Foreign Investment Review Act. So Austin warned "Joe" Greene that if Brown was indeed about to sell, the size of Home Oil made it quite possible that the only buyer with sufficient resources to entertain the deal might well be an American company, and he asked the minister's authority to talk to Brown and find out what he had in mind.

Brown was in hospital when Austin first called him, but he agreed to see him after his release and they met at Brown's home on August 5, the day after his mother's funeral. Brown confirmed that his financial situation made it imperative for him to take in a partner, if not sell control of Home, but said he had not yet made any commitment to anyone. Austin told him the government would not like to see a major Canadian resource company such as Home fall under American ownership, and asked Brown to keep him informed about his negotiations with potential buyers, which Brown agreed to do. Austin also suggested that perhaps Polymer, the government-owned petrochemical complex in Sarnia (now Petrosar), might be interested in making an offer for Home. Brown was surprised at this suggestion, but he told Austin he expected to be in Toronto with Ross Phillips the following week, and if the Polymer people were interested either he or Phillips would be glad to talk to them.

Brown and Phillips flew to Toronto on Monday, August 10, and settled in to the Royal York Hotel. Brown's doctors had opposed the trip, but he insisted on making it. When Neil McKinnon had finally returned his call on July 24, Brown had explained almost apologetically that he had been in hospital with a heart attack but promised he would be in Toronto to discuss his position well before the August 20 deadline set by the bank. He had also arranged to see Crockett and Nicks at the Bank of Nova Scotia, to try to persuade them to give him the time he desperately needed by taking over his loan from the Commerce. He wanted, too, to see another potential buyer who had expressed an interest: Edmund C. Bovey, an old school friend who was now president of Northern & Central

Gas Ltd., a rapidly expanding natural-gas distribution company based in Ontario.

It was an exhausting week for Brown, an endless round of meetings that sometimes went on long into the evening. He thought he detected a softening in the Bank of Commerce's attitude, a hint that August 20, after all, might not be an immutable deadline. But he was disappointed with the Bank of Nova Scotia's initial coolness to his suggestion that they take over his Commerce loan. His talk with Ed Bovey seemed promising, however. They met along with Brown's old friend, Jack McCausland, of Wood Gundy, and Bovey was interested enough to suggest that he come out to Calgary at the weekend to follow up their talks.

Ed Kennedy, of Lehman Bros., was in Toronto that week, too, and he told Brown that the Bronfman interests in Montreal had been in touch with him and might be prepared to make an offer for Home. Brown also talked to his old friend Jim Kerr, who said TransCanada would be interested in discussing a deal, and to Orin Atkins, who once again assured him of Ashland's continuing interest.

By now, at Austin's suggestion, the cabinet had authorized Polymer to open negotiations for the purchase of Home, and Brown, accompanied by Phillips and his Ottawa lawyer, Ross Tolmie, had a preliminary session with a couple of Polymer executives, Ralph Rowzee and Stan Wilk, which Austin also attended. Rowzee and Wilk were given some figures and promised to get in touch again within a few days.

On balance, it had been an encouraging week—but it was too much for Brown. When he returned to Calgary at the weekend he suffered another heart attack. His planned meeting with Ed Bovey was cancelled and on August 18 he was readmitted to hospital. When he emerged again, on August 27, it was under sentence of death. Scrawled on the desk pad he always kept beside his bed, almost lost among the rows of figures and the names of people he had called that day, or planned to call, was this chilling note: "A lot of kidney damage; outlook one or two years."

Brown told hardly anyone about this diagnosis. His sister Lois knew. So did his pilot, Don Douglas, who during the years of ferrying Brown all over the continent, often at only a half-hour's notice, had become a close friend and valued confidant. Douglas knew perhaps better than anyone the perilous state of his boss's health, and Brown once told him, "If I should die on the road, don't you ship my body back on an Air Canada cargo flight. Bring me home in my own plane."

Ahead of Brown there still lay months of brutal strain, during which events several times conspired to force him into a labyrinth from which there seemed no escape. The men he dealt with during those months realized he was a sick man—there were times when a nurse followed him around with oxygen tanks in case he collapsed. But only Brown himself knew his days were numbered, and his resolution never wavered. He was fighting now not for his own life, but for his family: he knew that if he died before he could straighten out his affairs Genny and their three daughters would be left penniless.

His most pressing worry had been eased before he left hospital. Two days before its August 20 deadline, the Bank of Commerce relented and agreed to give him more time, and on the same day Arthur Crockett told him that the Bank of Nova Scotia, which had initially refused his request, had now changed its mind and would take over his Commerce loan, provided he would make a definite deal for the sale of his assets within ninety days. This meant that after all the paper work was completed and the loan was transferred he would owe the Bank of Nova Scotia the staggering sum of $24 million. But at least it was a breathing space.

This decision by the banks may have been affected by the government's interest in Brown's affairs. Theoretically, if the Bank of Commerce had actually called Brown's loan at that time and taken over the shares he had pledged as his collateral, it would have been left with, if not control of Home, at least a major interest in the company. There were rumours, in fact, that both banks had turned down offers for the shares they held as collateral. And Jack Austin had called both Arthur Crockett and Larry Greenwood, president of the Bank of Commerce, informing them of the Polymer approach and hoping Brown would be given time to consider any offer the government-owned corporation might make.

Representatives of Polymer met Phillips in Toronto to get more information on Home while Brown was still in the hospital, and the government had a report on the Home-Cygnus group prepared by the Price-Waterhouse accounting firm. But the day after Brown returned home Roger Hatch, a vice-president of Polymer, called

Ross Phillips and said his company, a Crown corporation, did not feel it could recommend the purchase to the cabinet. As a large buyer of crude, Polymer had thought there might be some advantage to owning its own source of supply, but in fact it could not have assured itself of lower prices, for instance, because of the Alberta government's system of allocating all the province's production among the various refining companies. After making its evaluation, Hatch told Phillips, Polymer felt that it could not justify the purchase on a strictly commercial basis.

Jack Austin called Brown on September 1 to tell him the cabinet had met and discussed Polymer's report. "Situation not happy," Brown's note on the call said. "Polymer advised Home not their cup of tea. . . . Cabinet will not interfere with decision. . . ."

This outcome disappointed Austin, who saw the prospect of acquiring Home as an opportunity to establish a government presence in the oil industry. Had the deal with Polymer gone through, Home would have been the nucleus of a government-owned oil company, along the lines of the giant British Petroleum. But, as Austin told Brown, with Polymer out of the running there did not seem to be any vehicle the government could use to make the purchase.

Brown, according to his note pad, "told Austin that this decision cleared me with regard to any responsibility to govt.—he agreed." Austin, whose career in the government service was later acknowledged by his appointment to the Senate, told the author this was not so, that at all times he told Brown the government was still interested and wished to be kept informed about the progress of his search for a buyer. Brown undertook to do that anyway: further on in his notes he wrote, "Austin asked what I was going to do now. I told him that I had several possibilities, would think about it and keep him informed."

The two spoke again on September 3, when Brown noted: "Austin still interested—didn't have vehicle. Trudeau and Greene want to be kept informed. Who is negotiating now? . . . If sale to non-resident then they would try to counter-bid. With Polymer out what vehicle could be used? Govt. could take money from treasury and finance Eldorado [the Crown corporation that mines and processes uranium]." Austin called again next day, and Brown noted that while the government would not interfere if he was able to find a Canadian buyer, it was "reserving position *re* foreign buyer". The note ended: "Told Austin in light of his efforts I would not do a deal without informing him."

That same week, representatives of Ashland Oil were in Calgary gathering information to enable Orin Atkins to make Brown a firm offer for his Cygnus shares. Atkins and his Canadian lieutenant, Earl Joudrie, lunched with Brown—who was still at home in bed— on September 2, and it seemed they were in agreement on at least the outline of a deal that would suit both parties.

Meanwhile, at the office that afternoon, Ross Phillips received a telephone call from an official of the Toronto Stock Exchange, who told him there was a rumour on Bay Street that the CPR was about to make a public offer of twenty dollars per share to Home share-holders in an attempt to take over the company, or at least to secure a major interest in it. Phillips had always been afraid something like this would happen. Cygnus controlled Home by holding 43.6 per cent of its voting shares, but that holding amounted to only a little over 14 per cent of the total number of Home A and B shares outstanding. So a company with sufficient resources to make an attractive public offer for those shares—even if it did not succeed in purchasing enough Class B to wrest actual control from Cygnus— could have seriously undermined Brown's position by acquiring such a large equity in the company that other potential buyers would have backed off, reluctant to become involved in the struggle. The premium value of his control block of Cygnus would then have been severely diminished, if not destroyed.

And Phillips thought his worst fears had been confirmed a few minutes later, when he received another long-distance call. Norman Alexander, managing director of the Winnipeg-based financial house Richardson Securities, told him he wanted to see Brown and would be in Calgary the following day. Phillips tried to dissuade him. Brown, he explained, had only just left the hospital and he was still confined to bed. But Alexander was insistent. He had urgent business, he said, and it was important that he see Brown right away.

Phillips picked him up at his hotel next morning and drove him to Brown's house, fully expecting to hear that the battle was over and Brown had at last met defeat. But when Alexander sat down beside Brown's bed and disclosed his mission Phillips was able to relax: he was an emissary not of the CPR but of Brascan, the Canadian multi-national corporation that began life as an electrical utility company in Brazil. And Brascan, he said, was interested in making an offer for Brown's shares of Cygnus.

Thereafter, Brascan representatives spent several weeks going over the figures with Phillips but in the end they could not agree with the valuation Brown put on his shares.

Brown was not unduly concerned. He still felt that the Ashland deal would be the best one for him, as well as the shareholders of Home, but in view of the government's interest he continued to hold discussions with potential Canadian buyers. Oakah Jones, president of the Consumers' Gas Company of Toronto, flew to Calgary to talk to him on September 11—it was the first day Brown had been allowed downstairs since his second heart attack—and Brown promised that Phillips would supply him with some financial information about Home. But it was a promise made without much enthusiasm: he had not warmed up to Jones when they had met on earlier occasions and had no desire to deal with him.

On the whole, the negotiations that seemed to hold out most promise were those with Ed Bovey. Northern & Central Gas (now Norcen Energy Resources Ltd.) was an outgrowth of Northern Ontario Natural Gas, a utility company formed to supply several communities in northern Ontario with gas when it became known that the TransCanada pipeline would be taking that route. It had expanded by purchasing controlling interests in Greater Winnipeg Gas and Gaz Métropolitain in Montreal, and had also acquired ninety per cent of the outstanding common stock of Canadian Industrial Oil and Gas, a medium-sized production company based in Calgary. Ed Bovey and Spencer Clark, Northern & Central's chairman—who like Bovey had known Brown since their school days—proposed a two-stage deal under which Northern & Central would buy enough of Brown's Cygnus stock, at $15.50 per share, to give it control of Home, and would later merge Cigol and Home to create what would have been by far the largest Canadian-controlled oil and gas producing company.

Bovey and Clark had several meetings with Brown, and executives of Home and Cigol met frequently over a period of weeks examining each other's operations. But they were unable to reach agreement on the respective valuations of the two companies—an issue Bovey wanted resolved before he went through with the first stage of the deal. Also, Brown wanted to remain chief executive officer of Home after the merger, and Bovey and Clark were reluctant to accept that: they had full confidence in Ed Galvin, president of Cigol, and his management team, and were unwilling to subordinate them to Brown.

Then, on October 22, Brown received a written offer from Orin Atkins which, without mentioning a specific price, essentially met his conditions for the sale. Ashland offered to buy half his Cygnus shares immediately and take an option on the rest exercisable on his death or at a prior date to be mutually agreed upon; and to advance him a substantial loan to rescue him from his financial difficulties.

As he had expected, it was by far the best offer he had received, and none of the Canadian companies which had expressed an interest in dealing with him was prepared to match it. So in December Brown called Jack Austin and requested a meeting with him in Ottawa. Austin had by now decided the Department of Finance should become involved in the issue, so he arranged for the meeting to be held in the office of Simon Reisman, its deputy minister, on December 17. Brown was accompanied by his lawyers, Earl Lomas from Calgary and Ross Tolmie from Ottawa, and the representatives on the government side included Marshall Crowe, deputy secretary to the cabinet, who later became chairman of the National Energy Board.

According to an account of the meeting written by Lomas afterward, Brown opened the proceedings by saying that, as Austin knew, he had negotiated with several Canadian companies over a period of six months but had not received an acceptable offer from any of them. He therefore proposed to make a deal with a foreign buyer along the lines of Ashland's offer, which he outlined to the meeting without disclosing its source.

Austin and Reisman both asked why no Canadian company had been prepared to offer as much as the foreign buyers who had contacted him. One reason, Brown said, was that the foreign companies realized they would be acquiring control of a very valuable asset, worth about $300 million, and were prepared to pay a premium for it, whereas some at least of the Canadian buyers had under-estimated the value of Home because of the currently depressed price of its shares on the open market. In addition, he said, foreign companies operated under more favourable tax laws, which would enable them to write off any interest charges they incurred in borrowing money to make the purchase—an option which, under the Canadian tax regulations then in effect, was not open to a Canadian buyer.

Reisman asked how much difference this would make in hard cash. Brown estimated that while he expected to receive $26 million in the transaction, the net cost to a foreign buyer able to take advantage of its own country's tax laws might be as much as $6 million less than that. This would appear to have been an exaggeration but Brown was trying to make his case look as strong as possible. And at least partly because of the attention focused on this aspect of Canadian tax legislation by the Home case, the regulations were changed a year later to permit Canadian companies deductions for interest charges similar to those available in the United States.

Brown then told the meeting he intended to offer the terms he had just outlined to several prospective foreign buyers during the following weekend, and he would be expecting their replies early in January. He would accept whichever deal had most to offer the shareholders of Home and Cygnus. Austin once again asked Brown to keep him informed about the progress of his negotiations, and Brown agreed to do so—though Reisman, who seemed to think Brown had already done all he could to meet the government's wishes, asked Austin why he had made that request. Austin replied that he had to keep his minister informed.

Discussing the tenor of the meeting later, Brown, Lomas, and Tolmie unanimously agreed that Austin had given no indication that the government had any further plans to acquire Brown's position in Home. They concluded, also unanimously, that Reisman had no further interest in the matter; that Austin had to keep Joe Greene informed but it was unlikely that he had any further interest; and that Brown was free to make whatever deal he could with a foreign purchaser.

Brown had prepared a brochure setting out the terms he wanted, and between December 19 and 21 he handed over copies of it to Hudson's Bay Oil and Gas, a company jointly owned by the Continental Oil Company of the United States and the Hudson's Bay Company; Great Plains Development, the Canadian subsidiary of a British company, Burmah Oil; and Ashland Oil of Kentucky—though it was virtually a recapitulation of the terms he had discussed with Orin Atkins and was fairly confident he would accept.

These were the three foreign buyers who had expressed most serious interest in the deal, though Brown had received several other approaches from American companies, including one from Texaco and another from Fred Hamilton, who had revised his initially poor opinion of Brown when he got to know him better. In the end, only Ashland remained in the bidding and by early January both sides were working out the formal details of the transaction.

Brown kept in touch with Austin, who now explained that while he might have gained the impression from the meeting in Reisman's office that the government was no longer interested in his affairs, this was not the case. Some newspapers had been criticizing the government at around this time for its delay in announcing its policy on foreign investment, and Austin told Brown that pending receipt of the Gray report the cabinet would not want a major Canadian company to fall under American control. After all, he reminded Brown, there was a precedent for government action in its intervention the previous year to prevent Stephen Roman, of Denison Mines, from selling his uranium interests to a U.S. buyer.

Brown was well aware of this precedent—the unsuccessful $100 million damage suit Roman brought against Prime Minister Trudeau and Joe Greene as a result was still pending. But he also had independent legal opinion that no matter how much the government might regret the sale of Home to a foreign buyer there was no legislation in existence under which it could be stopped. He also considered his impending deal with Atkins to be in effect the "Canadianization" of Ashland Canada, and he was convinced the government would ultimately recognize that it was in the national interest: other refinery and marketing companies were virtually all under foreign control and the new, larger company he would continue to run would bring welcome new expertise under Canadian control.

However, he had felt it his duty to co-operate with the government all along, and he now conceived the idea that a three-way deal, introducing another Canadian partner to the transaction, might meet the government's objections to a deal with Ashland alone. So he asked Ed Bovey to meet him and Orin Atkins in the Château Laurier on Sunday, January 17. At that meeting, Atkins offered Bovey half of his deal: in other words, Ashland and Northern & Central would combine to buy out Brown. This would reduce the "American content" of the deal, and the new company that would result from a merger of Home, Cigol, and Ashland Canada would be by far the largest Canadian-based independent, the only one even remotely able to compete in size with Imperial Oil.

After some consideration, Bovey said the three-way deal would not fit in with Northern & Central's general corporate philosophy, nor could he see how it would resolve the difficulties he and Brown had had in reaching agreement on a two-way deal. So he turned down the offer and he and his party left the meeting.

Brown was now satisfied he had no alternative but the deal he had worked out with Atkins. He shook hands all round and went to bed, leaving the lawyers on both sides to frame the agreement in suitable legal terms. As the night wore on, the shirt-sleeved lawyers realized they needed a typist to enshrine their legal language in a formal letter of intent that Brown and Atkins could sign next morning. The hotel was unable to supply one at that late hour on a Sunday night, so Earl Joudrie put on his coat, stepped out into the all-but-deserted Ottawa streets and somewhat nervously began to accost any woman who looked as if she might be able to type. Eventually, after half an hour or so, he stopped a young French-Canadian girl heading home from the movies. She dubiously agreed to accompany him as far as the hotel lobby, where Joudrie assured her she would find the assistant manager of the hotel waiting. The assistant manager set the girl's quite natural fears at rest and escorted her up to the lawyers' suite, where she spent a harried but well-rewarded night typing repeated drafts of the desired letter.

In essence, it spelled out a deal in which Ashland Oil of Kentucky would buy 665,231 Cygnus B shares from Brown for $10 million—approximately $15 per share—and advance him an immediate loan of $16 million, secured by 400,000 shares of Home. Ashland would also be given an option to buy the rest of the Cygnus B voting shares Brown controlled but did not actually own—692,383 shares he had placed in trust for his family—the option to be exercisable after ten years or on Brown's death, if that occurred first.

Then, as the second stage of the deal, Home would acquire Ashland Canada, on mutually acceptable terms. The merged company would retain the name Home Oil and Brown would be its chairman and chief executive officer, exercising a form of shared control over its affairs: he would be in charge of Home's day-to-day operations but subject on major decisions to the approval of the board of Cygnus, to which he would appoint four directors and

Ashland three. Major decisions, under a voting trust agreement, would need the approval of at least five members of the Cygnus board. In practice, therefore, Ashland would have a form of negative control over the new company—but so would Brown, in that two of his votes would be required for any major decision. And he was confident he would not be just a figurehead, that Atkins' ideas and objectives coincided with his own, and that they would work together without any difficulty.

Brown and Atkins checked the somewhat imperfectly typed letter of intent next morning, and each signed it. In accordance with normal business practice, they considered it to be, if not the legal consummation of the sale, at least a commitment morally binding on both sides. They then left for the airport, but on the way Brown stopped off at Joe Greene's office to pay what he considered a courtesy call, to show him the letter that would at last enable him to extricate himself from his financial plight and continue at the head of Home.

Atkins remained outside in the car waiting for Brown—until he, too, was summoned to the minister's office. There, Joe Greene repeated what he had just told the ashen-faced Brown: that the government had no intention of permitting the deal to go through as planned. The cabinet proposed to study it thoroughly and consider all its ramifications in the light of the new legislation then being planned to cover foreign ownership of Canadian companies. And in the meantime neither Brown nor Atkins should make any announcement about their negotiations.

Earl Lomas, who had been waiting in an outside office, was shocked at Brown's defeated appearance when he emerged from his talk with Greene. Brown had called a meeting of the directors of Home for that evening at the Royal York, hoping to disclose the successful conclusion of his long negotiations, and they flew to Toronto in an atmosphere of deep gloom. There, after Brown had made a brief report to his board on his meeting with Greene, he retired to his suite—but not to rest.

David Campbell, an engineer who had been acting as a consultant to Brown during some of his talks with potential buyers, was with him in the suite. He recalls that Brown couldn't sleep, but spent the night pacing the floor, occasionally shaking his head and muttering repeatedly, "What are they trying to *do* to me?"

Looking back over his career, he had ample reason to reflect bitterly on governments and all their works. It was government action, for instance, that had wiped out his appliance business overnight so many years ago. Then, as he saw it, he had built the company whose purity the government was now trying so nobly to protect with scant assistance from successive administrations which had invariably favoured the international oil industry over domestic producers by repeatedly turning down his plan for a pipeline to serve the Montreal refinery market. Instead, he and the rest of the Alberta producers had always been told to sell their surplus oil in the United States—which did not always want it but took it because it seemed to have a better understanding than Ottawa itself of the strategic importance to Canada of having a healthy domestic oil industry. Likewise, governments had repeatedly turned down his pleas for changes in Canadian tax law to enable domestic companies to compete on equal terms with their U.S. competitors. Then, not so long ago, this particular government had come up with a fatuous set of recommendations for "tax reform" which would have virtually forced him to sell Home to an American company. Now, when he was faced with ruin, it had backed him into a corner by waving the Canadian flag in his face.

Brown knew that if and when the news leaked out that he was not going to be permitted to sell to a foreign buyer, his bargaining position would be destroyed. In the meantime, each week that passed without a solution to his problems plunged him deeper into debt: the interest charges on his loans now amounted to the terrifying sum of more than $6,000 a day.

As if all this were not burden enough for one man, even a man in full health, the Royal Canadian Mounted Police had recently called on him back in Calgary and told him two prisoners about to be released from penitentiary had been overheard hatching a plot to kidnap one of his daughters for ransom. Bodyguards had moved into his house, his children were being escorted to and from school every day by Mounties, and his telephones had been tapped by the police in an attempt to intercept and perhaps trace any threatening calls. Happily, no kidnap attempt was ever made, presumably because the plotters became aware of these precautions. But it would have been a harrowing time even for a father without all Brown's other problems.

A lesser man would undoubtedly have broken under the strain. Instead, on the morning after his sleepless night, Brown began to try to pick up the pieces. Ross Phillips had flown back to Calgary the night before after the busy weekend in Ottawa. Brown called him and told him to catch the next plane back to Toronto. Then he revived the negotiations by summoning Atkins and Bovey to his suite and telling them, "Okay, we've got to make this a three-way deal."

Thus began a solid week of meetings in the Royal York during which the figures were rehashed again and again and Atkins, to demonstrate his confidence that the deal would be beneficial to all three parties, proposed to Bovey that if he were not satisfied with the way it was working out after two years he could buy out Ashland completely at Ashland's cost plus interest.

Once again, Bovey concluded that the three-way deal would not be to Northern & Central's advantage—among his problems was how Cigol's earnings could be "passed upstairs" to its parent company. But he followed up the sessions by making Brown yet another offer for a two-way deal.

Brown, still convinced Ashland should be in the deal, saw Greene again in Ottawa on the morning of January 28 and reported that he was not having much success with his negotiations. Greene heard him out but ended the meeting by reiterating his position: the government would approve a two-way deal between Home and Northern & Central, or even a three-way deal bringing in Ashland, too—though in that case it must look as though a Canadian company had acquired control of Home; a two-way deal between Home and Ashland would not be approved.

Brown flew straight back to Toronto for yet another meeting that afternoon with Ed Bovey. Once again, he tried to persuade Bovey to enter the three-way deal. Ashland, he pointed out, had stood behind him from the start of his troubles and he still wanted to honour his commitment to Orin Atkins. Bovey repeated his arguments against the three-way deal and the conversation then turned to his latest proposal for a two-way deal involving Home and Northern & Central.

Brown noted that Bovey's latest offer said nothing about his own position, the one he had insisted on all along: that he would continue as chief executive officer of the new company. Was that an oversight, he wondered? No, Bovey said, the executive committee of Northern & Central had approved the offer exactly as it was written. Brown then asked why he was not acceptable as chief executive.

Bovey hesitated and Brown repeated his question. Embarrassed, Bovey replied that some of Brown's deals "had not sat well with the financial community". Brown bristled. "In that case," he said angrily, "my answer is NO, capital N, O."

Regretfully, Bovey rose to leave, shook hands with Brown, and said he hoped there were no hard feelings. "I'm sorry," Brown replied, "but I can't acknowledge that."

Both Brown and Atkins were still receiving legal advice that despite Greene's warnings there was no existing legislation the government could use to prevent them from making their deal. When Bovey left, Brown picked up the phone, called Orin Atkins, and suggested their lawyers begin immediately to draft the definitive documents covering the sale.

Next day, when he told his old friend "Scotty" Shoults what he had done, Shoults counselled caution. What, he asked, if in spite of Brown's legal advice the government *did* ban the sale to Ashland? Brown should not have cut off Northern & Central so hastily. Perhaps he, Shoults, should contact Ed Bovey, try to heal the breach and see if he would agree to resume the talks? Brown saw the wisdom of Shoults' advice and magnanimously enough, when Shoults reached him, Bovey agreed to meet Brown again a couple of days later, on Sunday, January 31. So the two sides began yet another attempt to reach the agreement that had eluded them for so long.

Up to now, the months of negotiation, and the government's intervention, had passed without public notice. Rumours that Home was in trouble and Brown might be contemplating selling his interest had been reported in a few newspapers during 1970, but there had been no headlines. That happy situation was about to change.

When Joe Greene had told Brown and Atkins on January 18 that they should not say anything about their proposed deal he had placed Atkins, in particular, in an impossible position: Ashland was bound by law to observe the U.S. Securities and Exchange Commission regulations and file an immediate report on any corporate development that might affect its shareholders, and the negotiations Atkins had engaged in with Brown certainly came under this heading. When, on February 1, the financial news service Dow Jones got wind of the report he had been forced to make to the SEC, Atkins had no alternative but to confirm that he had made an offer for Home.

Published in Canadian newspapers on February 2, his statement prompted the leader of the New Democratic Party, Tommy Douglas, to rise as soon as the House of Commons met that afternoon in an attempt to force a special debate on the issue. His motion was denied the unanimous consent it needed, but when the question period began Joe Greene admitted in response to the Leader of the Opposition, Robert Stanfield, that he had discussed the proposed deal with its principals and had "urged upon them the desirability of maintaining a majority Canadian ownership and Canadian control" of Home. "To date," he continued, "the president of the Home Oil Company has clearly displayed his very keen interest as a Canadian citizen in maintaining a majority interest in Canadian ownership. Under the laws that exist, I will, to the best of my ability, continue to maintain the position that this major Canadian oil company should be retained as a Canadian company."

Under further questioning outside the House, Greene was reminded of the firm action the government had taken in the Denison case. This time, he said, he was using the "silken glove" rather than the "iron hand". A reporter asked the obvious question: would the government use legislation to stop the sale? "I have no authority at this time to so state," the minister replied. "The government has not decided, although it's not beyond the realm of the possible."

It is a moot point, of course, whether retroactive legislation affecting an individual's property rights can ever be written by a hand clothed in a silk glove. At any rate, by this time Brown was feeling more than ever like a man being clubbed by a mailed fist. He saw the minister again next day, but could only report that his latest round of talks with Bovey had again failed to find a mutually acceptable basis for a deal.

Greene's statement in the House had finally put Brown's troubles into the headlines, and as he emerged from the minister's office press photographers who had been waiting outside levelled their cameras. Earl Lomas threw up his hand protectively, trying to shield Brown from their lenses, but a photograph on the front page of that afternoon's *Toronto Daily Star* showed a haggard Brown, his once-boyish face somehow collapsed and jowly, heavy pouches beneath his eyes, the ebony hair greying now, and thinner. He looked above all like a man who badly needed rest. But there was to be none.

He flew that afternoon to New York, where still another ordeal awaited him: an interrogation by SEC lawyers. The previous

September, Brown had realized that his Arco shares were not likely to recover while the many problems on the North Slope remained unresolved, and that he had a better chance of recouping his losses by owning shares of Home, whose financial performance, thanks to the remedial measures initiated early in 1970, was now beginning to improve. So he had instructed his brokers to sell his Arco shares—gradually, so as not to disturb the market—and buy Home Class A non-voting shares with the proceeds. Between September 1970 and January 1971 he increased his Home holdings by 385,000 shares.

Since Home shares were listed on the American Stock Exchange, this subjected him to the SEC's regulations requiring him to file reports on such major transactions. Because of his illness and all his other concerns, he had been late filing these reports and when Ashland's filing disclosed his negotiations with Atkins the SEC became suspicious that his share purchases were somehow linked with the Ashland offer. The American Stock Exchange suspended trading in Home shares on February 2 and Brown was ordered to appear before the SEC to explain himself.

The lawyers grilled him for almost three hours in what Earl Lomas, who accompanied him to the hearing, described later as "a most direct, uncomplimentary manner". Both in person, and in a written submission prepared by Richard Pettingill, his U.S. lawyer and a specialist in SEC procedure, Brown explained his situation: the heavy losses he had incurred on his Arco purchases and his belief that his best chance of recouping them was to switch to Home shares. He told his questioners his Arco shares had been pledged as collateral with the Bank of Commerce and the Bank of Nova Scotia, and both banks had agreed to release them so that he could exchange them for Home shares. There had been nothing under-handed about his purchases, and he had bought only non-voting shares, through normal brokerage channels. Eventually, the SEC accepted his explanation and took no punitive action against him—but the interrogation had been punishment enough.

As he walked from the hearing room, Brown almost collapsed and Lomas had to help him to a nearby bench. Concerned now, the SEC officials thought he was having a heart attack and wanted to summon an ambulance. Brown waved them aside weakly, asked for a glass of water, and took a couple of the heart-stimulant pills he always carried with him. But it was almost an hour before he felt strong enough to get up and return to his hotel.

At Joe Greene's request, he had agreed to meet Oakah Jones of Consumers' Gas in Toronto the following day. When he got back to his room he called Greene and told him he would have to postpone his meeting with Jones and return home to Calgary to rest. Greene, who had left the floor of the House to accept Brown's call, had survived a heart attack himself and he was immediately sympathetic. Of course the meeting would have to wait, he said. Then he told Brown that Prime Minister Trudeau had telephoned Ed Bovey earlier that day, February 4, to ask him whether there was still any chance that Northern & Central could reach an agreement with Brown. Bovey had replied that as far as he was concerned the door was not closed. The Prime Minister had then said the government would certainly be pleased if an all-Canadian deal could be worked out and had asked Bovey to meet Brown once again, this time in the presence of Greene. Brown agreed to attend such a meeting as soon as he was well enough, and suggested Greene make the arrangements for it through Ross Tolmie.

It took place amid great secrecy in a suite rented by Brown at the Hotel Vancouver on February 12, after Greene had addressed a luncheon meeting of the local branch of the Canadian Club. Earl Lomas and Ross Tolmie accompanied Brown, and Ed Galvin, president of Cigol, attended with Bovey. And once more the positions of both sides were recapitulated, with Jack Austin trying desperately to persuade them to come to an agreement. Eventually, Bovey and Galvin left with a promise to submit another offer. And before Brown returned to Calgary he had a visit from Norman Keevil, of the Teck Corporation, the Vancouver-based mining company, who expressed his interest in joining the ranks of potential buyers of Home.

Greene had managed to shake off the reporters before going to Brown's suite and the meeting did not make headlines. But the issue had resurfaced in the press a couple of days earlier, when Tommy Douglas had once again tried to force a special debate on it in the House. On this occasion, Mitchell Sharp, who was Acting Prime Minister in Trudeau's absence, refused to give an undertaking that the government would prevent the sale to Ashland. Asked why it had not moved decisively to halt the sale, as it had Roman's proposed sale of Denison, he replied, "In that case, there was no problem with respect to constitutional authority." The case of oil was not quite so clear-cut as it had been with uranium, and he thought the provinces might object if the federal government tried to assume complete jurisdiction over the oil industry.

It now looked as though the cabinet, despite Greene's firm warnings to Brown, might be less than unanimous on whether it had the authority to block the sale. But if Brown took any comfort from Sharp's statement it was short-lived. A few days later, on February 18, the full-scale debate Tommy Douglas had demanded got under way at 8 p.m., and Orin Atkins and Earl Joudrie, looking on from the visitors' gallery at the invitation of Joe Greene, sensed that the mood of all parties in the House was in favour of government action to prevent their deal with Brown.

The cabinet had finally resolved that morning not to permit the sale, but Greene did not enter the debate to announce this until almost 11:30 p.m.—to the annoyance of some members, particularly when they learned that he had given a television interview earlier in the evening which had been broadcast on the 11 p.m. news, before he rose to speak. Confident that most of the MPs who would speak in the debate, particularly the New Democrats, would be pressing for prompt government action to stop the sale, Greene presumably wanted that lesson to register firmly in the minds of his visitors. And if he had spoken at the beginning of the evening there would probably have been little if any debate for Atkins and Joudrie to hear. For his statement seemed to satisfy the House that the government would somehow make sure Home remained in Canadian hands.

The minister had to resort to some fancy political footwork when members challenged his earlier statement to the House that no agreement had been signed between Home and Ashland—the letter of intent of January 18 was now public knowledge, having been disclosed in Ashland's filing to the SEC. Greene professed to be unsure of the legal definition of the term "letter of intent" and said he had understood that "the document to which I was privy was one which stated terms that would form the general basis for an agreement if one were later entered into."

The members let this pass and for the most part listened in silence as he traced the history of Brown's attempts to sell his Cygnus shares and the government's intervention to try to assure that the purchaser was Canadian. "I am confident," he said, "that the House *does* have power to prevent any transfer of property in Canada, constitution or no." As long as Canada operated under a private enterprise economy, "private citizens who are dealing with their own assets should be given the maximum liberty to deal with those assets under the law." But he thought that "the rights of property, over the years, are becoming less, *vis-à-vis* the state." In modern society, for instance, there were zoning by-laws that restricted the ownership of property and anti-combines laws restricting the rights of corporate owners. He thought the House would agree that such laws "should be used only as a last resort if the intention is to prevent a private transaction which is carried on in good faith and which is perfectly valid under existing legislation."

And in Home's case, he did not think it would be necessary to use the law. "I have been confident," he went on, "from the nature of the discussions I have had both with the vendor, Mr. Brown, with the Ashland company and with potential Canadian buyers that we can work this out together in confidence—because that is the only way in which such transactions can be carried out—so as to maintain this as a Canadian company without any legislation being passed which has a retroactive aspect to it. That might be necessary if things go wrong—if I turn out to be wrong as an intermediary of the government and as an intermediary, as I understand it now, for the will of Parliament, because it is quite clear tonight that this Parliament is determined that the company be maintained as a Canadian company...."

Having clearly intimated that the government would not shrink from retroactive legislation, the minister now backed away slightly. Doug Rowland, an NDP member from Manitoba, wanted a cast-iron guarantee that whether or not the negotiations in which Greene was engaged were successful, Home would remain Canadian. Greene said that what the government would do if no Canadian company matched Atkins' offer to Brown "cannot be communicated this evening," because "there is no decision yet on what we will do in the event that my confidence in the likely success of these negotiations proves to be misplaced."

That the government had another ace to play before resorting to retroactive legislation became clear early in March, after Brown had reported to Greene that the final offer from Ed Bovey was "not in the same ball park" as the one he had received from Atkins, and that in fairness to him Bovey had withdrawn all his previous offers and notified him formally that Northern & Central had no further interest in the deal.

Brown and Lomas were in New York on Friday, March 5, when they received a call from Jack Austin. The government, he said, had decided to buy Brown's interest in Home Oil and at that moment a team was being put together for negotiating purposes. Brown, Lomas, and Ross Phillips should therefore be in Ottawa next day to begin discussions.

Annoyed by the peremptory nature of the summons, Brown told Lomas there was no need for Phillips to be brought from Calgary yet, but he and Lomas flew to Ottawa that night. Next morning, Lomas walked into a meeting room as Brown's sole representative —to find himself confronted by a team of about twenty lawyers, investment advisers, and representatives of the Energy, Mines and Resources and Justice departments. Austin asked where Phillips was and Lomas replied that he would not be there. At that time, some press reports were still suggesting that Home—rather than Brown personally—was in financial trouble, and the government representatives wanted to make sure they were not buying a bankrupt company. So when the meeting ended for the day Austin phoned Phillips and asked him to come to Ottawa, immediately, armed with full details of Home's position.

After calling Brown to discuss this unusual summons, Phillips took an overnight flight to Ottawa and he was present for the resumption of the talks on Sunday when Austin told Brown he had set up a confidential meeting for him with Joe Greene the following evening in Toronto, where the minister was to make a speech. Anxious to keep the meeting secret, Austin made the arrangements for it himself, but he flew to Toronto with Brown and Lomas in the Home jet and drove downtown with them in the chauffeur-driven car Brown maintained in Toronto. The suite he had booked for the meeting was in the Royal York, where Brown's visits—and tips— had been a legend for years. To avoid detection, Austin led the way into the basement of the hotel through a side door, but a car despatcher who held the door open for them promptly recognized Brown and greeted him by name—as did the elevator operator. And later, when Joe Greene had joined them, a room-service waiter delivering coffee recognized Brown and gave him a warm welcome —completely ignoring the federal Minister of Energy, Mines and Resources.

Brown opened the proceedings by stating for the record that he had not come to Toronto for the purpose of negotiating a transaction with the government—he did not want any more trouble with the SEC and strictly speaking the government's decision to make an offer for Home should have been reported to its shareholders immediately. He also explained that when he had received no acceptable offers from Canadian buyers he had told the lawyers to go ahead with the Ashland deal under the impression that while the government would not be happy it would not actually oppose it.

Greene interjected to deny that he had ever given Brown that impression. But, he said, the government realized that because of its decision to block the sale to Ashland or another foreign buyer some potential Canadian buyers might feel they did not need to deal with Brown fairly. Consequently it had been decided to make him an offer that would match Ashland's as closely as possible.

Greene said the government's determination to block the sale had been forced on it by the public of all provinces, including Alberta. Brown challenged this, reminding the minister that he had recently seen Harry Strom, the Social Credit premier of Alberta, who had expressed his support for Brown's cause and had been quoted in a CBC interview as saying that Canadians were unduly concerned about the dangers of foreign ownership of domestic industries. Strom had pointed out in that interview that Alberta's prosperity was due almost entirely to development fostered by foreign investment, and had questioned the fairness of telling the owner of a company who had found a good buyer for it that the sale could not go through because of the nationality of the buyer.

This was not the only expression of support Brown had received since his troubles had become public. Senator Harry Hays, the doughty ex-mayor of Calgary, had encouraged him privately in his lonely stand against apparently insurmountable odds, and had spoken out publicly in his favour. Continued government "meddling" in Canadian industry, Hays had told the Meat Packers' Council of Canada, would lead to "mediocrity", and people such as Brown should have the right "to sell where they want to". The government, he had warned, "must be very careful not to kill the goose that laid the golden egg."

The respected Montreal financial columnist John Meyer had also written in *The Gazette*: "No investor is prepared to take a position in an enterprise and subsequently expand it over the years without the assurance he can dispose of it to the highest bidder in the open market." He thought both Brown and Stephen Roman would recognize the merit of government intervention if a clear-cut case for the national interest had been made. But, Meyer went on, "That case has not been made. What is being experienced here is a retroactive application of a new set of rules based on political sentiment. Canadian assets are not compromised by foreign ownership, not as long as the use of these assets is subject to Canadian law—as they most assuredly are. The government's intervention in Mr. Brown's affairs will have long-term consequences which cannot now be visualized but which will be most assuredly detrimental to future investment in Canada. . . ."

Buoyed by these and other assurances of support he had received privately, Brown made one last attempt to persuade Greene to permit him to go through with the Ashland deal which, he told the minister, he and Atkins had hoped to conclude later that week. Home's acquisition of Ashland Canada, he said, would be very beneficial to Home's shareholders. He showed the minister figures worked out by Lehman Bros. and another Wall Street firm, Dillon Read, which indicated that the new company would have a sizeable increase in cash flow and net earnings per share. Also, with assets approaching $500 million, it would be big enough to compete with the larger international companies on the Canadian scene and this would be a tremendous base for growth, either through exploration or through further acquisitions.

The minister's only response to this glowing picture was the acid comment that Home and Ashland had shown tremendous optimism in going ahead with those studies in view of the government's opposition to the deal. (In fact, they had been undertaken as part of the attempt to reach a three-way agreement including Northern & Central.) Brown pleaded with Greene again, saying the deal would not be detrimental to Canada. On the contrary, it would reduce Ashland of Kentucky's net interest of 89.5 per cent in Ashland Canada to a mere 36 per cent in the new company, which both he and Atkins thought would drop even further as time went on. Surely, he asked, this figure would be well within any guidelines the government might introduce for the percentage of foreign ownership permitted in a Canadian company?

No matter, replied Greene. However low Ashland's percentage ownership went, it would still be in effective control of Home, and this the government could not permit. From then on, the meeting resolved into a discussion of how the government's purchase of

Home could be accomplished, and how it would be announced to the public.

The vehicle chosen by the cabinet to make the purchase was Eldorado Nuclear Ltd., and for the next ten days Brown's team met almost continuously with Eldorado officials in Ottawa to work out details of the offer. By 4 a.m. on Friday, March 19, the lawyers acting for the government had drawn up definitive documents that met all the requirements of Earl Lomas and Dick Pettingill, acting for Brown, and Ross Phillips and Ron Coleman, representing Home. In essence, Eldorado agreed to pay Brown $11.4 million for his own Cygnus shares and $10.9 million for those owned by his family trust. And he would continue as chief executive officer of both Home and Cygnus.

The documents were then sent to the printer's to be readied for signature, and plans were made for Joe Greene to announce the consummation of the deal late that afternoon, after the stock markets had closed and just before the House adjourned for the weekend. Brown was expected in Ottawa from Toronto early in the day and it was anticipated that the documents would be ready for him to sign well before the minister's announcement. But an overnight snowstorm closed down commercial air traffic between Toronto and the capital and Brown's Gulfstream ii—which incidentally had become one of the bones of contention during his negotiations with some potential buyers, who shied away from his extravagant style—was in the United States undergoing maintenance. So Brown called his friend Jim Kerr and borrowed the TransCanada plane, which delivered him to Ottawa early in the afternoon. There he found that because of a delay at the printing press the agreement was not yet ready for his perusal.

Ross Phillips had gone for a walk on the Sparks Street mall and he returned to the hotel at about 4 p.m. fully expecting that Brown would have signed the agreement and that henceforth he and his colleagues at Home would be civil servants—a prospect none of them found appealing. Instead, he discovered that the documents had just been delivered to Brown—and the deadline for Greene's announcement in the House was now only about half an hour away.

His lawyers had assured Brown that the Eldorado offer contained substantially all he needed to match the Ashland deal but that there were a few points he should consider carefully before putting his signature to it. He began to leaf through the printed sheets but suddenly thrust them aside and said, "I've come too damn far in life to sign everything away in half an hour. Tell them I won't sign today. I want the weekend to consider it."

Greene's statement was hastily cancelled and Brown told his aides to return to Calgary. He himself flew to Toronto alone, and none of his associates know even today how he passed that weekend. He probably talked to Orin Atkins, because he had not yet finally abandoned hope that somehow he might arrange a three-way deal involving Ashland. And he might have been encouraged by others among his friends to reject the Eldorado deal in the expectation that a private Canadian buyer might yet make him an acceptable offer. Just the day before he went to Ottawa, while Phillips and the lawyers were putting the finishing touches to the Eldorado agreement, he had met with Alf Powis, president of Noranda Mines, a company which had participated in some of his ventures as a shareholder in Alminex and was at that time seeking new investment opportunities in the oil industry. Powis had said he would like to follow up their talk by examining Home's financial position and this new approach might have been enough to overcome Brown's reluctance to sell Home to the government.

Like Jim Lowery before him, Brown had always opposed any government involvement in private business, particularly the oil business. He may have decided as he contemplated his situation that weekend that it would be too great a break with his principles, too much of an embarrassment, for him to have to admit to his friends that he had sold out to the government to bail himself out of trouble. At any rate, on Monday, March 22, he flew back to Ottawa and turned down the Eldorado offer. He met Greene in the Château Laurier with Jack Austin, Marshall Crowe, and William M. Gilchrist, president of Eldorado. There he once again recounted the history of his attempts to sell his Cygnus shares and read a statement in which he said that the government had at all times been "helpful in aiding me in finding a compatible Canadian buyer". All these attempts had failed, however. And while he admitted that the Eldorado offer was fair and generous as far as money was concerned, "it in no way matched the Ashland deal." While it left him in nominal control of Home, it gave him no contractual right to be involved in the selection of its board of directors, all of whom could be appointed by the government—even though his actions as chief executive officer would be subject to the sanction of that board.

Consequently, he said, "after careful and thoughtful consideration I have decided I would prefer to deal with the private sector. The Eldorado deal offers nothing for the shareholders of Home. . . . I now intend to try to put a consortium of Canadian and American companies together to see if I can accomplish my desires and still keep Home's control in Canada."

All through the months of Brown's travail, the people at Home— from the executive floor down to the lowliest employee—had been anxiously awaiting the outcome of his struggle, not knowing from one day to the next when they might wake up to find they had a new boss, or no job at all. But by now they were becoming somehow numbed, inured to the apparently endless suspense.

Nevertheless, Brown's closest associates within the company, such as Bob Campbell, Ross Phillips, and Ron Coleman, were surprised and puzzled by the apparent anticlimax after his rejection of the government's offer, the seeming lull in all the frenzied activity of the recent past. Behind the scenes, however, Brown was still casting round desperately for some solution to his problems.

Ashland's offer remained open to him. Orin Atkins—while his position was more than a little exposed, since his company depended heavily on crude imports from Canada controlled by the government he ran the risk of mightily displeasing—had no intention of leaving his friend "twisting slowly in the wind", as the Watergate phrase later had it. The negotiations with the Teck Corporation were still going on, though Brown eventually rejected its offer as impossibly low, and Alf Powis of Noranda Mines still seemed interested and had requested an outline of the terms Ashland had offered. Also, the persistent Oakah Jones continued his attempts to overcome Brown's refusal to consider Consumers' Gas as a serious potential buyer for Home.

Ross Phillips had sent Jones an outline of the Ashland offer on February 11, and Jones had several meetings with Brown and Atkins in an attempt to work out a three-way deal involving Home, Ashland, and Consumers'. But none of the proposals Consumers' had made seemed to Brown to come to grips with his situation— until he sat down with Jones alone, on some date neither apparently recorded, and suddenly realized he had been mistaken in his initial antipathy toward him.

The two men could hardly have been more of a contrast. Jones, thirteen years older than Brown and at six feet considerably taller, was a pillar of the Anglican Church, conscientiously civic-minded, a man who might take an occasional drink but who frowned on excess of any sort. A rock-ribbed Boston Yankee, he had left school at sixteen and become a self-trained accountant and trouble-shooter for Stone & Webster, the leading firm of engineers and consultants in the energy field. He had been running Oklahoma Natural Gas in Tulsa in the early 1950s when he was brought to Toronto to head Consumers' just as "nature's wonder fuel", natural gas, was about to make its appearance on the Toronto scene.

Consumers' had been founded in 1848—a few years before the North American oil industry took its first faltering steps out of the Enniskillen gum beds—with a charter empowering it to manufacture coal gas to light the night-time streets for "the citizens of Toronto and the village of Yorkville". When Oakah Jones took over, it was still a conservative Toronto company whose plant and mountainous pile of coal was a none-too-popular landmark at the foot of Parliament Street. Oakah Jones, and the sales campaign he initiated for the natural gas which TransCanada PipeLines was about to bring from Alberta, transformed it into a province-wide utility operation with assets of more than $444 million and about 28,500 shareholders. In the process, Jones himself became one of Toronto's foremost public figures. He took out Canadian citizenship because he didn't aim to live anywhere he couldn't vote, became chairman of the board that planned Toronto's centennial celebrations, and, as president of the city's proud Canadian National Exhibition, earned the soubriquet "Mister CNE".

Bob Brown, a much less disciplined figure in private life, also preferred to remain out of the public eye. While he took his civic responsibility seriously and gave away hundreds of thousands of dollars to charity, his benefactions were almost invariably anonymous. But when he sat down face to face with Jones he found they shared at least one characteristic—a capacity for shrewd, tough, but straight bargaining. Perhaps a faculty perceived in Jones by the geologist and Home director Bill James played some part in the success of their personal negotiations. "Oakah," James told this author, "could play people like a banjo."

At any rate, when the two men took each other's measure the difficulties that had appeared to stand in the way of a deal between Home and Consumers' swiftly melted away. Some of the potential buyers Brown had dealt with had been leery of his personal style, fearful that if he remained at the helm of Home they would have scant control of his conduct of the company's business. Jones—and in this he shared Orin Atkins' sentiments—admired Brown and respected his ability; he made it clear he wanted him to stay on and convinced him they could work effectively in tandem. So the bargain was struck.

Brown said nothing about the deal to his own aides until Jones, who played his cards close to his vest, had had a chance to spring the news on his board of directors. In the words of one of his former associates, "Oakah always liked pulling rabbits out of the hat." And when he finally told his board that Consumers' was about to buy Home, it was obvious that he and Brown had settled the essentials of the deal between them. It remained only for the lawyers to draw up the papers embodying their agreement, which they did in Earl Lomas's office in Calgary over the weekend before the annual general meetings of Home and Cygnus, which had been called for April 23, 1971.

The atmosphere of secrecy was such that when Ross Phillips joined the lawyers in Lomas's office he parked his car several blocks away and slipped in to the meeting feeling like a character in a spy novel. And during the few days immediately before the annual meetings one group of Brown's executives worked far into the night on a speech he would never give, while Phillips and Coleman, like conspirators in a plot, put together the real one behind closed doors.

The Consumers' directors approved the final agreement on Wednesday, April 21, and a relieved Joe Greene ended all the suspense when he rose in the House next day to announce that Home Oil would after all remain in Canadian hands.

On Friday morning, Bob Brown, looking old beyond his fifty-seven years, explained the transaction to his shareholders in a voice so subdued he could hardly be heard. Consumers', he said, would pay a total of $20 million for the Cygnus B voting shares controlled by him and his family. The payment took a complicated form: it amounted to just under $10 million for his own 665,230 shares, which worked out to $15.03 per share;[1] then—instead of the loan included in the Ashland deal—Consumers' made a prepayment of $7.6 million ($11 per share) for the 692,384 shares owned by his family trust, which it contracted to buy for a minimum of $14.45 per share at the end of ten years, or on Brown's death, if that occurred first; that meant a future payment of at least $2.3 million—

more if the market price of Cygnus B shares had risen above the $14.45 level when the deal was completed. In addition, Consumers' received a ten-year right of first refusal on Brown's 390,366 Class A shares of Home, and undertook to lend Cygnus $2.5 million.

Brown told the shareholders of both companies he would remain as president and chief executive officer of both Cygnus and Home Oil, with an employment contract assuring him of substantially the same terms he had enjoyed in the past, including his use of the Gulfstream II. Oakah Jones became chairman of both companies, three directors of Cygnus and five of Home retired to make way for Jones and his nominees on both boards, and changes in the company by-laws provided for the form of "negative control" of Home's activities envisaged in the agreement with Ashland.

An era had ended, for both Home and Bob Brown. But the beleaguered Brown, against all the odds, had managed to escape the bankruptcy that had threatened him ever since he lost his last gamble with the hidden history of the earth, on the frigid North Slope of Alaska.

Epilogue

Bob Brown lived for only eight months after signing his deal with Consumers' Gas. But they were months during which, outwardly at least, nothing seemed to have changed. Since he had always before run his own show, there were many who feared he would be unable to work in tandem with Oakah Jones, but the expected friction never appeared to develop. Instead, associates of the two men were surprised to see them becoming good friends, and whatever direction of Home's affairs Jones exercised behind the scenes he accomplished with a very light rein.

The company expanded its exploration activities during 1971 into the Arctic Islands and the Mediterranean, where it entered partnerships to drill off-shore wells east of Malta and off the west coast of Italy. Brown's main enthusiasm had now become the North Sea, and he made frequent visits that summer to England, where the government was accepting applications for exploration blocks to be issued in the Fourth Round of North Sea licence awards. There was a shortage of off-shore drilling rigs at the time so Home, anticipating that it would receive more licences, became a twenty per cent partner—with another Calgary company, Bow Valley Industries, and two Norwegian firms—in the construction of a $32 million self-propelled, semi-submersible drilling vessel, the *Odin Drill*.

Oakah Jones accompanied Brown on some of his business trips, and he raised no objection that September when Brown arranged one of his typically sumptuous parties to celebrate the official opening of the gas plant in England, expensively designed to meet the specifications of the Gas Council and blend with its beautiful surroundings in the Vale of Pickering. A special train took a distinguished array of guests north from London to Yorkshire and after Her Majesty's Lord Lieutenant for the North Riding, the Marquis of Normanby, had declared the plant open, Brown entertained scores of local and national dignitaries at a reception held in a mammoth marquee, gracefully lit by crystal chandeliers.

Jones seemed to find the production end of the industry more fun than presiding over the somewhat circumscribed activities of a utility company, and he took a lively interest in Home's affairs without treading on anyone's toes. Not that he had any reason to be displeased with the company's performance. Thanks partly to a twenty-five-cent-per-barrel increase in the price of oil at the end of 1970, its gross revenue for 1971 rose by more than fourteen per cent, to the record total of $34.2 million. And out of the seventy-eight wells it drilled during the year, fourteen were completed as oil wells and fifteen as gas producers.

Brown's confidence in Oakah Jones as a partner grew with the passing months, and as Home's fortunes continued to improve he regained much of his old buoyancy. By the end of the year, his personal financial situation had been restored to what was for him normal: he had a substantial bank loan but it was more than covered by his assets. The money he had received from Consumers' for his Cygnus shares had not been enough, of course, to completely pay off his huge debt to the Bank of Nova Scotia. But by the time the deal went through he had had a rapprochement with Neil McKinnon and the Bank of Commerce had lent him the extra $9 million he needed to settle his Nova Scotia loan in full. As collateral, Brown pledged some of the 390,000 Class A shares of Home he still owned, which were worth more than $13 million at the going market price. Those shares, when Home made the new discoveries he was confident lay ahead in the North Sea, would rocket upwards, and all would be well again.

On New Year's Eve, Brown picked up the phone in his Palm Desert home and called a few close friends to wish them a happy new year. Earl Lomas recalls that he was "just effervescent with confidence". He spoke glowingly of the new horizons he saw opening up for Home Oil and warned Lomas jokingly, "You and I are going to have a very busy 1972."

The first item of business for Brown during the busy year he anticipated was a meeting scheduled for the afternoon of January 4 in the Toronto offices of Wood Gundy. During 1971, the measures instituted in 1970 to restore Home's working capital position had continued. A further 100,000 shares of TransCanada PipeLines had been sold, for instance, providing $3.3 million to be applied to the reduction of the company's bank indebtedness. And Consumers' had increased its holding of Class B shares of Home by purchasing blocks previously held by two of Home's subsidiaries, Foothills Oil and Gas and Coastal Oils, which contributed a further $9 million to the company's funds. Now, to retire its remaining bank loans, it was planned to market a $25 million issue of convertible debentures —the first such issue it had sold in Canada since 1964—and the meeting at Wood Gundy's offices had been called to make the final decision on the price at which this issue should be offered to ensure its success.

Brown had recently suffered a slight stroke which had left him with a barely noticeable weakness of his right arm. Now, feeling somewhat under the weather after his celebration of the holiday season, he flew to Toronto on January 3, to be sure of getting a good night's sleep before the next day's meeting. That evening, watching the late-night TV news with his daughter Pamela, then aged twenty, and his pilot, Don Douglas, he suddenly slumped over in his chair, the victim of another, catastrophic stroke. Douglas laid him on the floor and gave him mouth-to-mouth resuscitation, but knew he was dead before the ambulance arrived to take him to hospital.

Next day, Douglas performed his last duty to the boss who had become his close friend, and flew his body back to Calgary in the Gulfstream, the warrior slain on the field of combat borne home on his shield. Of all the tributes paid to his memory, R. A. Brown, Jr., would probably have most enjoyed the last line of an obituary written by the respected oil reporter Les Rowland in the industry journal *Oilweek*: "We can only imagine that Bobby is still scanning the scene from his next incarnation," Rowland wrote, "although it's possible he may be too busy making a farmout deal on the golden pavements."

Brown's closest associates, stunned by the news of his death even though they had half-expected it for several years, assumed that the meeting planned to price the new bond issue would now be postponed. But Oakah Jones was a trouper firm in the traditional belief that the show must go on. "I know how badly you guys feel," he told Phillips and Coleman, "but there must be no uncertainty. There is a complete transition settled here and it's taking place." So he added the title of chief executive officer to his chairmanship of Home, presided over the meeting as arranged, and the issue was successfully marketed a month later.

In the eight months since the sale of Home to Consumers' the staff had remained largely unchanged, except for the departure of Bob Campbell. As soon as Brown had completed his negotiations with Consumers', Campbell had resigned his post as executive vice-president and accepted the invitation of Ian Sinclair, chairman of the CPR, to become chairman of Central Del-Rio Oils (which was later merged with Canadian Pacific Oil and Gas to form Pan-Canadian Petroleum Ltd., of which Campbell remains chairman). Presumably after consultation with Oakah Jones, Brown had not appointed a successor as his right-hand man but had split Campbell's duties between Ross Phillips, who was promoted to senior vice-president, finance, Maurice Paulson, who became senior vice-president, operations, and Ron Coleman, now vice-president, secretary, and general counsel.

After Brown's death, Consumers' Gas continued to expand its holding in Home Oil. It bought all his shares from his estate and made a public offer to buy all the outstanding shares of Cygnus Corporation for $8 per share, which resulted in its acquiring more than ninety per cent control of that company. And when Oakah Jones took Brown's place at the helm, running Home through Phillips, Paulson, and Coleman, they found him just as decisive and ready to consider plans for the company's expansion as Brown had been. As an accountant and utility-company executive, Jones had a reputation for financial conservatism, and his personal style was the antithesis of Brown's: once, when a meeting in his luxurious suite in New York had dragged on well into the evening, Brown was appalled to discover that Jones, who wanted to return to Toronto that night, had no plane reservation but planned merely to go out to the airport and stand by for an economy seat, because as a "senior citizen" he qualified for a fare discount. Brown tried to persuade him to fly back in the Gulfstream, but Oakah demurred. He would not even permit Brown to summon his private limousine and chauffeur to take him to the airport. "I'll just grab a taxi," he said.

With this background, Brown's aides were prepared for some resistance when it became time to submit costly exploration projects to their new chief executive officer. But whatever private qualms he might have felt about investing millions of dollars without any guarantee of at least some return, Jones quickly grasped that speculating on exploration was essential to an oil company and during 1972 he sanctioned a twelve per cent increase in the exploration budget, which had been severely cut back after the headlong plunge into Alaska. More than $10 million was spent during the year, and the search for new oil and gas was stepped up in Alberta, the Arctic Islands, and Atlantic off-shore regions of Canada, and in the Mediterranean and North Africa.

Soon after Brown's death Home obtained the rights to two more exploration blocks in the Fourth Round of North Sea awards, for which high hopes were held, and a seismic program was undertaken with a view to drilling them in 1974. But otherwise there was bad news from England. First, one of the two wells supplying the Pickering gas plant began to suck up water and had to be shut down temporarily while the engineers tried to analyse the trouble. Then Earl Beatty, chairman of Home Oil of Canada Ltd., entered hospital for what was expected to be merely exploratory surgery for a circulatory problem. He never recovered from the operation and died in June. These troubles necessitated several visits to England by Oakah Jones—and his staff was amused to discover that some of Brown's style was beginning to rub off on their new boss: while in London he took the palatial suite Brown had favoured at the Inn on the Park.[1]

Eventually, Earl Beatty's position was assumed by a leading British industrialist, Lord McFadzean, chairman of the British Insulated Callender's Cables group and a director of many other companies, including the Canadian Imperial Bank of Commerce. But Jones took his time appointing a new president for Home. While there was no shortage of applicants for the post, he ran the company himself for more than a year and a half after Brown's death and then evidently decided he could do no better than continue to rely on the staff Brown had built up. In August 1973 Ross Phillips was appointed to the presidency, though Jones retained the title of chief executive officer. Soon afterward, however—on Thanksgiving Day, 1973—Oakah Jones collapsed and died while planting a shrub in the garden that was his chief hobby outside his office. He was seventy-two.

So ended the era of strong personal control of Home Oil by one dynamic, dominating figure. Henceforth the company would be run, like most other large corporations nowadays, by a professional management team which—since the modern oil business, despite its size and complexity, is still a form of legitimized gambling—was charged with the formidable responsibility of exercising entre-preneurship by committee. Ross Phillips became chief executive officer; Maurice Paulson executive vice-president and general manager; Ron Coleman senior vice-president, secretary, and general counsel. And to replace Jones as chairman the directors elected Anthony G. S. Griffin, a Second World War corvette commander, whose experience in the insurance and financial fields made him a valued director of a long list of major companies, including Consumers' Gas.

The new team had hardly taken over when the whole industry was revolutionized by the Organization of Petroleum Exporting Countries' sudden quadrupling of the price of oil at the end of 1973. The repercussions of this historic event, which transformed the economy of the western world, are still playing themselves out, and their ultimate effect on international politics and the balance of power cannot even now be calculated. But in Canada they led to new government intervention in the oil industry on a scale that Jim Lowery and Bob Brown could have imagined only in their worst nightmares.

This trend had begun even before the OPEC price increase, when mining companies' balance sheets began to be bolstered by "windfall" profits arising from increased world prices for metals. It was widely felt both outside and within government circles that these profits could not in conscience be permitted to remain in the hands of the mining industry. This belief, founded in considerable part on sheer indignation, was strengthened by the huge leap in the price of oil, and there began an unseemly scramble for the lion's share of the bonanza, with the provinces on one side, the federal government on the other, and the oil companies sandwiched between them.

Alberta and the other resource-producing provinces believed that whatever windfall profits were about to be made should go to the provinces owning the resources from which they came. But when they tried to translate this belief into practice by steeply increasing the taxes and royalties levied on mining companies and oil producers, the federal government perceived their action as a sneaky attempt to pillage the federal treasury and announced that in future the companies would not be able to deduct the increased levies when calculating their federal tax.

Trying to insulate Canadian consumers from the new world price of oil—at that time $11.70 per barrel—Ottawa also held the price to Canadian producers down to $6.50, but imposed a federal tax of $5.20 per barrel so that the United States would have to pay the full OPEC price for oil from Canada. The revenue thus gained was earmarked to subsidize the oil imported to eastern Canada from Venezuela and the Middle East—a flight of funds from the country which recalled to more than just those in the oil industry Bob Brown's long and fruitless campaign for a Montreal pipeline.

The new Canadian price, set early in 1974, was $2.70 above the 1973 price of $3.80 per barrel, which in normal times would have been a satisfying increase of seventy per cent. But the companies found the increase more than wiped out by the combination of higher provincial taxes and royalties and their inability to deduct them for federal tax purposes—a form of double taxation under which they were faced with paying tax on money they had not in fact received. In some cases, the government "take" threatened to exceed one hundred per cent of companies' profits.

During 1974, out of a gross revenue of $79.5 million, Home paid governments at various levels $31.3 million in royalties, taxes, and other payments directly related to its petroleum production, and a further $17 million in income taxes. And like other companies it was compelled to compensate for its higher tax burden—which approached an extra $5 million—by reducing its capital spending.

By far the major item of so-called "discretionary expenditure" in an oil company's budget is the amount it sets aside to search for new reserves of oil and gas. As Home's financial position had improved, it had stepped up its spending on exploration considerably—by 72 per cent in 1973 and 56 per cent in 1974. But during 1975 it spent less than half of what it had originally budgeted: $20.2 million, a sharp drop from the $31.4 million spent the year before.

Such cutbacks were general throughout the industry and since they came at a time when inflation had doubled exploration costs in just three years their effects were magnified and the level of activity in the oilfields declined disastrously. Drilling rigs with no work to do packed up and left the country by the dozen, and industry spokesmen were once again faced with trying to instil in the public consciousness the message they had been labouring to get across since Lowery's day: that while it was not certain new reserves of oil and gas existed in Canada, it *was* certain that none would be found unless someone had the money to go out and look for them. Fortunately, the realization that dead geese lay no golden eggs sank in, the various governments involved settled their differences, and the tax "take" was adjusted to a level more commensurate with what the traffic could bear. As the carrot replaced the stick and new exploration incentives were introduced, the companies began to plough their so-called "windfall profits" back into the business and the search for new reserves was resumed on a larger scale than ever. Home's exploration spending bounced back to $36.4 million in 1976, and that figure was more than doubled during 1977, reaching $75.3 million, out of a gross revenue that had by now climbed to $139 million.

At first, the trend of preceding years continued and most of the discovery wells yielded gas, rather than oil. But the rewards of perseverence became apparent in 1977, when Chevron Standard disclosed that it had made what was soon hailed as the most important oil discovery in Alberta for more than a decade, in the West Pembina area, west of Edmonton. It is not yet known how West Pembina will compare in productivity with earlier discoveries such as Redwater, Pembina itself, and Swan Hills. But what excited the industry and sparked yet another Alberta oil boom was that the discovery was made at around 9,000 feet, almost twice the depth of the other wells in the Pembina field, in rock of the Upper Devonian age known as the D-2 Nisku formation, which occurs at Leduc at around the 5,000-foot level. The significance of this was that such reefs had only previously been found at shallower depths and much further to the east, so the Chevron discovery raised hopes that other deep new fields might be found in the future.

Before 1977, Home held interests with various partners in 41,800 acres of land in the general area of West Pembina. By the end of the year it had increased that holding to 111,600 gross acres, and by the spring of 1978 it had made three promising oil discoveries.[2]

Unhappily, this success at home has not so far been matched by the company's ventures overseas. The trouble encountered at the Pickering gas plant early in 1972 proved more serious than anyone realized. It turned out that the two wells serving the plant, as sometimes happens, had tapped not the rich reservoir originally thought to exist but a badly fractured limestone structure. The gas which flowed so promisingly at first had been held in "traps" among the fractures and as it was extracted, reducing the underground pressure, it was replaced by water making its way up through the fractures from below. The plant struggled on for a couple of years but both wells eventually stopped producing and it had to be closed in 1974. When no more gas supplies materialized in the area it was dismantled and in 1978 work was under way to restore the site to farmland.

Further disappointments were in store in the North Sea, where drilling on the two blocks awarded to Home in the Fourth Round failed to find oil or gas. By early 1978, Home had completed all the obligations it had incurred in England and the North Sea up to and including the Fourth Round of licence awards and the United Kingdom office was closed. But the company still held the rights to two exploration blocks awarded in the Fifth Round in 1977.

The well drilled off Malta also proved to be dry, as did others drilled subsequently off Italy and in Tunisia and the sultanate of Oman. But gas was found in the Gulf of Thailand and Home persevered in its search for overseas reserves. In 1978 it was drilling in the Timor Sea, north of Australia, and negotiating for exploration rights in New Zealand and Vietnam.

The mid-seventies also saw a considerable expansion of Home's activities in the United States, where the success of its storage and marketing operations provided funds for an exploration program that has so far resulted in oil and gas discoveries in Louisiana, Texas, Oklahoma, and Wyoming. With land holdings of more than 1.5 million acres, the company budgeted $18 million for its U.S. exploration activities during 1978.

Exploration, of course, is only one of the ways—and the riskiest —by which an oil company can expand its reserves and production. The other is by acquiring other companies, and Home's management was able to examine that course as the remedial measures instituted in 1970 to restore the company's financial fortunes took effect. These measures, and the higher prices for oil and gas, greatly increased the company's cash flow during the seventies. Among other things, they included the sale of most of the shares in other companies bought in Bob Brown's day. By 1974, for instance, Atlantic Richfield shares had recovered to a price level that permitted Home to begin divesting itself of the 475,000 shares it had been holding unproductively since the height of the North Slope fever. The sale of 174,000 Arco shares during the year brought in $16.4 million, a welcome addition to the company's funds even though it meant a loss of $3.9 million on the transaction. The following year, most of the rest of the Arco shares were sold, together with a further 314,000 shares of TransCanada PipeLines, and the company's revenue benefited to the tune of $29.1 million.

Before his death in 1973, Oakah Jones, displaying a bullish tendency his aides had not expected, sanctioned the purchase of three blocks of shares in Scurry-Rainbow Oil Ltd., a Calgary-based company about one-seventh the size of Home, formed in 1954 by the amalgamation of two companies each of which had through the years absorbed several smaller companies going back to the early days of the industry in Alberta. Having thus accumulated eighteen per cent of Scurry-Rainbow's outstanding shares, Home early in 1974 made a public offer of $27 per share for the rest. The offer was briefly and unsuccessfully resisted by Scurry-Rainbow's majority shareholders in the United States but by June Home had acquired control, with 85.6 per cent of the outstanding shares. The purchase cost a total of $59.3 million, and it was a reflection of Home's restored stability that Ross Phillips was able to obtain the Canadian Imperial Bank of Commerce's assurance that the required loan would be available merely by picking up the telephone and making one call.

The acquisition of Scurry-Rainbow brought Home new oil and gas production in western Canada, exploration acreage in Canada and the United States, and potentially valuable coal-mining properties in Alberta and British Columbia. Scurry-Rainbow also held rights to an exploration block in the North Sea which were not highly regarded at the time but on which three marginally economic oil discoveries were made in later years. At the time of writing, it was not known whether these would eventually become commercial wells.

In subsequent years, Home failed in a similar attempt to acquire control of Canadian Export Oil and Gas Ltd., but in 1978 it succeeded in acquiring control of another Alberta-based company with oil and gas production and exploration acreage in both Canada and the United States, Bridger Petroleum Corporation Ltd.

The acquisition of Bridger was a milestone that would have delighted Bob Brown and staggered the imagination of Jim Lowery: it brought Home's net assets, for the first time, to more than half a billion dollars.

A mere generation earlier, the operations of Home Oil and Federated Petroleums were being conducted by a handful of staff in a few rooms on one floor of the old Lougheed Building. Now, Home and its subsidiaries employed more than nine hundred people, and its head office occupied the top fourteen floors of one of Calgary's newest skyscrapers, a thirty-two-storey black-glass tower rising from an office-shopping complex which embraces a 2.5-acre indoor park graced by thousands of tropical trees and plants, a mile of pathways, pools, and waterfalls and fountains.

Had Bob Brown lived to move into the tower-top executive suite he could, from a window facing north, have looked down on the six-storey Brown Building, whose construction he had supervised with such loving, almost child-like pride. And Jim Lowery, had he been given a window facing east, could have seen far below him the grey stone pile which in his day dominated the low Calgary skyline: the Palliser Hotel, scene of so much of his spirited wheeling and dealing.

Somehow one wishes both men could have lived to savour their achievements from this lofty height. As it turned out, their quest for the hidden treasure of the earth did not bring them great fortunes: while both lived well, it was as often as not by courtesy of their bankers. But the amassing of wealth seems to have been only an incidental to their ambitions. Jim Lowery was fond of quoting the old bromide "I don't want to be a millionaire; I just want to live like one." And in that, for at least a part of his life, he succeeded.

Bob Brown, more intense than Lowery, would not have made a remark like that: he certainly did want to be a millionaire, and never doubted that he would become one. But he, too, was driven more by a general ambition to succeed—to be a leader, to build something big and lasting, something that would earn him the respect of his peers—than by the mere love of money. As the geologist Bill James once said of him, "In the days of Kublai Khan, Bob would have had the stately pleasure dome." And one imagines that while he would have been well pleased with the top floors of the Home Oil Tower, he would have considered their eminence merely a springboard to higher things.

Jim Lowery, whose ambition was more relaxed than Brown's, not quite so all-consuming, would probably have taken just as much pleasure from the fact that in 1978 Home No. 1, the Section 20 well whose drilling he supervised half a century ago, in his high field boots and rough work shirt, was still producing a modest flow of gas from the Mississippian lime of Turner Valley, where it all started.

Directors of Home Oil Company Limited Through the Years

E. T. Bishop* (1929–30)
S. Burke* (1929–41)
A. G. Clark* (1929–30)
C. V. Cummings* (1929–34)
J. W. deB. Farris* (1929–38)
G. S. Harrison* (1929–35)
R. H. B. Ker* (1929–51)
J. R. Lowery* (1929–53)
F. R. Macdonald* (1929–31)
W. H. Malkin* (1929–41)
F. Mannix* (1929–30)
W. C. Shelly* (1929–31)
N. Spencer* (1929–41)
J. W. Stewart* (1929–38)
J. W. Troup* (1929–30)
E. G. Hanson (1930–52)
The Rt. Hon. A. Meighen (1930–31)
G. M. Bell (1930–36)
The Hon. P. Burns (1930–31)
G. Farrell (1930–35)
J. C. Gage (1930)
A. L. Hager (1930–41)
V. W. Odlum (1930–40)
A. B. Singleton (1930–36)
V. W. Smith (1930–35)
W. J. B. Wilson (1930–34)
M. W. Doherty (1936–38)
W. B. Farris (1938–42)
W. A. Akhurst (1938–41)
L. D. M. Baxter (1939–52)
H. Greenfield (1939–47)
H. R. Milner (1939–53)
M. M. Porter (1939–51)
R. W. Ward (1939–52)
E. E. Buckerfield (1942-51)
M. A. Dutton (1947–71)
J. W. Moyer (1951–68)
J. B. Weir (1951–52 and 1955–72)
R. B. Curran (1951–52)
R. A. Brown, Jr. (1952–72)

R. Will (1952–71)
A. Clark (1952–59)
A. H. Williamson (1952–61)
E. F. Davis (1954–71)
B. W. Gillespie (1955–64)
W. A. Rockefeller (1955–64)
R. M. Brown (1955–66)
R. W. Campbell (1959–71)
M. C. Govier (1960–65)
W. F. James (1961–77)
P. M. Fox (1964–77)
G. H. Thompson (1961–71)
H. I. Price (1964–77)
A. J. Walker (1965–71)
R. St-Laurent (1966–77)
J. B. Sangster (1967–71)
M. A. Cooper (1967–76)
The Earl Beatty (1967–72)
H. J. Howard (1969–71)
O. L. Jones (1971–73)
F. W. Hurst (1971–73)
J. C. McCarthy (1971–75)
H. E. Langford (1971–77)
J. Innes (1971–76)
The Rt. Hon. Lord McFadzean (1972–77)
B. A. Carlisle (1977–   )
G. W. Carpenter (1973–   )
G. E. Creber (1975–   )
J. D. Gibson (1971–   )
A. G. S. Griffin (1973–   )
The Hon. H. W. Hays (1972–   )
H. F. LeMieux (1976–   )
P. L. P. Macdonnell (1975–   )
W. D. C. Mackenzie (1976–   )
M. P. Paulson (1973–   )
R. F. Phillips (1973–   )
A. R. Poyntz (1977–   )
A. M. Shoults (1975–   )
W. H. Zimmerman (1972–   )

*Directors of original company, before change in charter.

Notes

Chapter One

1. Ottawa seems to have had a change of heart later. In 1904, to encourage the discovery and production of petroleum, it authorized a "bounty" payment of 1.5 cents a gallon to producers of crude oil. A total of $3.38 million was paid out between 1905 and 1924, all to Ontario producers. There was still no eligible production of crude oil in Alberta.

Chapter Two

1. In 1887, the Dominion government began to retain the mineral rights to all Crown land sold or homesteaded. Settlers who bought their farms from the CPR, or one of the other railroad companies which had received land grants to subsidize their construction, originally received the mineral rights as well. But from 1902, with few exceptions, the railroads also reserved the mineral rights when selling their land.

Chapter Three

1. Land in western Canada is divided into townships six miles square, each containing thirty-six numbered sections. Each section—640 acres—is divided into sixteen legal subdivisions of forty acres each. A quarter-section thus contains four LSDS. Townships are numbered in ascending order from the U.S. border and located laterally in "ranges" numbered westward from meridians established at intervals on lines of longitude.

Chapter Four

1. There is no record of what happened to the rotary rig rented by Home from British Petroleums, but the original well diary found among Lowery's papers shows that a standard cable-tool rig was used on Home No. 1.

Chapter Five

1. Canada's oil imports in 1928, stated in gallons here, amounted to just over 19.4 million barrels. During 1977 the country imported 240 million barrels, at a cost of $3.2 billion.

2. The English company became almost moribund as the mortgages were paid off—until the 1950s, when it was bought up by land developers and became quite active building shopping plazas and housing estates in the postwar English real-estate boom.

Chapter Six

1. Through the years, the company recouped about $110,000 of this sum from the re-sale of some of the shares it had bought, so its venture into gold mining incurred a loss of slightly over $100,000 —though by the time the final tabulation was made prosperity had returned and the Home treasury was well able to stand it.

Chapter Eight

1. Wendell Farris was the brother of Sen. J. W. deB. Farris, an early member of the Home board who resigned when he was appointed Chief Justice of the B.C. Supreme Court.

Chapter Nine

1. Home–Millarville Nos. 20 and 21, wildcats sunk to almost 10,000 feet during 1945 on the northern and western edges of Home's property, turned out to be dry—"dusters", in oilfield terminology. But the geological information they supplied helped to delineate the full extent of the company's underground reserves and paved the way for the siting of the subsequent eighteen wells.

2. Anglo-Canadian Oil was a successful Calgary company founded between the wars by an ex-Mountie named Phil Byrne, who after the failure of a later series of wildcat ventures committed suicide in tragic circumstances. After passing through several hands its control ultimately went to Shell.

Chapter Ten

1. During that same year, 1938, a German company, Tropicorp, wrote to the Alberta Petroleum Association—R. A. Brown, Sr., was its president at the time—offering to build a pipeline from Calgary to Vancouver for $16 million, in return for the right to buy the oil it would carry. Brown rightly concluded that with war

clouds gathering the proposal had little chance of acceptance. He showed a somewhat less sure grasp of world politics on his return from London in 1939, when he told reporters, "There will be no major war in Europe in 1939."

2. He was not the only one to think so. Also about to be demobilized from the navy, where he had served aboard oil tankers, was Jack Hamilton, an Alberta farmer's son who had sweated to put himself through a diesel mechanic's course in the depths of the Depression and had been lucky enough to hire on as a warehouseman with Brown, Moyer & Brown. When he wrote home from Halifax asking about job prospects Hamilton received a reply from his old superintendent, Ole Nevra, suggesting that since he had worked his way up to Chief Petty Officer he would be wise to stay where he was or find some comfortable job in the civil service, since everyone knew Turner Valley would be played out within a couple of years. Hamilton returned to his old job anyway and in due course became production superintendent himself.

Chapter Eleven

1. A lawyer handling R. A. Brown, Sr.'s, estate was surprised to find he owed no gift tax: whenever he had settled shares or money on his wife or children—Bob, Lois, and his youngest son, Ronnie—he had been careful to declare the gifts and pay the tax on them in full. Another lawyer who once suggested to the Chief that he could avoid paying tax by transferring his domicile, and his capital, to the Bahamas, as other Canadians much richer than he had done, was taken aback by his indignant reaction. "I made my money in this country," the Chief said, "and that's where it and I will stay, whatever tax I have to pay."

2. It seems likely that Brown's buying did force the price of Home shares upward. They sold at a low of $10.75 and a high of $17 during 1950, and a low of $13 and a high of $18.25 during 1951. Thereafter they started to fall, and it was 1957 before the 1951 high was reached again.

Chapter Twelve

1. Both Brown and Curran secured legal opinions at the time that this bonus would be free of tax. But in 1957, long after Curran had left Home and returned to the U.S., the Exchequer Court ruled that it was, in fact, taxable.

2. Several productive fields were eventually developed in the Williston Basin, but the rosy expectations of the early days were not fulfilled. The renewed pace of oil exploration prompted by the energy crisis, however, has led to a new boom in the area in recent years, and promising discoveries have been made—some of them on land given up by Brown.

Chapter Thirteen

1. Blundun went on to become a president of the Canadian Figure Skating Association and in 1967 he was appointed a judge by the International Skating Union in Davos, Switzerland. He has judged at world championships in Yugoslavia, France, and Japan and was general chairman of the world championships held in Canada in 1972.

Chapter Fourteen

1. Regent Refining, previously known as Trinidad Leaseholds, was a subsidiary of the major British oil company in the West Indies, Trinidad Oil Company, which was in turn a subsidiary of Central Mining and Investment Corporation,' a London-based South African gold-mining company. At this time, Regent had a refinery at Port Credit, Ontario, fed by oil from Trinidad, and about five hundred gas stations in Ontario, plus a few in Quebec.

2. One of Home's partners on this bid was a U.S. company with a fascinating history. Kern County Land Co. of California was founded in 1874 by a couple of Kentucky entrepreneurs named James Ben Ali Haggin and Lloyd Tevis, who had been drawn to California by the gold rush. The pair participated in the development of scores of mines from Alaska to the Andes, including the Anaconda copper mine and the Homestake, the richest gold mine ever found in the U.S. Starting with 400,000 acres in the San Joaquin Valley, including most of the land on which the city of Bakersfield now stands, their company expanded until it held more than 2,800 square miles—an area twice the size of Rhode Island—on which it raised cattle and grew everything from alfalfa to potatoes. The discovery of oil on its property after the First World War multiplied its assets and it diversified into mining and manufacturing. And in 1958, perhaps noting Alminex's profitable connection with Home Oil, it negotiated an agreement with Brown under which it put up twenty-five per cent

of Home's exploration costs in some areas and ultimately shared in about two hundred Home wells. Kern County was later absorbed by the huge U.S. company Tenneco, and its Canadian holdings found their way into the Canada Development Corporation.

Chapter Sixteen

1. By 1960, the original three-storey Brown Building was too small for Home's growing staff, some of whom had to work in rented space in other buildings. So Brown raised it by six storeys, at a cost of more than $1 million. As usual, he wanted everything to be the best. The ninth, or executive, floor drew on exotic materials from around the world: Yellow Rosa Marittinia, a marble-like lava rock quarried in southern Italy, was used to floor the foyer; the walls were variously panelled with Macassar ebony from Indonesia, Paldao wood from the Philippines, and Rhodesian walnut; and the drapes in Brown's office were flecked with gold and silver, and produced—in the words of a brochure he issued at the time—"by a secret screen printing process originated by Mariano Fortuny of Venice".

Chapter Seventeen

1. A couple of years later, Home bought out Union Petroleum, and in 1974 it acquired similar salt caverns at Conway, Kansas, which gave it about five per cent of all liquid petroleum gas storage in the United States.

2. As it happened, Union Gas and Consumers' Gas did discuss the possibility of a merger on several occasions during 1967 and 1968, and one of the reasons for Union's withdrawal from the negotiations in 1969 was Consumers' purchase of such a large block of shares from Brown while the talks were going on. Consumers' later tried to acquire control of Union by making a public offer for its shares, but the takeover was blocked by the Ontario government.

Chapter Eighteen

1. The purchases were actually made through Home's U.S. subsidiary, Home Oil Co. of Canada, which was later merged with Union Petroleum (the liquid petroleum gas wholesaling and storage company) to form the current Home Petroleum Corporation, based in Tulsa, Oklahoma, and Houston, Texas.

Chapter Nineteen

1. Cygnus B shares closed the day before the deal was announced at $7.12, so that in effect Consumers' paid Brown a premium of more than one hundred per cent to gain control of Home. There was some criticism that this price was not offered to all Cygnus shareholders, the prevailing opinion in the United States and Britain being that control of a company is an asset that ought to be owned equally by all its shareholders, not merely those in control, and that even in private takeover bids whatever offer is made to the controlling shareholders should be extended to all other holders of shares. A committee of the Ontario Securities Commission which reported on the question early in 1970, however, had concluded that the adoption of this convention in Canada would reduce the incentive for private entrepreneurs to found and develop businesses badly needed by the country. Second thoughts prevailed, and in 1978 the Ontario Securities Act was revised to provide that anyone purchasing control of a company at a premium by private agreement with a controlling shareholder must offer the same price to minority shareholders. As this book went to press, the change was expected to come into force early in 1979.

Epilogue

1. Jones hardly ever used Brown's Gulfstream II. He was opposed to the whole idea of company aircraft—not only on the grounds of extravagance but because of the danger of accident: he did not like his senior executives flying together at any time. The Gulfstream was sold in September 1972, though the Home fleet, indispensable to the company's wide-ranging operations, continued at various times to include smaller craft such as Cessna 180s, de Havilland Beavers, Queen and King Airs, and, later, a Lear jet.

2. Late in 1977, Chevron alleged that Home used confidential information improperly obtained from Chevron and initiated legal action laying claim to all Home's interests in formations of the Upper Devonian age in the area. Home announced that the claim, which its legal counsel considered without merit, would not deter the company from pursuing its exploration activities in West Pembina. The case was still pending as this book went to press.

Index

308 / The Treasure-Seekers